T0354809

Praise for The Divine Journey and Janet Myatt

"*The Divine Journey* offers you a comprehensive and in-depth exploration of spirituality and metaphysics and I believe takes this field to the next level of understanding. I have had the privilege of studying with Janet and know that she truly walks her talk."

Kate Mackinnon, author of *From My Heart and Hands*

"*The Divine Journey* truly connects you to the higher consciousness thought, it contains many excellent tools for the light-workers of the world to work with on their spiritual quest."

Amanda Romania, author of *Akashic Therapy*

"We need every voice tuned to the Divine presence in all of us. Use Janet's joyful, wise words to tune your heart to the divinity you are and have always been. As a friend and sister seeker and teacher, I've been looking forward to reading her book and I'm glad you have a copy in your hands!"

Laura Hansen, best-selling author,
Hand Me a Wrench, My Life Is Out of Whack

"*The Divine Journey* successfully translates complex spiritual concepts into logical, practical guidance that can be used to help explain how one can develop and grow their own spiritual path."

Peggy Prien, client

"Janet creates a welcoming environment for you to explore, learn, and begin to understand this wonderful, yet at times difficult, journey in a comfortable and effective way."

Tammy Campbell, client

The Divine Journey is awesome! The information provided is interesting, clear, concise, and fun to learn. Full of golden nuggets of wisdom, powerful meditations, and new approaches that support you on your journey back to wholeness.

Eugene Vodovoz, client

"I truly appreciate Janet's help in walking me through the areas I am blind in, so that I can see a little more each time. If everything is a grand puzzle, I'd want to ask for another's opinion every once in a while. How does the puzzle look today? That is the value and the reason for seeking Janet and continuing with her type of help."

John Quartieri, client

"Working with Janet, I always get the message that who I am is valuable — as a spirit and as a person. I learn that accessing and understanding myself as a spirit is straightforward and powerful. People who see me afterward say, "You look so good! What have you been doing?"

Susanna Schweickhardt, client

THE DIVINE JOURNEY

Awakening to the Creative Process of Life

Janet Myatt

BALBOA.
PRESS

A DIVISION OF HAY HOUSE

Balboa Press books may be ordered through
booksellers or by contacting:

Balboa Press
A Division of Hay House
1663 Liberty Drive
Bloomington, IN 47403
www.balboapress.com
1 (877) 407-4847

Print information available on the last page.

ISBN: 978-1-5043-6863-6 (sc)
ISBN: 978-1-5043-6864-3 (e)

Balboa Press rev. date: 12/15/2016

CONTENTS

For Spiritual Seekers everywhere,
may your light shine bright.

I Am Love

Word & Music by Janet Lee Myatt © 2001

Come walk among the rocks with me
I won't let you fall
I'll bind your feet if they should bleed
But I won't let you fall
Come dance among the stars with me
I'll be the rhythm in your soul
I'll be the sound, I'll be the symphony
That guides you as you go

I am love, and I am here
I am here, and I am love

Come sail the ocean deep with me
In your sails, I'll be the wind
I'll be the endless bounty of the sea
And by your side at journey's end

I am love, and I am here
I am here, and I am love

When the stars were formed
You and I were made
Nothing you can do
Will make my love go away

I am love, and I am here
I am here, and I am love.[1]

---

[1]   Myatt, Janet Lee. "I am Love." *Tattooed Heart.* 2005

1

PREFACE

Throughout my life, I have often found myself wondering, "Why is life so hard? Why am I so powerless? What is the true meaning of life?" Whenever life got really hard for me, I would turn inward for answers because I often didn't understand the answers being offered up to me in the external world. As a child, I used to go to Bible study at my neighbor's house. I had such a strong affinity for Jesus that I felt I knew him personally. But what I learned at Bible study often made me feel bad, as if I were responsible for things completely outside my control. How could I have been born *bad*? How could an innocent child who hadn't done anything yet be a *sinner*? How could I turn the other cheek when people were so mean and hurtful? What did it mean to do that? Why do we have to die to get to heaven, and why did the missionary keep saying only certain people could go? It seemed inherently wrong and unfair. So, I drifted away from Christianity and resisted the word *God* for many years. However, I did continue to have an internal relationship with Jesus and with something within me I couldn't quite name.

As an adult, I have found myself continually drawn to esoteric, occult, and mystical books that attempt to explain the complex universe. The subject is so vast and complicated that I often felt overwhelmed trying to figure it out, and I often walked away from these books exasperated because the information was so foreign to me and challenged many of my most basic beliefs at first. But I would always return because something deep within me yearned to understand. And, slowly but surely, the information began to take meaningful shape in my mind and tell me a story that has changed the way I understand myself and my reason for being here.

One of the most important shifts I had to make in my mind revolved around understanding the evolutionary nature of the Creation. Coming to understand that there are various states of consciousness and that God exists in a variety of ways helped me reconnect with God in a way that moved me out of my ego's belief that God was "out there" sitting in judgment of me. I was finally able to see for myself how God exists within me personally and exists in all things without separation. This led to further shifts. For instance, I came to understand that I was the creator of my life, but I still felt baffled by how powerless I remained. My question for many years was, "If I'm the creator of my life, why aren't things going the way I want them to?" Why were there still so many things I couldn't change? I eventually came to understand that the problem was stemming from an internal point of view that was immersed in beliefs that sit in opposition to the greater truth of who we are, how we got here, and what we're here to do. These foundational beliefs held an enormous energetic charge in my mind, and they worked as "givens" in my life. I came to understand that I was—and continue to be—on a journey to learn about how the forces of creativity within me work. This opened me up to investigating the thoughts and feelings that have created limitations in my life over and over again. Slowly, I have gained valuable insight into this divine journey, and I embrace the work of freeing myself from layer after layer of distortion and to reveal more and more of the divine Self at work in my life.

The journey of awakening to our inner divinity is no small task! It's a long journey and requires an unyielding commitment to continue to unravel the many layers of our distorted thinking so that we may move our identities out of our fearful patterns and remember ourselves as we truly are. And who are we? I'm discovering the beautiful reality that we are Spirits clothing ourselves in matter for the purpose of expressing God in a tangible way. Well, then, who is God, and how does God relate to each of us? There is no shortage of ideas in the world about God and how God relates to us, and I imagine all those ideas hold a key that we can eventually learn how to use to uncover our own answers. I don't claim to know everything or really much of anything about God, for God is vast and ultimately unknowable to us here in our human form. But I do know that changing my mind about God and how God relates to me has led to a profound healing.

I want to share with you as much of this information as I can in the hopes that it will serve you in the same way. The subject is rather complex and abstract; thus, talking about it is very much like assembling a jigsaw puzzle. The overall picture is slowly revealed piece by piece in a manner that is not particularly linear or predictable. I will be introducing concepts and terms that may be unfamiliar at first, so I want to point out that there is a glossary in the back of the book. Also, you will see notes inserted along the way that I hope will help clarify things as much as possible.

Additionally, the purpose of this book isn't to tell you "how it is" but rather to present ideas and experiences that can serve as a catalyst for your discovery of your own answers. Let me state up front that while I've endeavored to present this information in as straightforward a manner as I can, it will not be an "easy read." Many of these concepts are at first quite foreign to us and challenge us in profound ways. The good news is that the challenge in and of itself is sufficient unto the day. For it is in our struggle to understand ideas that feel new to us that we stimulate our intuitional mind and consequently access new levels of awareness within ourselves. If we consider all ideas and concepts that currently exist in the world as possible tools for understanding and not as the absolute and undiluted Truth, we can begin to work differently with ourselves. So, I encourage you to be patient and remain open to considering the value of the ideas presented, especially when they challenge you. If they add value and improve the quality of your experience of life, great. If not, let them go and continue to seek out ideas and concepts that will.

Road Map

In Part I, we'll take a look at the design of the Cosmos and our part within it. We'll gain a better understanding of who we are and why we're here. In Part II, we'll examine how our thoughts color our perception and change our personal reality. This will help us better understand our suffering and give us some important clues about what we can do to heal ourselves. In Part III, we'll consider key steps we can take to transform our reality and come to work consciously within the greater field of life and carry out our part of God's plan. In Part IV, we'll tie everything together as we consider the Seven Rules for Inducing Soul Control. At the end of each chapter, you will find chapter exercises to help you process the material and discover your own answers. Finally, in Part V, I have included several powerful meditations in Appendix A to help get you going if you're new to meditation. Appendix B contains my personal story, which I've included to give you an opportunity to know more about me and how I came to do what I do. Appendix C includes an index of concepts, an index of the diagrams in the book, the glossary, and the Works Cited.

In my own process, I have learned that it is necessary for me to take the time to stop and reflect on what comes up whenever I encounter new ideas, especially those that I most resist. I have found that the inflexible areas in my mind tend to stand between me and something vitally important that I am trying to remember or realize. So, I encourage you to notice your reactions (both positive and negative) to the ideas presented here, as this will give you an idea of where you might want to investigate further both in your personal meditation and quiet reflection space and in other writings and spiritual teachings. I have also found that it's often helpful to take notes and write down questions as they arise. This creates a strong focus for deeper inquiry. More than once, I have heard the following saying: "Prayer is when you talk to God, and meditation is when you listen." [2] It's important to do both because this activity in and of itself is the bedrock of the divine journey. Also, in my opinion, information alone will not help us create a transformational change in our lives. In my experience, we learn by doing, and this can be achieved only through "right practice" and application of the truths and principles in our daily lives.

I also recommend that you reread this book (and/or sections of it) again and again as you navigate your way through the process of awakening. Each time you read it, you will find that you

1. Understand something that you didn't before,
2. Have gained awareness and expanded your consciousness, and
3. Discover the next nugget to explore further.

Sources

With the exception of the Bible and possibly *A Course in Miracles*, many of the source materials that I refer to in the book may not be familiar to you. Like both of the above, many of these lesser-known sources are also divinely revealed, most of them within the past 150 years. (This means that the information was communicated from a divine personality, or group of personalities, through a human channel.) I have occasionally included quotes from some of these sources because they hold words and statements of power. I encourage you to ponder them, to dwell on them, especially if you don't understand them at first. There are layers of meaning to be found in them.

---

[2] Robinson, Diana.

Real-Life Stories

At certain points in the book, I have included real-life stories from both my own life and those of my clients to help illustrate and clarify a concept. The names of the people whose stories are shared here have been changed to protect their privacy. No one's story has been included without his or her direct consent and final approval. Those who agreed to share their story did so out of a joyful willingness and desire to be of service to others in the hopes that their story will inspire others to take this transformational journey into the Light, Love, Power, and Presence within us and all around us.

Part I: Cosmic Design

In the resulting explosion of creativity, psychic universes were seeded, each seed an indivisible bit of aware-ized energy with its own unique perspective and filled with the same exuberant desire to know and to love that had given it birth.[3]

To extend is a fundamental aspect of God which He gave to His Son. In the creation, God extended Himself to His creations and imbued them with the same loving Will to create.[4]

So God created man in his own image, in the image of God he created him; male and female he created them.
Genesis 1:27

---

[3]   Ashley, Nancy. *Create Your Own Reality, A Seth Workbook*, p. 10.
[4]   *A Course in Miracles* (ACIM), p. 17.

Chapter 1 ~ In the Beginning

A New Idea of God[5]

I was profoundly affected by the Seth books written by Jane Roberts when I was in my twenties. Seth was the first one to teach me that we are immortal spirits having physical experiences, not physical bodies having spiritual experiences. He explained that we got here by choosing to be here, choosing to incarnate into physical bodies. He taught me that we are all the creators of our own reality. This was such a staggering idea for me at the time because I felt so powerless in my life. It seemed crazy, and it made me feel a dragging sense of responsibility for things that felt completely out of my control. At that time, I could identify myself only through my ego, and my ego believed God was separate from me. And if God was

---

[5] NOTE: Over the course of my life, I have used many different names for the all-encompassing, unifying, loving, divine Presence called God by the Christians and Jews—for example, "Source," "All That Is," "Supreme Being," "Creator," "Universal Mind," and "Deity." All these names stand for the same thing to me. And I have referred to God as both Him and Her along the way. However, for me, God is neither male nor female because God is formless, a creative intelligence and loving presence who had nothing to do with separation of any sort. To keep things less confusing here, I have decided to keep it simple and most often refer to Source as God (but you will also see all the terms mentioned above when it serves to make things easier to understand). And I will be using the male pronoun rather than switching back and forth between male and female. Please feel free to substitute in your mind whatever word creates within you the strongest experience of unconditional love.

the Creator of everything and He was "out there," how could I also be a creator?

In those days, I didn't have a clear sense of myself as a divine spirit, even though I'd had communication from spirits, so I knew they existed. Within my own personal experience, I had an awareness of *something* that most people called "God," so I felt He must exist somewhere. But I didn't understand all the teachings and trappings that surrounded that word and felt rather alienated from it at times. I'd heard "the Voice" at various points in my life and concluded that something bigger than me was talking to me. But I still thought of this "something" as being completely separate from me. Eventually, however, I began to wonder why my experiences of God were internal rather than external. If He was out there and separate from me, why did I experience God internally? This got me thinking. Why do we believe we're separate from God when we really aren't? I have come to understand that we think we're separate because we've forgotten that we're not. And we have the free-will authority to think whatever we choose to think. So, in a nutshell, separation is an experience based on an *idea*—nothing more—that we have taken so seriously that our entire identity is based on it. Thus, it's no longer an idea we're willing to move out of readily.

Imagine your mother falls and hits her head. When she regains consciousness, she has no idea of who she or anyone in the family is. She doesn't remember you or that she's related to you. Does that make her no longer your mother? Is she no longer a member of your family? Of course not. *You* know she is still your mother. *You* know she is still a member of your family. *You* know you came into this world through her. Just because *she* doesn't remember it doesn't mean it's not true.

I have found that it's the same with God and us. We come from God, and God is always within us. But because God made us in His own image, we have *free will*. We can create whatever we want, even spiritual amnesia. This doesn't negate

God from God's perspective, only from our own. God's point of view is holistic. It includes everything. Our point of view is individual, and we contribute our point of view to God's experience of Himself.

The Big Bang

Let's go back to the beginning (relative to our point of view). As I thought about God being whole and complete, I wondered what kind of creations would result from that wholeness and completeness. Why create anything new if you're already everything there is? What I saw was that God creates because God *is creative*. Furthermore, all that creativity needed to be expressed and *experienced*.

Figure 1: Big Bang

We can actually understand this from our own experience. For example, you can imagine all kinds of things. You can *see* them vividly in your mind's eye. You can envision every little detail about something. The only thing you can't do in your imagination is *experience* it. Thus, if it's an idea that excites you, you want to experience it. You want to give it form; you want to move it from a subjective experience in your mind to an objective experience. I imagined writing this book long before I sat down and wrote it. The imagined version was an idea full of *unexpressed potential*. Because it was not yet manifested in the physical world, I could only subjectively experience the potential of the idea. But the idea was compelling enough to motivate me to sit down and do the work of actually writing it so I could objectively experience it in a material form.

Seth teaches in his books that it was like this for God. Simply put, before the Big Bang, God was full of ideas that yearned to be expressed. Thus, God *existed* as the Formless One, the Source of the three primary creative forces of will, love, and intelligence but did not yet *experience* these forces *in action.* He did not yet experience these creative ideas because they were still unformed, unactualized bits of potential. They existed as creative forces or pulses that had not yet been put into play. But it was God's desire or will to express and experience Himself; thus, the necessary coupling of latent and active forces within Him ignited and resulted in the Big Bang. The activated forces of will, love, and intelligence exploded. Universes were born and seeded with the same creative forces and inherent desire to experience creativity.

In this way, everything created in the Big Bang is an extension of God and remains a part of God, imbued with the same creative forces of will, love, and active intelligence. Every spark of life has within itself the divine potential and inherent drive for self-consciousness or self-awareness. This innate potential drives each spark to find ways of individuating to experience a sense of self, or a particular point of view, within the larger point of view. Nothing in all the universes is truly separate from God. In other words, a "son" of God is but the Father in some form of manifestation. Father and son are in no way separate and can never be so. Thus, every "son" or Divine Spark in the Creation is an extension of God and contains the exact same forces inherent to God. These differentiated expressions create individualized points of view, but all points of view are simultaneously experienced within the collective cosmic consciousness of Source or All That Is. The Seth teachings refer to this phenomenon as "Separateness Within Unity."[6] I prefer to use the term *differentiation within unity* and avoid

---

[6]   Ashley, p. 10.

the word *separation* altogether. On the macrolevel, we are all One—and that oneness is God—and God is experiencing everything wholly and simultaneously. On the microlevel, we are individual spirit-personalities experiencing our own point of view in conjunction with everyone else. The experiential aspect of God expands and evolves as a result of this cocreative experience. In this way, God experiences His creativity through what He creates. Because we are made of the same stuff as our Father, we also experience ourselves as creative entities, and we learn and grow through our creative experiences.

Hinduism teaches us that this process of exploding into creative activity is cyclical and evolutionary. When God is active, He is manifesting or expressing Himself objectively. When He is passive, He is dormant or unrevealed. Objectively, we see evidence of this cyclical creative activity on the cosmic physical plane of the universe we live in. New stars are born, and old stars die out. Whole solar systems come into existence and then fade away. Various levels and sectors of the Grand Universe are in various stages of activity or dormancy. From a human perspective, these alternating periods last for an extraordinarily long time—literally trillions of years and more. For instance, one "day" of Brahma (an active period also called an age) is equal to 4,320,000,000 human years.[7] And one night of Brahma (or an inactive period) is equally long. According to the Hindu teachings, an age ends when the creative mandate for that part of the creation has been fulfilled.[8] The creative mandate for any given age is different from one age to the next, and we cannot possibly hope to understand the overall interconnectivity of the entire plan from our distinctly small point of view. The reason I find it helpful to ponder this idea of the cyclic nature of God's creativity is that it is consistent with our own experience. Thus, as above, so below. We, too, move

---

[7] Bailey, Alice. *A Treatise on Cosmic Fire*, p. 39.

[8] Astronomically speaking, an age (in our solar system) consists of "that portion of time which intervenes between one conjunction of all the planets...at the first aspect of Aries, and a subsequent similar conjunction. (Ibid)

into objective forms, and we move out. Understanding that we exist either way is essential to opening up our consciousness awareness of who we really are and what we are doing here, and it is one of the main points of this book.

Divine Spark

Although there is only one All That Is, each of us exists as a divine spark (or creative extension, or son) within this Oneness. We all derive our "beingness" from this same Source and at the unity level we experience at-one-ment. Each divine spark, or son of God, is imbued with the same creative potential as the Father who created him. And each seeks to express his divine will, love, and intelligence and add to the Creation. In the material universe, this involves a process of differentiation during our descent into material form and a process of integration during our ascent out of form.

We have been given everything we need to create and the free will to do it. We start out, then, as unlimited, formless divine potential without a definite sense of self, and we slowly begin to differentiate as we descend into denser levels of material substance—matter being the creative building blocks of the universe. As Spirit, we *clothe ourselves* in various grades of matter to create forms through which we can express creatively. For now, I will skip the earliest ages of material creativity, which encompass an epic journey through the mineral, plant, and animal kingdoms, and begin our discussion at the point where we as Spirit individuate in the human kingdom. Once this individuation process occurs, we

1. Become "self" conscious—aware of ourselves as thinking, feeling, creative beings;
2. Learn about our creativity through the process of activating, developing, and eventually mastering the three primary creative forces inherent to us— intelligence, love, and goodwill—and

3. Develop and improve the inherent qualities of matter to better reflect our divine nature in objective, material form.

Matter provides the fundamental building blocks we use to create forms in the physical levels of the universe. As creative expressions of God, we—the indwelling spirit—remain immaterial even when we are actively revealing ourselves through the forms we've created. The incarnated personality (spirit clothed in material substance) is an extension of the soul. The human soul is a type of actively evolving consciousness that creates and expresses through these forms. It's important to distinguish between spirit, consciousness, and matter. And we will be exploring this point in more depth as we go along, because it is our confusion over this distinction that ultimately gave rise to our suffering.

So, we are creators in training at the beginning of our journey, full of potential and becoming actively creative. When God becomes creatively active, He extends Himself or reveals Himself through His creations. The same desire to express or extend that exists within God the Father or Source exists within His creations (God the Son, or the Divine Sparks), too. This drive motivates the Sons/Sparks to seek out ways to differentiate and explore their creative potential. Simply put, within each of us is the same stuff as God, and we are here to figure out how that "God stuff" works. Each divine spark begins as a free-standing creative entity with the potential to become an active, manifesting Creator. As creative expressions of God in action, each divine spark is imbued with a personality status and operates as a unique point of view *within* the larger lens of Source (or All That Is). At this point, I am using the term *personality* to symbolize

1. The bestowal of a state of personalized existence within the Whole gifted with the latent ability to organize a collection of qualities and to act independently as a self-conscious being, and

2. One who has been imbued with an actual fragment of the Father and given the opportunity to become aware of that gift and to merge with it over a course of evolutionary experience.

This state of being is the gift God bestows on us as His divine sons when He is in an active state. Each son exists as a fractal of the whole. Thus, His loving, intelligent will to actively create is our innate spiritual heritage. Understanding this symbiotic relationship draws us closer to our actual identity as the Sons of God, or God in action.

The Tree of Life

The concept of the Tree of Life reveals this principle of differentiation within unity beautifully and simply and also shows us how there are various levels of consciousness within the Creation. Imagine entering a beautiful garden full of light and love. As you enter, you become aware of the Presence that dwells in the garden, and you begin to fill up with a sense of returning home. As you look down, you notice you are on a path that leads to the center of the garden. Follow this path until you come to the Tree of Life—an enormous tree made of Light and radiating Love. This tree is the symbol of all Creation; it contains everything that exists. Sit down now at the base of the tree and rest your back against the trunk. Gaze up and notice all the many branches and countless leaves. Recognize that each of us is a leaf on the tree. Notice that the tree would be incomplete without the leaves, and the leaves wouldn't exist without the tree. Be aware that at no time are the leaves separate from the tree; in reality, they are not separate from one another because they all exist on the tree together as a whole. However, each leaf has its own place on the tree, its own unique point of view within the collective point of view of the tree as a whole.

As you look at the tree, focus now on the branches. Notice that there are large main branches coming off the trunk and smaller branches stemming off the main branches. Once again, pay attention to the leaves and notice that they stem off the smaller branches. Everything works together, but there are different parts of the tree and they each serve the whole in their own way.

In just this way, the Creation as a whole is multifaceted or multilevel. There are creations within the Creation that all serve specific roles and functions within the whole. The tree grows and forms from the trunk outward in successive phases of creativity (from our point of view). The main branches can be likened to High-Level creative beings that have the ability to create the smaller branches and the leaves that stem from them. In other words, they have creative input on how those branches form and how they work in the overall creation. At this very high level, these creative entities are all working cocreatively with one another and within the larger point of the view of the Creator as a whole. There is no delusion of a separation from the Creator or from the whole at that level, but there is autonomy. As the branches get smaller, the individuation process intensifies and narrows, yet all remains connected to the whole.

There is a hierarchy of creativity within the Creation. There are beings, or creative personalities, that exist in states of consciousness far greater (or broader, or more universal) than the consciousness we are familiar with in our daily lives as incarnated beings. In our example, the leaves encompass distinctly smaller, more differentiated points of view than the branches, and the branches have a relatively smaller point of view than the tree as a whole.

The point of all this is that at the incarnational level of existence, we have a relatively small and individuated point of view of ourselves and one another. At the same time, in cosmic reality, each of us simultaneously has access to a much larger point of view at all times. Thus, it is only a matter of focus. What are you focusing on in your life? Is it the feeling of being small and separate from everyone else, or is it the bigger picture of God-within-you and how you fit into the larger scheme of things?

The movement from at-one-ment (at the tree level of reality) to individuation (at the leaf level) serves an evolutionary purpose. When we first emerge in the mind of God, we are merely unlimited, untapped *potential*. We are minicreators in training, and the creative process is firing up as God becomes active. We have unlimited potential, but it is latent. Our task is to develop our potential through actively creating in the realms of material substance. By actively building forms to express through, we get feedback on the quality of our creativity. As we do this, we learn about the forces inherent within us and learn to master these forces over time. So, let's take a look at the three primary creative forces more closely.

Three Primary Creative Forces

Let us start with the understanding that the creative forces within God contain the master pattern or blueprint of all material reality.[9] Understanding God as a trinity is a useful way to comprehend the three primary forces of Creation:

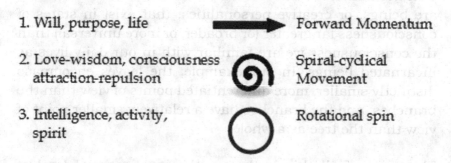

1. Will, purpose, life — Forward Momentum

2. Love-wisdom, consciousness attraction-repulsion — Spiral-cyclical Movement

3. Intelligence, activity, spirit — Rotational spin

This is also known as the Father, Son, and Spirit.

---

[9]   *Urantia*, p. 8.

First and foremost, it is important to remember that these three forces work together as one. Just as we have different parts of our brain that perform different functions, these functions work collectively and as a whole. Thus, within these creative forces is one unified purpose. The entire Creation works together in an integrated fashion, and this "establishes the peace of God."[10] This means there is no conflict between the forces of Creation as a whole. God's will is *good*will, and there is an overriding order to all things.

Figure 2: Trinity

Once again, we are looking at the concept of differentiation within unity. Each force serves a distinct purpose but works cocreatively with the others. Everything in the universe reflects the cocreative principle of the Trinity, and this provides us with an important clue in understanding what we are here to learn.

God the Father—Divine Will

Let's start with the first creative force of divine will, also known as God the Father in Christianity and the First Logos in Theosophy. As we just discussed in the Big Bang section, manifesting an idea starts with a desire to express it. Desire is *will* turned outward. The Father aspect of God is the personalization and activation of divine *will*. He is first in the triple forces of God. He is the parent, the initiator, and the directing force of creativity. *Will*, then, is the prime force from which all things are directed. *Will* is the outbreath and the in-breath of God. It creates and it destroys. The out-breath is God in action or manifestation, and the in-breath is the withdrawal from manifestation and a return to inactivity. God exists (and we as extensions of God exist) whether there is a

---

[10]   *ACIM,* p. 39.

form of expression or not and whether He is manifesting an idea or withdrawing from an idea, just as we exist whether we are expressing ourselves through a physical body or have withdrawn from it. With His will, God creates and destroys, *but He exists either way.* God's will is that which directs both of these activities. And we, as his children, are also directors of will. We create forms of expression and we destroy them, but we *exist* either way.

The intelligent, loving will of the Father is the *igniting* energy of the universe. This powerful creative energy is at the center of all things and is *absolute intention* and *the drive to extend, express, and reveal.* It is the creative ignition switch, and central axiom or organizing principle of the Cosmos at large. This energy is inspirational and unifying and is the source of what we know of as "God's will." As His children, we have within us the free use of this same force of will. At all times, we are God in action whether we remember this or not. Therefore, we are employing our will at all times whether consciously or unconsciously. Our entire life is the result of the creative choices we have assertively made or passively been unable to make (thus making us the effect of other people's choices) and is a reflection of how we are directing, or failing to direct, our will. As creators-in-training, we may not always be using this force well, but we are using it, or failing to use it, nonetheless and are learning about this force through our experiences. When we learn how to align our will with the greater unified loving, intelligent will of God the Father, we come into sync with the greater good of God's plan and the peace and *goodwill* of God is established. We experience a glimmering of what this alignment is like when we feel deeply inspired, creative, and powerful and our life flows from a higher power manifesting with ease, certainty, and abundance.

The Father is the Source of our beingness and is *That* which granted us with the potential for personality status. What does it mean to have a personality? To answer that, we must turn our attention to the second force: God the Son.

God the Son—Personification of Love-Wisdom

The Son is the personification or the embodiment of God and is an expression of His loving, intelligent will. Because we *are* the sons of God, these are our innate qualities. In the physical realms of the universe, we are learning how to reveal these qualities in material form.

The Sonship as a whole is composed of all the Sons of God existing within the Mind of God. God distributes Himself into the Sonship gifting each Son with a *specific existence* that can come only from Him. In this way, God the Son is the "spiritual personalization" or *revelation* of God the Father. For now, let's define personality as *a self-aware collection or organized pattern of qualities and characteristics, an essential uniting principle that underlies all subjective experience and knows itself to exist.* The Father has instilled Himself within us, and we could not exist without Him or outside Him. However, God in His *pre-personal state as Source did exist without us.* This means that even when God is not actively revealing Himself through His sons, He still exists. *The Urantia Book* tells us that God exists outside His current creation (because He is absolute infinity); therefore, there are "places" (for lack of a better word) beyond the edge of the Grand Universe where He is Present but nothing is manifest. He is existentially present but not experientially present. My analogy is that the manifested Grand Universe is the Tree of Life, and everything around the Tree is the unmanifest where God is still Present. However, within His creation, He is personally distributing Himself within every son. Hence, a reciprocal relationship springs up between God the Father and His Sons. Only as Source is God inherently eternal in that He had *no beginning* and *has no end.* Immortality (to exist without end) is the *destiny* of the sons of God. But they were created. That is, they have a *beginning*; there was a time when they did not exist. Never, however, did Source not exist.

Janet Myatt

The Urantia Book is quite definite about this. It states that the sons of God are gifted with a pre-personal "Thought Adjuster" by God the Father at the time of our conception in His mind. And we become eternal only if and when we develop our minds to the point where we can merge with the divine Thought Adjuster within us. When this merger happens, the Thought Adjuster (an aspect of God the Father) becomes personal through us (the individuated personal son), and we become eternal through this conscious merger with God the Father within us. Another way to say it is that the personality consciousness of the human being becomes an activated Son of God when we awaken to our Spiritual essence and identity. Jesus refers to this in a conversation with his disciples. At this point in his life, Jesus was already what is called by the Theosophists an "Ascended Master." This means he had already merged his human consciousness with his indwelling Thought Adjuster or personal fragment of God the Father when he says,

> "I am the way and the truth and the life. No one comes to the Father except through me. If you really know me, you will know my Father as well." John 14:6-7

> Don't you believe that I am in the Father, and that the Father is in me? The words I say to you I do not speak on my own authority. Rather, it is the Father, living in me, who is doing his work. Believe me when I say that I am in the Father and the Father is in me; or at least believe on the evidence of the works themselves. John 14:10-12

Jesus points out that the only way to know ourselves truly and live as divine beings is to awaken to the fact of our existence within God as a divine expression (a Son) of the Father. And we can't really know God except through the Sonship experience. Furthermore, as sons, we are inherently of the Father, for He dwells within us.

In summary, then, the ascending Sons of God (those entities who develop into Creators through their experiences in material existence) start as pure Spirit containing pre-personal Thought Adjusters, which contain the yet-to-be-manifested *potential* of Divine Mind. The Sons of God are destined to activate and actuate this potential in the material realms through

- Their activity in matter,
- The development of their ability to be in loving contact with greater levels of intelligence, and
- The discovery of their divine purpose within the Creation.

The soul is the middle principle of the divine Self containing both our potential in the early stages *and* our activated abilities in the later stages of our evolution. Once we fully merge consciously with our soul and become soul directed, the gift of personal existence as divine beings given to us by the Father is made actual. It bears fruit. From there, the divine Son continues to expand and eventually emerge as a fully realized Son of God and divine creator in his own right.

In this way, God actively *reveals His identity* through His son, and the nature of that identity is love, intelligence, and goodwill. Where the Father aspect of God is universal and all encompassing (He is the entire Tree of Life), the Son is individualized and distinguishable in comparison to the whole. In this way, the Son is akin to the branches and leaves on the Tree of Life. However, at all times all parts of the tree exist within the whole and the whole always contains all its parts.

And while each son is distinguishable and contributing to the whole in unique ways, there is really only *one* Son (also called the Sonship), and we are all differentiated manifestations of the Sonship. Furthermore, the Son *is* the Father *in action*. There is no separation between Father and Son. Another

Janet Myatt

interesting way to understand this concept is to look at it the way Jesus describes it in *A Course in Miracles* when he says, *"If all His creations are His Sons, every one must be an integral part of the whole Sonship. The Sonship in its oneness transcends the sum of its parts."*[11] This is another way of understanding the concept of differentiation within Unity or the at-one-ment and the interconnectivity of the entire Creation.

Figure 3: All That Is

When Moses asks God for His name, God says, "I am that I am."[Exodus 3:14] When we get the inflection of this phrase right, we can begin to understand what He is saying. Try saying it this way out loud: I am *that* I am. What does this tell us? I saw for myself in a deep meditation one day that God the Father encompasses *everything*— He truly is All That Is. He extends beyond my horizons in all directions without beginning or end. The Son, on the other hand, appeared to me as a distinct light within this endless field of creative force. I heard His voice saying, "I Am." From this experience, I was able to see for myself how the Son *is* the *Word* of God—the *manifestation, the expression of God*, just as *The Urantia Book* says, *"the divine Sons are indeed the 'Word of God'...God speaks through the Son."*[12] And as I continued to meditate on the Son, I saw that *every* divine spark in the Creation was also sounding "I am."

In the beginning was the Word, and the Word was with God, and the Word was God. He was with God in the

---

11   *ACIM*, p. 33.
12   *Urantia*, p. 111.

beginning. Through him all things were made; without him nothing was made that has been made. In him was life, and that life was the light of men.^{John 1:1-4}

When we speak, we are *expressing* something. We are putting a thought or feeling into form, bringing it to life with our breath, and releasing it out into the world. By giving voice to our thought we are revealing it; we are manifesting it, or making it known. For instance, when we communicate out loud with others, we enter into a relationship of speaking and listening, of giving and receiving, and yet nothing is lost and everything is gained. When we share an idea with other people and they take it up in their mind, we don't become separated from the idea and the idea does not become separated from us. It doesn't leave our head as it enters another person's mind. Instead, the idea *grows* through the act of sharing; it expands and becomes *greater* than before. Because this is so, it is vitally important for us to consider how we express ourselves. When we "sound our word"—that is, use our life—correctly, we reveal our divinity. When we sound our word incorrectly, we obscure our divinity. Through the process of our evolution, we learn the difference. We learn to be the embodiment of love and light, which is our natural or original state.

The nature of love is to extend, connect, and share. Love and light are synonymous; light shares the same qualities as love, and vice versa. Light is the objective visible manifestation of love, which is a subjective experience. Love and light emanate, attract, radiate, and extend. Because our true nature is inherently loving, we intuitively seek to connect and share. Just like ideas, when light connects with light, nothing is lost or traded; instead, the light is magnified. It becomes brighter and extends farther. As we learn how to extend our love unconditionally into the world and seek out and acknowledge the light and love in all our brothers and sisters, we understand our true nature and the creative process of divinity. We awaken to the greater truth of who we all are and arrive at at-one-ment. Thus, the qualities of unconditional

Janet Myatt

love, forgiveness, and compassion are important qualities we learn to activate within ourselves as we become all that we are meant to be. As we become aware of this creative power within us, we gain the wisdom of God and activate our fullest creative potential. Jesus teaches us this in his sermon on the mount when he says,

> You are the light of the world. A town built on a hill cannot be hidden. Neither do people light a lamp and put it under a bowl. Instead they put it on its stand, and it gives light to everyone in the house. In the same way, let your light shine before others, that they may see your good deeds and glorify your Father in heaven. Matthew 5:14-16

The Father and the Son are two inseparable aspects of God in relationship with one another. God shares His love with and through His sons. This act of sharing reveals the creative nature of God and that the Word of God is love. Together, the Father and the Son establish the fellowship of God and the cocreativeness of the universe can be seen. Therefore, when we consciously live in loving relationship with one another, we come to recognize ourselves as whole. We have within us the innate ability to know ourselves to be both unique *and* indivisible from God and one another and, in so doing, acquire the wisdom of God. The *forms* through which the Sons of God reveal themselves may look different from one another. But differentiation is not separation. God expresses this way and that way, but it is always God doing the expressing.

We, the Sons of God, are thus the revelation of God the Father *in action.* Jesus repeatedly makes this point in his ministry:

- The Father and I are one. *John 10:30*
- If you really know me, you will know my Father as well. *John 14:7*
- Anyone who has seen me has seen the Father. *John 14:9*

Upon awakening to our innate divinity, we come to know ourselves fully as the Sons of God in action. We understand that, regardless of race, religion, or any other apparent divisions we experience in the external world, we are all One. When we live from this activated spiritual point of view, we fully participate within God's overall plan, creativity, and will. We are all instruments in the symphony of the Cosmos. Each one of us is a working part of the whole, cocreating with one another and with the Father (or the unified point of view) to manifest the music of His creativity. We can fully trust that our role and our divine creativity exist within the larger context of God's loving, intelligent will and that all is well.

God the Spirit—Active Intelligence

> The divine Sons are indeed the "Word of God," but the children of the Spirit are truly the "Act of God."[13]

The very instant that the divine forces of will and love come together as a full-fledged idea to be executed, the activating and actuating force of the Infinite Spirit, springs into existence.[14] The Spirit is Divine Mind—the executer of the plan, the universal manipulator of energy.[15] The Infinite Spirit is the revelation of God's intelligence in action in the universe. It is the aspect of God that executes the Father's plans and designs the environments within which His creations can experience themselves and evolve. The Infinite Spirit is also the bestower of intelligence to all things living, from the mightiest superuniversal Creator Sons to the minutest atoms of substance. It exists as a beneficent Presence in our minds and has oversight over the domain of the intellect. In this way, God as Spirit is knowable to us through our intuition

---

[13]   *Urantia*, p. 111.
[14]   *ACIM*, p. 90.
[15]   *Urantia*, p. 99.

and serves as a divine influence when we turn our awareness inward to seek the council of our inner wisdom.

The Infinite Spirit is the aspect of the Creator that organizes the Universe of Universes and ensures that His will is carried out. It is the vehicle through which God's will is administered and manifested in the universe. On its own, or in cocreative concert with the Father and/or the Son, the Infinite Spirit ministers, administers, and manifests God's will. Thus, the management and organization of the Universe is carried out by this aspect of God. This includes the creation of nonpersonalized things like matter, gravity circuits, the structural organization of the planets, galaxies, and universes, as well as certain personalities (beings) that minister to the evolving sons of God and oversee the management of God's plan within the Creation.

What an interesting and varied revelation of God. The Infinite Spirit is the *activator* of the universe and material reality, source of the mind and intellect, and the divine minister and uplifter of mankind. As the creative source of all the ministering agents of the Grand Universe, *The Urantia Book* teaches that Infinite Spirit is represented by a diverse group of ministering spirits, messengers, teachers, and guides.

To summarize, Infinite Spirit is

- The loving intelligence of God shared directly with all the creatures in the Creation through the agency of the mind,
- The source of intelligence in action in the universe,
- The manipulator and administrator of energy, and
- The source of atomic matter.

What can we learn about ourselves from understanding the Infinite Spirit and the creative force of *active intelligence?*

1. We have intellect—the capacity for rational thought, inference, and discrimination.
2. The Infinite Spirit works within our higher mind—the abstract, intuitive, illuminating superconscious mind—and serves to correct our thinking when we go astray.
3. The Spirit is always broadcasting higher-level thought patterns that we can tap into, and this helps us release the mental barriers that keep us unaware of ourselves as God in action.
4. The Infinite Spirit is the container of our intuition and higher consciousness.
5. The Spirit is That which manipulates energy to create forms (the divine Thinker within us) *and* that intelligence quotient within matter that enables it to respond to our creative demand. H. P. Blavatsky stated, "Matter is spirit at its lowest point of manifestation and spirit is matter at its highest [point of manifestation]."[16] This could also read as matter is intelligence at its lowest point of manifestation, and spirit is intelligence at its highest.

The Trinity

Each of the three qualities of God has a specific function and works in a particular way. Once God became active, all other forms of spirit personality became possible. The seeds of potentiality were put in place, and numerous types of divine personalities developed from these seeds. Everything created in the Universe stems from the Trinity in a successive line of creativity. This includes everything in the material (physical) and spiritual realms. The creative activity of the Trinity establishes the master blueprint on which all things are based.

---

[16] Bailey. *The Rays and The Initiations*, p. 264.

Janet Myatt

All divine spirit-personalities trace their lineage back to the original Trinity, including us. We can trace our existence back to our inception point within the mind of God because (and I can't say this enough) we are God in action or in active manifestation. The consciousness assigned to this physical lifetime is but one small aspect of a much larger, multidimensional self that rests within an even larger entity. This chain of creations-within-creations is reflected throughout the Grand Universe, and we will explore this more in our next chapter. What is exciting to note is that even at our smallest, we have within us the inherent qualities of God: divine will, love-wisdom, and active intelligence. We are creators and cocreators. We are, each of us, a unique creative expression or revelation of God. We remain connected to everything, even as we create and experience unique or differentiated forms of expression.

Chapter 1 Exercises

1. Sit quietly for a moment and imagine your soul patiently waiting for you to remember and attend to it. Focus your attention on this deep source of love and wisdom within you. Focus on your breathing for a few moments, and allow the body to decompress, let go, and relax. Focus on one thing that you are grateful for today, and allow that gratitude to flow through you. Open your hands in a gesture of receiving, and imagine golden light filling you up. Put your mind in a receptive state, and be willing to listen and receive. Ask for a deep experience of remembrance of who you are.

2. Can you imagine that you might actually exist even when there is no objective form of expression to define you? Can you imagine that you are pure consciousness and that you periodically use bodily forms to reveal yourself and then pass out of the form? What comes up for you when you consider this possibility?

3. What comes up for you as you consider the Trinity?
   - In what way do you see the force of will or purpose working in your life?
   - In what way do you see love-wisdom working within you or in your life?
   - In what way do you see active intelligence working within you or in your life?

4. The Father—Divine Will:
   - Can you think of a time when you aligned your will with the intention of serving the greater good of everyone concerned? What did you experience?

5. The Son—Love-wisdom:
   - When you think about diversity within unity, what comes up for you?
   - What does it tell you about yourself, others, and humanity as a whole?

6. The Infinite Spirit—Active Intelligence:
   - Reflect back and see if you can remember a time when you felt a divine Presence either within you or

around you. What stands out for you about those times?

7. Use the space below to write down your notes on chapter 1. If you have some questions, write them down and ask for divine assistance to help you discover your answers.

CHAPTER 2 ~ HIERARCHY OF CREATIVE ACTIVITY

Existential and Experiential

Earlier, when we talked about God in His original form (pre–Big Bang), we saw that He existed as the absolute—infinite, eternal, and without beginning or end. And this existential aspect of God fully desired to experience Himself. In becoming active, He distributed Himself through His Creation, and all other forms of spirit-personality became possible. The seeds of potentiality were put in place, and numerous orders of divine personalities developed from these seeds. What is important to note here is that everything created after the Big Bang is *evolutionary*. The beings that dwell within the created universes are both *experiential* (i.e., they experience themselves as unique personalities with unique points of view) and *evolutionary* (i.e., they change, grow, and evolve in response to their experiences).

The *experiential* aspect of God is evolutionary (God as He is present within all His creations). The *existential* aspect of God is not evolutionary. In this way, after the Big Bang, God became present in two ways:

1. *Existentially*: God as He has always existed. Limitless, eternal, perpetual, ceaseless, endless, complete, perfect, and absolute. The aspect of God that is infinite, not subject to limitations or conditions of space, time, or circumstance. Also sometimes referred to as Source or the Godhead.

2. *Experientially*: God as He exists within the evolutionary universes of time and space. Evolving and finite. He is in the process of personally observing, encountering, and undergoing a process of growth and change that is subject to limitations of space, time, and circumstance. The God of time and space is destined to become infinite (limitless), and this potential exists within Him and develops in accordance with the evolution of consciousness happening within the Creation as a whole.

"Supreme Being" is one of the titles *The Urantia Book* uses to refer to the *experiential* form of God, and I find it quite helpful. It helps us distinguish this personal form of God from the existential pre-personal aspect of God. The Supreme Being *relates* to us and *experiences* through us. He is within us, and we are within Him. He is the synthesizing Deity Who encompasses and ensouls all Creation. He is greater than the sum of His parts and is an evolving Being in His own right. Everything that exists within the manifesting universe exists within Him and is an extension of Him. This makes him a very personal aspect of God. He is a

Figure 4: Supreme Being

"living and evolving Deity of power and personality."[17] However, in this form, He is not yet fully existential. He is not yet complete or infinite (without limitations) because He is not yet done creating. New branches are being added to the tree, and all the leaves are still developing their potential. An important point to consider is that each of us is an irreplaceable part of the Supreme Being. This means that you, as one such irreplaceable part, are an aspect of the Supreme Being, and

---

[17]   *Urantia*, p. 1268.

that aspect can be fully revealed only through you. Therefore, each of us has a spiritual responsibility to learn how to fully express our divinity. As we do, the Whole is revealed.

The physical universe is constantly expanding and contracting, and new universes are being born as older ones settle into full fruition of Light and Love. Just like His creations, the Supreme Being is still evolving and growing in experience because *we* are still evolving and growing in experience. And this process of change and growth occurs over time. This is the distinguishing characteristic of the experiential aspect of God. The Supreme Being, then, is a work in progress within the Grand Universe, and the Grand Universe is always changing. New stars are being born, and old stars are dying out. Epochs of evolutionary growth are beginning in one part of the universe and ending in others. His destiny, like ours, is perfection, but His present experience "encompasses the elements of growth and incomplete status." [18]

I want to include the following quote from *The Urantia Book* because it contains a powerful statement that is worth understanding:

> *If man recognized that his Creators—his immediate supervisors—while being divine were also finite, and that the God of time and space was an evolving and nonabsolute Deity, then would the inconsistencies of temporal inequalities cease to be profound religious paradoxes.* [19]

When we understand this statement, we realize two important things. First, any inequity that exists between the sons of God exists only temporarily and is a reflection of the stage of evolution each one is in. Second, God exists within us, even when we are not yet perfect, because God in His experiential

---

[18]   Ibid.

[19]   Ibid.

37

form in the evolutionary universes is also growing and changing in response to the processes of creativity.

An example of the first statement can be seen here on Earth. We can see that some people are farther ahead in the evolution of their consciousness than others, most likely because they've been at it longer. Because God's creativity happens in waves, there are old souls, new souls, adolescent souls, and so forth. Each soul is where he or she needs to be and working on what he or she needs to be working on at any given point. At all times, we remain brothers and sisters in God and coexist within the Sonship as whole. From a cosmic point of view, all roads lead us forward (even the ones that seem to be leading us away), and it is not for us to judge one another's progress but instead to be of service in whatever manner serves the highest good of the Whole.

The experiential aspect of God is built on the partnership between the Creator and his sons—"God and man in association."[20]This relationship fulfills the Father's desire to express and experience His creativity. My original worry and confusion over perfection stemmed from a misunderstanding of God and a lack of awareness of how time and space work in connection with God. Now I understand:

1. God is present both existentially and experientially; He *is* and He is *becoming*.
2. God is *both* perfect and evolving. This evolution is happening perfectly within the goodwill of God the Father.
3. All of us—no matter where we are in the process of our evolution—are unique expressions of God, and our ability to express our divinity fully is dependent on where we are in the process of our evolution.
4. God relates to us personally regardless of where we are in the order of things. There is no separation from God.

---

[20] Ibid.

Hierarchy of Beings

Here on Earth, many people are familiar with at least two types of beings—humans and angels—but there are others as well. All the various types of beings in the evolutionary universes are manifestations of God, and each exists at his or her own stage of conscious evolution and at various levels of experience. All beings descend in one way or another from the original Paradise Trinity [21] and serve in the Creation according to their design and in alignment with God's overall plan.

Let's take a brief look at some of the very highest levels of beings within the Creation. The Supreme Being, as we just discussed, is an experiential and evolutionary aspect of God that works within the entire Creation as a whole (at the Grand Universal level, or the Universe of universes.)[22] Ancients of Days, Eternals of Days, and Unions of Days are a few examples of beings that exist at the superuniversal level,[23] and the nature of their consciousness is quite different from our highly individuated point of view. On the Tree of Life, superuniversal beings would be akin to the first main branches stemming off the trunk, or the first generation on the family tree. These mighty Beings have administrative oversight over entire superuniverses and work to establish the will of God in the evolving universes of time and space

---

[21]   *The Urantia Book* uses this term to refer to the original Father, Son, and Infinite Spirit of all Creation. The Paradise Trinity exists at the center of the Grand Universe, and they are the First Cause and Center, the Second Cause and Center, and the Third Cause and Center. This means they are the cause of all creation and exist at the center of all things.

[22]   Grand Universe: All That Is. The entirety of all Creation, all the seven superuniverses combined plus the original central universe that exists at the hub of the wheel of spiraling superuniverses.

[23]   Superuniverse: There are seven superuniverses that spiral around the central universe. They are composed of a vast number of smaller local universes.

(see figure 5). The Seven Master Spirits that surround the throne of the Paradise Trinity each oversee a particular superuniverse, and that superuniverse is greatly influenced by their inherent nature (see figure 6). Elohim and Tertiaphim are angelic beings that exist at this same level. The Avatar of Synthesis is a group consciousness that comprises all the levels of consciousness within our superuniverse that exist between us and the Trinity.

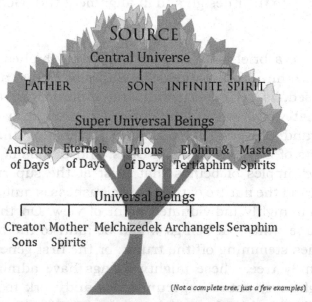

Figure 5: Family Tree of Grand Universe

Another example of superuniversal beings are the Creator Sons, who create local universes and are akin to grandsons of the Paradise Father. Creator Sons have the ability to create local universes in the same way that the Trinity created the central universe. They possess the same type of spiritual ability as God the Father to distribute themselves into the sons they create in their own universes. A Creator Son functions *as the Father* in His own local universe, because He is the direct Father of those who dwell there. Now, this gets a little tricky to explain, but I think it's worth noting.

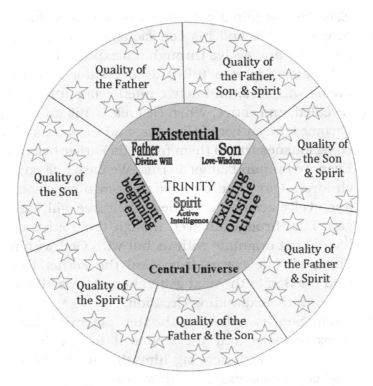

Each Spirit is a manifestation of an aspect or combination of aspects of the Paradise Trinity.

Each superuniverse is greatly influenced by the nature of the Spirit that ensouls it.

Figure 6: Seven Spirits that Surround the Throne

1. Any Son of God is a son because the Father gave him life. Thus, a son exists because the Father *is in him*.
2. A son gains personality status from the Father when the Father distributes Himself into that Son. Thus, all potential for self-consciousness originated in the Father and is passed on to succeeding generations through the descending Sons of God.
3. All sons are made of the same stuff as their father and can create using the divine forces of will, intelligence, and love.

4. Each Son is gifted with free will and has the ability to use his life and his consciousness to express his creativity and evolve through his experience.

5. A Creator Son is a full-fledged creator with all His divine will, love, and active intelligence fully evolved, revealed, and active. When He creates his universe, He becomes the Father of His sons, and He passes life and consciousness on to them from His Father before Him.

6. Even we human beings do this. We pass Life on to our children. Our children have their own consciousness and evolve according to use of their free will. But they gain Life through us even though the Source of that life did not originate with us but with God-within-us.

7. Thus, all Life comes from God the Father through God the Son to the next generation of sons all the way through the expanding Creation.

8. Each Son is gifted with the potential for self-consciousness and the free will to use it for the purposes of experiencing himself, but the Source of that consciousness came from God.

9. Here at the lowest levels of self-consciousness, our sphere of influence is limited. As we learn to become more self-aware and activate more of our divine potential, our consciousness expands, and so does our sphere of influence.

We exist within one of the great Creator Sons as a part of His creation. And we have the potential to evolve someday to this lofty place, too, if we choose to follow that evolutionary route.

From the superuniversal level, many different types of beings descend and ascend in the hierarchical structure of the Creation. And each of these different types of being is operating at its own level of evolution. For instance, a Galactic Logos is a divine entity that ensouls and oversees the evolution of an entire galaxy or sector of solar systems. He is more fully evolved than a Solar Logos (an entity who ensouls a solar system) and consequently has a larger sphere of influence and is operating on a higher plane of the Cosmos. However, they are both mighty divine beings who operate at the Deity level of consciousness, and they work cocreatively to carry out God's Plan. Using the body as a metaphor, you can imagine that a Solar Logos works as an atom or a cell within the larger body of a Galactic Logos. Looking the other way (into smaller spheres of influence), a Planetary Logos ensouls and oversees the evolution of a planet and exists as a cocreative atom or unit within the Solar Logos. Human beings (at our divine God-self level) exist as atoms within the Planetary Logos. This downward and upward chain of continuity continues from the Paradise Trinity all the way through the various levels of creation to us and back.

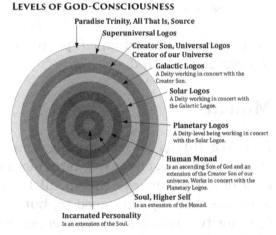

Figure 7: Levels of God Consciousness

I share this with you because, for me, it helped put the universe into a whole-new perspective. There is just so much more going on than what we're experiencing here as human beings on planet Earth. There's so much to look forward to, and I believe knowing this can give us the incentive to awaken to our true divine nature and get on with the business of evolving our consciousness. But more importantly, the creative process of emanation or self-distribution is the same throughout all the levels of the Creation, so it is helpful to understand it because it also applies directly to us. This will become clearer as we go along. These are just a few examples of the great variety of the Sons of God that exist in the Grand Universe, and all these beings can trace their lineage back to the original Trinity, including us through our relationship within our Creator

Son, which we will look at next. Various schools of thought have different names for these levels of personality and even categorize the levels slightly differently. However, the point is

- There is a hierarchy of creative entities or beings,
- There is a continuity of interconnectivity throughout this hierarchy, and
- Everything and everyone is contained within God as a part of this creative process.

Despite these distinctions in purpose and design, there is no separation from God.

Monads

To make things less confusing from here forward, I have opted to use the gender-free term Monad to refer to the divine level of consciousness within all human beings. I know it may take some getting used to, but in the end it is a useful term for two reasons, First, it is gender neutral (versus Son of God). Second, it doesn't include the words spirit, soul, or personality, which already have a lot of mixed meaning associated with them and are used to refer to other levels of consciousness later in the book. Monad is a Theosophical term meaning "unit of consciousness" and can be applied to any creative entity within the Creation. For the purposes of this book, however, I will use it to refer to only a human being's God-self.

Within the hierarchal structure of the Creation, human Monads exist within the Creator Son of our universe. The Urantia Book teaches us that each universe is ensouled or embodied by its own Creator Son, and each Creator Son is in every way God to all that dwell within that universe. Creator Sons are mighty cosmic beings of perfected light and love who fully express and reveal God. And just like His Father before Him, a Creator Son distributes Himself into His creative expressions—His sons, His offspring. Examples of the Creator

Son's offspring include (but are not limited to) the Deity-level planetary and cosmic beings that ensoul planets, solar systems, and constellations as we just described, as well as the human Monads—the ascending Sons of God operating in the human kingdom on planet Earth. It is this latter group of beings I am referring to when I use the term Monad. Synonyms for Monad include Divine Spark, Spirit-Personality, Spirit, and the I Am Presence. But just to reiterate, I am using the word Monad to refer to the highest level of our consciousness, to our inception point in the mind of God, our purely divine God-self.

When a Creator Son (offspring of God the Father and God the Son) joins with a Mother Spirit (offspring of the Infinite Spirit), a local universe is made. In other words, when divine will and divine love are ignited into intelligent action and activity, systems of creativity manifest, or come into being. Local universes are populated with a wide variety of creative entities in precisely the same way the Trinity did it when the central universe was formed—that is, through the process of divine Self-distribution and differentiation. The Creator Son bestows or distributes unique parts of Himself on each of His sons. Over the long course of the evolutionary process within all the subsystems within a universe, all the Monads within the Creator Son ultimately work together within a local universe to manifest their Father's loving will. At this point, I am referring only to the Spirit aspect, or the life aspect of the divine Self, and not to the material or objective forms of expression we use in the physical levels of the Cosmos.

Human beings are distinct, objective manifestations who descend from their Monadic source. The human Monad as pure Spirit remains in a state of unified God consciousness. Human beings are aspects of the Monad working within material forms. Because the Monad is the God-self, it works as the Father or Source of consciousness within the microcosm that is the evolving human being. In keeping with the law "as above, so below," the Monad distributes its consciousness into differentiated forms of expression for the purposes of activating all its inherent divine potential through its creative experiences. At the incarnated level of experience, these forms consist of the etheric-physical, astral-emotional, and mental bodies that make up the evolving human being. We'll talk about these vehicles of expression in greater detail as we go along. For now, we're going to confine ourselves to an exploration of the Monadic level of consciousness.

At our Monadic level, we are "born" with unlimited creative potential. At the time of our inception, we are the following:

- Omniscient (all knowing)—We have awareness of the whole of God's intelligence because we do not yet have any part of our consciousness sitting in ideas of separation.
- Omnipresent (in all places at all times)—We understand ourselves to be present everywhere within the whole for the same reason.

But we are not yet omnipotent (all powerful) because we have not yet mastered all levels of Creation. Remember that we begin our ascension career in the lowest level of the Cosmos (the cosmic physical plane) and have a long evolutionary career ahead of us. We must first learn how to become self-aware as individuals and slowly expand our conscious awareness as we activate and make actual our divine potential. As we expand in awareness and mastery, we increase our divine creative power and sphere of influence. The Planetary Logos ensouling Earth, for example, moved through his individual (humanlike) evolutionary process many eons ago in another system in another part of the universe. His long career has led Him to this lofty state of divine power, and yet He still has ahead of Him ascending to the level of a Solar Logos and onward from there. By the way, ensouling planets, systems, and galaxies is only one of many career paths for ascending Monads. We don't all end up ensouling planets!

The creative process is threefold: involutionary, evolutionary, and ascending. During the involutionary phase, the Monads learn how to merge with matter by slowly descending into the lowest levels of creation within the physical plane and building material forms. During the evolutionary phase, the incarnated personality working within the forms must learn how to activate the divine potential inherent within its consciousness through the auspices of cause and effect, as well as adapt the material forms it is clothing itself in until it can fully reveal its divinity in objective form.

Ascension is the process of harmonizing, integrating, balancing, and fully actuating and revealing our divinity as we move our consciousness back out of the material forms we've adopted and eventually return to pure beingness. At the completion of this divine cycle, the evolving Monad arrives at a new level of creative power and works at a new level in the universe.

At the lower individualized levels of the creation (the physically incarnated human level), we are not yet able to direct our creative forces fully in a manner that allows us to reveal our divinity objectively—or in material form. I want to point out that the evolutionary process is twofold. The evolving Monad is dealing with both the evolution of consciousness and the evolution of matter. Our consciousness evolves through our experiences in the material universe. And we in turn evolve the material substances we employ. We inherit from a previous age the matter of the system we incarnate into. As our consciousness becomes more organized, more in sync with the greater good, and more aware of our inherent divinity, we up-step the material we are working with over time. In this creative age, we are working to evolve both our consciousness and our material forms to such a degree that we may one day express and reveal ourselves as divinely loving beings in material form. We must work with the matter available to us in the system we exist within and through merging our consciousness with it, perfect it to such a state that we can exist within it and reveal ourselves without limitation. The way I see it, we are gradually working toward building vehicles of expression (bodies) that are made up of more light, and we will eventually no longer express ourselves through these dense physical bodies.

Matter is a manifestation of the third aspect of God: the Infinite Spirit. Life is a manifestation of the first aspect: the Father. And consciousness is a manifestation of the second aspect: the Son. We, the incarnated personality, are an extension of our Monad. As we grow in spiritual mastery, we activate and actuate our divinity in material form.

So, at the beginning of our creative arc into the physical plane of the universe, we are potential creators without any experience of ourselves as distinct beings yet. We have presence and intelligence, we are fully loving, and we have free will. But we have not yet individuated, even though we have each been given a unique spirit-personality and exist potentially as a specific point of view within the larger whole. Just as the newborn does not yet experience herself as separate from her mother, at our inception point in the mind of God, we exist as a unique being but do not experience ourselves as separate or distinct.

Various metaphors can help us better understand this concept:

- We exist as a note in the symphony of the spheres but know ourselves to be a part of the music as a whole.
- We exist as a spark of light in the constellations of the heavens but understand ourselves to be a part of the entire display.
- We exist as a thread in the tapestry of the universe but know ourselves to be one with the entire tapestry.
- We exist as a branch on the Tree of Life but know ourselves to be interconnected with the entire Tree.

Because we are sons of God, composed of the same trinitized creative forces as our Maker (will, love-wisdom, and active intelligence), the monadic level of our consciousness is internally driven to experience a sense of Self—a sense of its "I Am-ness." To do this, the Monad must move from the collective existential state of at-one-ment into increasingly individualized experiential states of consciousness that feel separate or distinct from the whole. And like his Maker, the Monad also individuates through extension or self-distribution into lesser (or more specific) forms. Thus, the note longs to experience its own musicality and add its own music to the symphony of the spheres. The spark longs to experience its own light and add its own constellations into the patterns of the heavens. The thread longs to weave and add its own designs into the tapestry of the universe. The branch inherently bursts with creative impulse yielding its own branches and budding with new leaves adding to the growth of the Creation. Throughout the individuation process, God the Father is expressing Himself—He is active. All His sons are God in action, God manifesting. Here in the physical level of the universe, the sons are developing the ability to reveal their full divinity in objective form.

Theosophy teaches us that once full revelation is accomplished, the creative goal for that evolutionary system is met, and the objective system flashes out of material existence. I imagine that when this happens, all the conscious beings within that system ascend and move on to higher levels within the Cosmos to continue along their evolutionary career path. The Logos ensouling that system also ascends, and the consciousness within the atomic matter of the system cycles into a passive or nonobjective state of relative rest or nonexpression until a new cycle begins. Atomically, the system departiculates as the energy of the system moves into balanced equilibrium. Duality no longer exists as the positive and negative charges merge and become once again one.

49

What this means for the human kingdom is that this inherent drive to discover and experience our own creativity slowly moves us from unity at the monadic level of consciousness into individuation at the incarnated personality levels and ultimately back to unity as a fully empowered creative Being. Throughout the entire evolution of our consciousness, the Monad remains within unity consciousness. But at the lower levels of expression, our focus moves our conscious awareness away from the collective into the individual and then, upon our return, back into the collective. We begin our individuation experience by slowly and gradually spiraling down aspects of our consciousness into matter, and then we return to unity through the process of ascension or withdrawal from matter. At the culmination of this creative cycle, we find we have developed into full-fledged Creators in our own right and sit within the Creation as mature Creators. And who knows what we do then? I imagine we start the process all over again. We, as Creator Gods, continue to add to the growth and evolution of the universe, for it is truly limitless and eternal.

This initial drive to individuate propels us to seek out the lower levels of consciousness where spirit and matter meet. This emerging desire to know Self and extend ourselves into our creative ideas is the will aspect of the Father igniting within us. And at the moment we awaken in the mind of our Creator, we enter into a state of recognition, communication, and relationship with our Father. The desire to relate, to love God and be loved by God, is the Son aspect awakening in us. As we develop our ability to express and reveal this loving nature objectively, we develop the wisdom of God. From this newly awakened

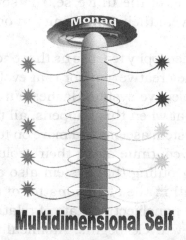

Figure 8: Multidimensional Self

desire to express and relate, we begin to create according to our own inherent design and to experience the first levels of individuality as the downward arc into material form begins. This impulse toward activity and the world of ideas is the Spirit aspect awakening within us. We become God in action. Thus, through our creative activity, lovingly applied, we learn to use our will wisely. We develop goodwill and learn how to reveal it in material form. Once committed to this process of evolution, we are restricted to this process of learning until we complete our task. As we move into more and more distinct forms, we move from our inception point in the mind of God into our multidimensional self, then our higher Self, and finally our individual human self. In this way, we move from unexpressed creative potential to expressed/applied creativity, to gain experience and evolve.

The creativity of the Monad works in the same way as its Creator—it is distributive, synthesizing, expressive, and evolving. The Monad encompasses and is the synthesizing source of life, will, and intelligence behind all human experience. On its own level of being, the Monad is the Father of the human personality. On the soul and incarnated personality levels of being, the Monad is the prodigal Son who leaves his father's home to journey into the lower three worlds of material form for the purposes of learning about his creativity and to activate his divine potential. The prodigal eventually returns to his home on the monadic plane once desire for form life is satiated and his divine virtues have been activated and developed.

Within the Monad, then, are increasingly individualized aspects of consciousness splitting off and descending into matter first as souls and then further splitting and descending into incarnated personalities.[24] In this way, the Monad is multidimensional—it exists in multiples dimensions of time

---

[24] Also called the personality-extension, the incarnated self, the human self, individual consciousness

51

and space simultaneously. We will explore these descending forms further in a moment. For now, let's continue to look at the overall creative process.

Making Choices

To move from the at-one-ment of Unity, where all possibilities exist at once, the Monad must focus its attention on specific possibilities and make a series of creative choices during its downward arc. For instance, imagine you are a bird flying in the air. Looking down, you can see the entire landscape all at once. If you want to land somewhere, however, you will have to choose a place and focus on it; you can't land everywhere. As you descend to your chosen destination, the details of the landscape become magnified and more pronounced. At the same time, the scope of what you can see becomes more limited. Furthermore, once you have chosen your destination, you have by default *not chosen* every other possible destination (for the time being.)

Elizabeth Clare Prophet[25] explained this process nicely with the following analogy. First, imagine a blank sheet of paper, and that piece of paper is God, or All That Is. As God becomes active, imagine a series of circles appearing on the paper as God begins to extend Himself into different points of expression. Each of these circles is a Monad (unit of consciousness). Notice that what is contained within the circles is the *exact same stuff* as the entire piece of paper. There is no difference in what exists within each circle; there are only different points of view. When you rest in God's unity point of view, you are fully experiencing all the points of view simultaneously. When you move your attention into just one of the circles, you are no

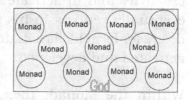

Figure 9: Monads

---

25 Prophet, Elizabeth Clare. Inner Perspectives: 6.1 Spiritual Alchemy & St. Germain.

longer directly experiencing all the other circles but are instead focusing on the experience contained within that one circle. Once again, the energy contained within that one circle is made of the same stuff the entire paper is made of; thus, you contain the exact same creative forces as your Maker: divine will, love/wisdom, and active intelligence (the Father, Son, and Spirit.) This triple force within you has the same will to extend, create, and experience.

During the downward arc, or the involutionary process, this desire motivates you to create more specific experiences (visualize smaller circles forming within the larger circle.) This process of individuation continues as you descend into matter (each of those smaller circles manifests even smaller circles.) As you narrow your attention into each smaller circle, your awareness of what that *specific* circle is experiencing grows, while your experience of the larger circles diminishes. However, at no time are you actually separate, and at no time does the life force within you cease to come directly from God. Even at the most distinct level of the smallest circle, you continue to be affected by the whole, for you are never an island.

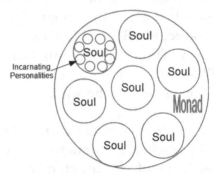

Figure 10: Souls within a Monad

I want to take a moment to point out that when you move your attention into just one of the circles on the paper, you move from *being all* to being in *relationship* with all the other circles and with the whole. In this way, we begin experiencing the love, or the Son aspect of the Trinity within us. The Father and the Son together form a *relationship* between intelligent will or intention and intelligent love or connectivity. And the Spirit aspect of God-within-us manifests and organizes the various vehicles through which we can experience this relationship objectively. We access our divine mind through the Holy Spirit (who dwells within our higher consciousness), and it is revealed through intelligent activity.

Theosophy teaches us that matter is a manifestation of the Divine Mind or Spirit aspect of God, and it is organized during this downward arc into progressively smaller units of consciousness. This drive toward individuation and differentiation continues until the units of consciousness we know of as atoms are so small and individuated that *self*-awareness is no longer possible. Thus, atoms have an inherent divine *consciousness* but not *self*-consciousness. The evolving Son must work with this energetic substance and organize it into cohesive, coherent forms that are capable of expressing a self-aware entity or personality. Thus, atoms are grouped together to form elements, and elements combine in various ways to form the minerals. Plants and then animals are formed out of these building blocks. Once an animal form is created that is sufficiently organized, developed, and evolved, the Sons of God descend into these forms and "wear" them. Thus, the human being is a Son clothed in matter. Where spirit and matter meet and merge, we begin to see the development of the soul.

Through this evolutionary process of merging with matter and developing forms that can ultimately reveal our divinity, all three of our inherent creative forces are developed and expressed in the fullness of time. *In this way, divine will intelligently expressed as love gains us the wisdom of the Creator.* You've heard the saying, "as above, so below." God, as a Trinitized force, expresses this triplicity holistically as the Creator and individually within each Monad. This pattern is repeated throughout all levels and dimensions in the Creation.

From whirling atomic particle to spiral-armed galaxy, the Creation Matrix is composed of the same pattern repeated across different scales and dimensions, uniting everything in one seamless dance, choreographed as one micro-macro movement 'in sync' with Itself.[26]

During the descent, the process of choosing more distinct points of view limits our awareness to such a relatively small field of consciousness that we eventually come to experience ourselves as quite distinct and separate from the whole. In this way, physical reality creates a plane of existence that is narrow enough for a creative entity to manifest effects that feel individual—and from those effects learn about itself. Many choices were made in the process of creating such a narrow field of play. These choices led us to focus on certain things at the expense of others, such as focusing on the lower levels of consciousness at the expense of the upper, focusing on forms rather than on energy or consciousness, and focusing on bodies rather than spirit. This focus gave us the ability to experience very specific effects, but it also caused us to lose our larger perspective to such a degree that we eventually forgot who we actually are and why we came to be here in the first place.

This is how we came to be in the position of misusing our creativity and setting our consciousness in opposition to God. Even this forgetfulness is a lesson to us about ourselves and the power of our creativity. For in the process of remembering, we deeply appreciate and understand what we are regaining for having experienced the loss of it. In this way, physical reality is our school, cause and effect is our teacher, spiritual mastery is what we are here to learn, and revealing our full divinity in objective form is our goal. Ascension is the work of reopening the lens we worked so hard to narrow in our descent. We free ourselves from the limitations of the choices we've made in the past by making new and different choices that reunite us with our God consciousness.

---

[26] Amoraea. *Divine Human Blueprint Course Manual.*

Try this on for size: First, sit quietly in a chair and focus on your breathing. Begin to move your awareness out of your body identification and into the breath. Allow yourself to see light within you, and grow that light with each in-breath until your entire body is filled with light. Begin to think of yourself as being the Light, and move your awareness more deeply into it. Now, repeat the mantra below at least three times, calmly, slowly, and with great enthusiasm and certainty:

I Am the Light of God

I Am the Love of God

I Am the Power of God

I Am the Presence of God

Wherever I Am, God is, and all is well.[27]

Before closing your eyes again, take a look at Figure 7 and allow yourself to ponder it a bit. Don't take too long but just long enough to tap your intuition. Imagine your consciousness beginning to expand from the smallest ring slowly out to the largest, stopping along the way to experience each expanding point of view. Don't worry about how to do it or if you're doing it right. This is merely an exercise to help us loosen our fixation on the smallest levels of our awareness and our habit of experiencing a sense of separation from God and from one another. Notice that you can travel in an upward spiral as you move from one ring into the next and ponder what that point of view might be like.

Close your eyes again. To help you move into the upward and ever-expanding movement of the spiral, imagine you are walking up a winding staircase. At each landing, look for a doorway. Open the door and move into the Light. Allow your

---

[27] This is my "I Am" adaptation of the Unity Prayer already noted by James Dillet Freeman.

imagination to create beautiful scenes that draw you in. You may notice a beautiful being of light and love welcoming you, or you may notice many different beings. At each stop along the way, ask for insight and for your mind to be healed of any sense of separation or aloneness.

You may eventually drift off and feel as though you've gone unconscious. That's OK. That's normal. Our mind can expand only so much at any given time, and it takes practice and persistence to build a bridge of consciousness into the higher realms. Just enjoy your experience and allow yourself to feel connected to God. Notice that you and God are one and that as you move into successive layers within the creative hierarchy, you become more interconnected to all Life, all the Creation. Allow your imagination to guide you, and have fun. When you feel complete with this meditation, generate a strong intention for establishing a "new normal" in your mind as you return your awareness to your body and to the room you're in. It's a new awareness that shifts your consciousness out of limiting definitions of self into ever-expanding definitions. Take a deep breath and fill your entire body up with golden light.

You exist within God, and God exists within you. No matter what level of the Creation you are operating within, you are ultimately connected to all the levels of consciousness within the Creation through your superconscious mind. As you open yourself up to this understanding, you discover you are not just a limited human being living in a physical body but are also a divine being.

I would like to point out that the Monad is our personal God, our personal Source of consciousness and life. Through the process of ascension (which is a series of large expansions of consciousness), we eventually integrate and merge with our monadic point of view and no longer know ourselves to be in any way separate from the whole. We do, however, take our power to manifest at the lower levels with us and remain knowledgeable about how to operate at those levels at will. As the Monad, we know ourselves to be God in action and are able to reveal our divinity in objective form. After that, we move through the higher planes of the cosmos, or the Creation. The Monads working through the human kingdom on Earth are all related to one another and work as one at the planetary level. We are a part of the collective consciousness of our Planetary Logos. He works cocreatively with His brothers (the other Planetary Logoi in our system) as a part of the collective consciousness of our Solar Logos. Our Solar Logos works with all His counterparts in the Galaxy as a part of the collective consciousness of the Galactic Logos; in turn, He works within His galactic group as a part of the collective consciousness of the Universal Logos or Creator Son. Once again, I bring this up to stress the point that we are all interconnected, and that we have different types of consciousness (individual and collective) depending on the plane of the universe we are operating on. [28]

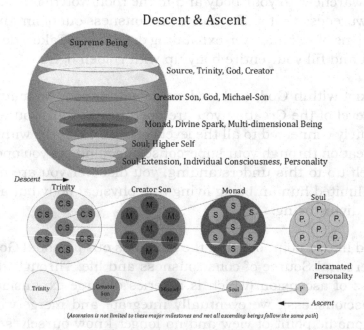

Figure 11: Descent & Ascent

---

[28] Logos: Deity, Divine entity, a deity level Son of God, a "Word" of God.

The Higher Self, Soul, and Causal Body

As we've seen, the Monad distributes itself into multiple levels of consciousness and creates various forms along the way. Each form serves as a vehicle for learning and evolving. Just as the Creator Son conceives of the Monad, the Monad in turn creates Higher Selves to express through, and each Higher Self creates extensions of consciousness that are able to incarnate into the physical planes for the same purpose. From this activity of interweaving the spiritual into the material, the soul (or causal body) is created. The experiences garnered through this weaving process create the causal plane. The purpose of the soul is to *cause* the divine potential lying dormant within the Monad to become activated and made actual through its experiences in the physical universe. The soul serves as a link between the incarnated personality and its indwelling God consciousness (the Monad).

The soul houses our creative potential during the portion of our evolutionary cycle that has to do with incarnating into physical forms, and it evolves as a result of our experiences in material form. The causal body is with us throughout our entire incarnational experience, but ultimately it is temporary. Just as all the physical bodies we live in during our various lifetimes are temporary vehicles of the soul, the causal body is a temporary vehicle of the Monad. Once all the potential housed in the soul becomes activated and actuated, the causal body is burned up, and the consciousness within it is drawn up into the Monad. In this way, the soul is an "experiential acquirement" that bridges the material mind of the incarnated personality with the higher nonmaterial mind of God.[29]

We access our God consciousness through our abstract mind or intuition. In this way, intuition is the language of the soul and connects us to the Creator and to everything in

---

[29] *Urantia*, p. 8.

the Creation. In *A Course in Miracles*, Jesus explains that it is through the active intelligence housed in our higher mind that we reconnect with the Holy Spirit within us, and through that connection we are returned or reunited with our God consciousness. This process enables us to overcome the erroneous, delusional thinking of the small self.

In sum, the soul is the body (or vehicle, or level of reality) through which the Monad dispatches specific aspects of its consciousness, known as soul-extensions, into multiple lifetimes to develop and activate all the creative potential housed there. In each lifetime, the incarnated level of the soul seeks to learn something, and it does this through the experiences of the portion of its consciousness assigned to that lifetime (i.e, the personality.) This process transforms our creativity from dormant to active, from potential to actual, and from existential to experiential.[30]

Evolution of the Soul

At the soul level, each lifetime is like a day in our life, and the soul progresses through the experiences of each lifetime. You might imagine that the soul is like a cluster of lights where each light is a latent spiritual ability requiring a level of spiritual mastery in order to turn on or become active. Our job in physical reality is to turn those lights on. This is done by learning the spiritual laws of Creation and learning how to use the creative power of our God consciousness properly.

Each lifetime offers up opportunities for spiritual growth. We face various tests, challenges, and lessons throughout our lives. When we tap into our intuition and learn how to respond from our God consciousness, we develop our spiritual capacities and grow in spiritual mastery. Any experience that fails to activate a divine quality does not affect the causal body, it only affects the personality level of activity. From

---

[30] Powell, A. E. *The Causal Body,* p. 8.

the soul's perspective, the experience either developed our divine potential or it didn't. All of our experiences are stored in our Akashic Records (which is why we can access past life memories) rather than in the causal "body," which is not really a body per se but a qualitative state of being. The records work like a library, but they are not divine mind. The causal body is more like a reservoir of latent and active divine virtues or qualities. During an incarnation, we have the opportunity to use the experiences and challenges we face to activate these virtues and express them in the dense world or fail to do so. In this way, we cannot hurt, damage, or pollute our causal body in the process of learning. We simply fail to completely activate a quality and must try again. We have a record of our experience to guide or hinder us depending upon how we relate to the information in the future. If our sense of identity is still wrapped up in the past experience, it will most likely hinder us. If we've moved out of the story and review it neutrally we may find the key to a current issue that holds a similar challenge.

Here's an example from my own life. As a child I was tormented by a recurring nightmare of being burned at the stake as a heretic by the Inquisition. This terrifying past-life memory was part of my unfinished business. This lifetime afforded me an opportunity to finish the work, but I didn't understand this for many years. My current personality subconsciously resonated with this fearful memory whenever I was in a position of wanting to speak my own truth, especially if I knew others would dislike it and particularly if it was spiritual in nature. When I realized this was an unresolved past-life experience that I needed to heal, I was able to move beyond the terror the previous personality experienced into the point of view of the soul. In meditation, I followed my spirit out of the "dead" body and merged with a higher level of being that filled my heart with unconditional love and forgiveness for everybody involved in the experience. I felt an especially deep compassion for the men who hated me so much they took pleasure in watching the pain and fear the personality experienced. I saw how terribly afraid and disconnected they were from love. Once I moved into this impersonal soulful place, the qualities of unconditional love, forgiveness, and compassion grew in the causal body. In that lifetime, those qualities were activated but not actuated on the dense plane. In this lifetime, I was able to access those qualities and learn how to bring them all the way through to the personality level.

Once we have learned our lessons, we are at last able to graduate from the school of physical reality. All that mastery is then employed directly by the Monad either in the worlds of dense form or elsewhere. This process takes many eons from our point of view because we understand things linearly and within the context of time passing. But spiritually, it is all happening here and now from the point of view of All That Is, or Source, which exists outside time and space. Thus, from the macrocosmic point of view, the continuity of life and consciousness is unbroken as one looks out into the evolving universes of time and space. Once again, as we climb up through the expanding levels of consciousness, we experience ever-widening at-one-ment within the greater field of life. This means, for instance, that at some higher point in our consciousness, we *know* that we and Jesus are *one*. We become fully aware that we exist within the Christ consciousness, and this consciousness exists within us. The same is true for Buddha and other great teachers, enlightened ones, angels, and ascended masters throughout the world religions. At the enlightened level of consciousness, we are one with the universe. We see clearly and know no separation from God and all God's creations. The purpose of the soul is to help us learn about creativity and the power of our minds. Everything we do and think teaches us our reality. When we align our minds with the inherent God consciousness within us, we begin to create according to God's plan, and we learn how to reveal our divinity. When this happens, Spirit is able to extend outward into physical reality unimpeded; God's creative design flows into the Monad, the Monad flows into the Higher Self at the soul level, and the Higher Self flows into the world through the incarnated personality via the soul. We evolve, the soul evolves, the Monad evolves, and God evolves through this experience.

What we choose to do with our consciousness in the lower three worlds is up to us; we have free will. We can pretend that we are not God and continue to create a false self to believe in and experience ourselves as separate from God if we want to. Or we can awaken to our divinity and set about aligning our consciousness with our soul purpose for this lifetime. It's up to us. What do we want to manifest? Do we want to manifest a life set in opposition to and/or ignorance of our God-self or a life restored to God's will which is, of course, ultimately our will, too? When we choose the latter, we begin to create the necessary pole-shift out of the man-made self that sits in apparent isolation from the spiritual self. As each individual does this, the collective whole—including humanity and all the lower kingdoms[31]—is healed. When we understand this, we realize that what we do with our life, with our creativity, and with our love affects not just ourselves and those around us but the Whole of humanity. A new level of spiritual ethics enters into our consciousness. In short, we transform our entire world.

As we've seen, within our own beingness we can trace our existence back to our inception point within the mind of God. The consciousness assigned to this physical lifetime is but one aspect of a much larger, multidimensional self that rests within an even larger entity, and so on. Even at our smallest, we have within us components of the Father, Son, and Spirit. We have will, we have love, and we have intellect. We have the ability to evolve, express, feel, experience, and think. We are creators and cocreators. We are, each of us, a unique creative expression of God, connected to everything and everyone yet

---

[31]   Lower kingdoms: 1) mineral, 2) plant, 3) animal. Middle kingdom: 4) human. Higher kingdoms: 5) Kingdom of Heaven (souls), 6) Monadic, 7) Logic.

sustain an "I Am" status within the universe, within the heart and mind of the Living God.

The Incarnated Personality

The personality level of creative activity is produced by an extension of lifeforce energy from the Monad and an extension of consciousness from the soul into the matter of the lower three planes producing the dense physical form, emotional sensitivity, and self-awareness. From one perspective it is accurate to say that each Child of God has one life if we understand this Child to be the Monad rather than the personality or even the soul. The Monad is the informing life of all that cycles into and out of apparent form on the physical plane. It produces consciousness on the mental plane and we call this soul. The soul is the source of consciousness of all that cycles into and out of apparent form on the planes below it. The personality is the meeting place of the consciousness of matter, the consciousness of mind, and the energy of life. It is here that life, mind, and form precipitate tangible expressions in a cyclical manner (which we call lifetimes) in accordance with the laws of the physical plane. Therefore, all of the personality "lifetimes" generated by the soul are cycles of creative activity pertaining to the same one life of the Monad. All of these lifetimes contribute to the cumulative activation, actuation, and revelation of divine qualities in the lowest, most individualized dimension of the cosmos – the dense physical. Over the course of an immeasurable amount of time (from our perspective,) the creative process we call reincarnation enables the Monad to eventually reveal its divinity in tangible form. This happens when the personality awakens and merges first with the soul and then with the monadic level of being. This awakening occurs through a specific series of initiations that are spread out over many lifetimes. Once the personality has established a continuity of consciousness with the Monad, new levels of creative activity open up and the Monad is free to move into higher levels of cosmic activity.

In practical terms, each personality experiences its lifetime as a separate experience from other lifetimes. And this is because the consciousness extending from the soul into the personality level of experience in any given lifetime is not exactly the same. The soul, being the first point of unity, is the aspect that maintains a continuity of awareness of all the personality lifetimes. Each new incarnation entails the manifestation of completely new vehicles of expression, thus the etheric-physical, astral-emotional, and lower mental bodies are definitely different from those manifested in previous incarnations. And, the extension of ego-consciousness streaming forth through the vehicles is particular to the current life.

Let's start by envisioning the soul as a bucket of developing spiritual intelligence. The bucket is the repository of the soul's activated spiritual abilities and qualities (all that has been developed,) and the soul's capacity (all that is possible but not yet active.) Each of the personality lives of the soul is a new and different dipperful of consciousness from the same bucket. Each particular scoop of soul consciousness sent into incarnation will include a unique combination of abilities and capacity (untapped potential.) Abilities will show up in the personality as talents, skills, and natural inclinations. The challenges the new personality faces in that particular life will indicate where development is needed. Over time, the bucket of soul intelligence becomes more highly developed and usually more well-rounded. Consequently, the scoops (lifetimes) do too. As a result, later incarnations reveal higher levels of spiritual mastery and coordination.

When the soul is ready to initiate a new personality life, a plan is formulated that will set the odds in favor of catalyzing in the personality the development of the intended soul qualities. The vehicles are designed to support the chances the desired growth can occur. And circumstances of birth into particular familial, ethnic, gender, and national lines are considered so that the highest probability is set to support the spiritual intention of the soul. All of this is part of the greater evolutionary plan for humanity as a whole. We are learning individually and collectively how to reveal the divinity of the soul and later the Monad in the lower three worlds.

To understand this idea of gifts and challenges further, we must understand the purpose of incarnation. In a nutshell, we are here to have experiences that will prompt us to activate our divine potential. Here in the world of duality, these experiences will be both positive and negative. When we understand that only the experiences that activate our divine potential have value to the evolving soul, we realize that the way we handle the challenges of our life is of the utmost importance. The way we think and behave—in essence, the focus of our attention in our life—creates certain effects spiritually. When the challenges in our lives serve to bring out our God consciousness, we find ourselves living in accordance with divine will and activating and developing our creative potential. Only the consciousness that comes up to a divine expression is absorbed back into the soul on the upper mental plane when we transition out of the physical body at death.

What is pertinent here is the understanding that all of the circumstances in our lives hold the seeds for spiritual development, each life serves a purpose, and there is an overall plan for our evolution that we can count on. Theosophy teaches us that through a long series of lives, man develops his three innate spiritual gifts: intelligence, love-wisdom, and will. First he acquires knowledge of physical life, physical love, and physical sacrifice. Once this knowledge is sufficiently in development, man begins to develop an awareness of love. He begins to cultivate a higher type of emotional intelligence (empathy, compassion, forgiveness, etc.,) and altruistic or unselfish love emerges. Also, aspiration, ideals, and a willingness to make intelligent sacrifices based on love comes into play. The first two evolutionary phases occur over an extremely long series of lifetimes. The final evolutionary phase is relatively short in comparison to the first two and deals with the development of divine will through sacrifice. In this phase, man learns to use his intelligence to dominate his lower nature, employ his will to lovingly be of service to others, and ultimately learns to sacrifice all that is currently known and loved to awaken to a higher state of beingness. [32]

The personality, then, is the most individualized level of creative activity. While it is a part of the monadic expression, in terms of consciousness and will, the personality operates independently of both the soul and the Monad until the path of return is undertaken. The personality has will, the ability to love, and the ability to think. It is free to create according to its own desires on the dense, astral, and lower mental planes of the cosmic physical plane. It learns about the quality of its desire-thinking through its experience with the results it produces. Through this process of cause and effect, soul qualities are eventually stimulated and consciousness evolves.

Before we go on to explore the incarnational process in greater detail, let's pause to consider the fact that healing from pain and suffering is not only possible for us but the personality can actually awaken to the soul and eventually move into that point of view. Once this is accomplished, that same soul-identified personality can continue to expand its awareness and eventually merge with the mighty I Am Presence of the Monad. This process of expansion into the soul and later into monadic consciousness is called ascension by some and initiation by others and it occurs in definite stages in a particular order. A critical factor in turning the personality towards the soul and onto the path of return is the dawning recognition that what it thinks and feels determines the quality of its experience. We'll be exploring this turning point in greater detail as we go along. For now, we can trust that

---

[32]   Cf. Bailey, *A Treastise on Cosmic Fire*, pp. 820-824

Janet Myatt

there is an overarching plan; a divine blueprint is encoded
within each of us and in humanity and the planet as a whole.
We can learn to make sense of things, we are learning how
to love, and we shall learn how to surrender our individual
will to the greater will of God. When we open our hearts and
minds to the peace, love, and intelligence of something greater
than ourselves, we discover first hand that there is no real
separation.

68

Chapter 2 Exercises

1. What happens to your sense of identity when you consider the idea that God exists within you personally and exists in all things without separation?
   - What changes occur in your consciousness when you consider this idea?
   - What happens to your sense of responsibility for your creativity and your impact on the world around you?
2. What is your understanding of the difference between the existential and experiential aspects of God?
   - How does this affect your understanding of your part and purpose in the universe?
3. What shifts within you as you consider the evolutionary nature of the Creation and the experiential aspect of God?
   - Does your idea of God change in any way?
   - How does this affect your relationship with God or your sense of the Divine?
   - Does your relationship with yourself change in any way?
4. What comes up for you when you consider the idea of a hierarchy of beings and the resulting concept of multiple levels of Deity expression ranging from the Supreme Being and other superuniversal beings and on down to human beings?
5. Can you imagine moving your sense of yourself into your purely spiritual aspect—the Formless One who creates forms, the Monad, the purely God-self?
   - What happens when you attempt to do this?
   - What ideas pop into your head?
   - What emotions get stirred up?
   - What beliefs get stimulated?
6. Monad, soul, personality—what purposes do you see each of these levels of creative activity serve?

CHAPTER 3 ~ INCARNATION

Incarnation is a creative process. It involves the manipulation by Spirit of energy, force, matter, and consciousness. When considering the incarnational process, it's helpful to gain an understanding of these factors and how they work together. Theosophists use the word *Spirit* to refer to that quality of deity that is a self-directed intelligent force and energy— that is, *That* which manifests, enlivens, and ensouls matter. Matter has its own sort of intelligence; it is responsive to and expressive of the Life force inherent within it, but it is not "self-aware" in the manner that human consciousness is. Human consciousness is a state that arises from the merger of spirit and matter. It is the result of the relationship between the two. The Monad (intelligent Life) enlivens matter (intelligent substance) and gives rise to the soul (active consciousness).

The creative process is happening all the time. We are creating our life every moment of the day, but we are mostly doing this unconsciously. We create, but we don't know *how* we create. This is because the human kingdom is the first (when looking from the lowest to the highest) to move into any kind of individualized conscious awareness, and we are still developing this gift. For instance, minerals form; plants grow; and animals are born, live, and die. All that creative living is done without individual self-awareness. Likewise, much of our human creativity is also taking place unconsciously. We're born, we age, we die, and we don't really know how this process came to be. Physically, our hearts pump, our lungs pull in air and push it out again, our brain processes stimuli, and we don't have to think about these things to make it so. Emotionally, we feel and respond; mentally, we think and form conclusions. But we don't know how all this works together. When it comes to understanding the mechanics of the creative process, we are still mostly operating in the dark.

This has given rise to many superstitions, false assumptions, wishful thinking, and other misunderstandings as we consciously strive to make sense of our experience. Science has made significant contributions in the past four hundred years and has done much to move us out of superstitious befuddlement, yet it has also "thrown the baby out with the bathwater" by focusing solely on the physical *effects* of creativity and blindly overlooking the spiritual *cause* in their investigative processes. Science is doing a great job of investigating the garment of God but completely ignoring That which created the garment and dwells within it. Nonetheless, much is gained in investigating the material "effects" of God's creativity, as it does drive one ever onward in search of the next underlying cause. Quantum physics is a fine example of science finally coming up against spirit and being forced to open that door.

So, how does the creative process of life in form work? How did we get here, and what are we doing? I won't begin to pretend that I know the answers to these questions, but I will endeavor to pass along some of the things I've learned and discovered about the creative process that have made a substantial impact on my ability to work more consciously as the creator of my life.

Translating Thought into Matter

Let's take a look at the process in terms of energy first. As we discussed in chapter 1, the creative *qualities* of God are triple: will, love, and intelligence. On the energy side of things, this correlates with force and forward momentum, attraction-repulsion and spiral-cyclical movement, and activity and rotational spin.

Father	Will	Force	Forward momentum
Son	Love	Attraction-repulsion	Spiral-cyclical
Spirit	Intelligence	Activity	Rotational spin

However, the *process* of creativity is dual.

- existential/experiential
- self/nonself
- spirit/matter
- active/dormant
- creative/destructive
- objective/subjective

Alice Bailey teaches us in her book *A Treatise on Cosmic Fire*[33] *that in the physical levels of the cosmos, it is the merging of the two opposite polarities of spirit* (positive polarity) with *matter* (negative polarity) that produces the evolving *son* (balanced charge). These two creative polarities of God merge together to reveal God in action, God in objective form.[34]

The masculine polarity of God is the electrically positive, active, assertive, and mobilizing aspect of God. It is the animating force that transforms the unmanifest to manifest, transforms what is potential into what is actual, and externalizes what is internal. In the atom of science, it is the positive nucleus. It is symbolized by the blade, or the upward-pointing triangle, as it is the rising force of will, love, and intelligence in action. The act of self-distribution that results in a Big Bang illustrates the masculine principle. God assertively distributes Himself into His sons, and the sons, in turn, distribute themselves into their various vehicles of expression. In terms of force, this is understood as forward movement.

---

[33] Bailey. *A Treastise on Cosmic Fire* (ATCF).

[34] In this sentence the word *spirit* refers to the Monad – the non-material Entity Who is a self-directing intelligent force and contains the energy of all three creative aspects. The word *matter* refers to the field of divine energy impregnated with intelligence but not with self-directing will.

The feminine polarity of God is the electrically negative, receptive, fertile, and generative aspect of God. It is the "mother" aspect of God, which produces the building blocks we need to precipitate forms. It is that which is bountiful, generous, plentiful, fertile, and nurturing. It is also the receptive aspect of God. On the form side of things, it is matter or the material building blocks of the universe. It is that which gives form to the thoughts the Thinker desires to express. When considering the atom of science, it is the electrons that orbit around the positive nucleus of any atom. In terms of force, this is understood as rotational spin. As a whole, these energetic building blocks of the Infinite Spirit exist in the Cosmos either in dormancy or in activity depending on whether the Father is in an active phase or a dormant phase of creativity. The feminine principle, symbolized by the chalice or the downward-pointing triangle, provides the receptacle or container for Spirit. It is the womb of life.

On the microcosmic level, the masculine, positive nucleus of an atom is the positive directing agent, and the feminine, negative electrons are receptive to the pattern being generated by the nucleus. Together, the two aspects precipitate the appearance of the atom—the form. This phenomenon of giving and receiving of positive and negative, of masculine and feminine, is referred to in esoteric writings as the Cosmic Marriage and also as the divine Hermaphrodite. We have seen that at each successive stage of the creative process in the Cosmos, this giving and receiving is reiterated. The microcosm is a reflection of the macrocosm. The divine parent (+) gives life and consciousness to His creations. His children, then, are the receivers (–). Each divine child from the mighty Creator Son to the human being in turn becomes the parent who gives life and consciousness to His creations. Thus, each succeeding unit of consciousness has both the positive and the negative attributes of creativity.

73

Janet Myatt

The Chakra System

So, let's zoom out a bit and take a look at how we build the forms we live in. This leads us into an exploration of the chakra system.

First of all, what is a chakra?

Basically, chakras are energy centers that run along the spine and up into the head. To a clairvoyant, these energy centers often look like spinning wheels of light. These spinning vortexes or wheels of energy create an electromagnetic force field within, and radiating out from, the body. This force field is called an aura.

What does the chakra system do?

The chakra system is a creative mechanism by which our Spirit is able to translate our thoughts and desires into form. To understand this, we need to reorient our thinking about who we are in relationship to our bodies, emotions, and thoughts. For the most part, we human beings tend to assume that we are our bodies and that it is the body that gives us life and identity. We also tend to believe that what we sense and feel is who we are. We think, "This is how I feel, so this is who I am." We also think we are our thoughts. "This is what I think, this is what I believe; therefore, this is who I am." But we are not our physical bodies, we are not our emotions, and we are not our thoughts. We are Spirit—the Formless One—who creates forms. We are the experiential quality of God that senses and responds—the mighty I AM. And we are the Thinker who has thoughts and ideas.

So, think about this idea for a moment. You have a house or a dwelling of some sort, right? And you live in that house and take care of it. It protects you and gives you comfort. But clearly you know that you are not your house. You are *you*, and you *live in* your house. It's not who you are. Extending our

74

metaphor further, you have a car. It allows you to get around in the world; it gets you from point A to point B. But again it's clear to you that *you* are not your car. You *have* a car. The same principle holds true regarding our bodies, or vehicles of expression here in the lower three worlds of:

- Objective appearance,
- Sentient response, and
- Intellectual activity.

We have three bodies or vehicles to express our creativity through, but we remain the nonphysical dweller within. These vehicles are

- The physical-etheric body,
- The astral-emotional body, and
- The mental body.

As we talked about in chapter 2, the soul on its own plane—the upper mental plane—sends an extension of itself into the lower worlds. Over many lifetimes, it learns how to appropriate each of these energy bodies and integrate them into a coordinated, dynamic, effective personality whole. Once this process is in good working order, the integrated personality takes on the task of connecting consciously with the indwelling soul. This contact leads ultimately to a conscious merging of the personality with the soul on its own plane. Once the soul-identified personality is in place, we seek conscious connection with the indwelling Monad and begin the second great merging process, ultimately to become a fully revealed Son of God in material form. This is an extraordinarily long evolutionary process. Because of this, it has been easy for us at the personality level to lose sight of the larger process we're involved in and to overidentify with our forms of expression, losing our sense of our true spiritual self in the process.

So, as we explore the energy side of things a bit more, let's work with the understanding that energy follows thought. The *thoughts* of the indwelling creative entity create the blueprints that the atoms conform to. Our thoughts create the patterns, and energy flows through the patterns to generate forms. It is in this way that spirit is able to build and embody forms. Let us further understand that energy is the effect or the activity of spirit. (I think that's an important point to ponder for a moment to see what comes forward in your mind.)

Setting up our train of thought here: Our thoughts create energetic blueprints, and the intelligent energy in matter responds to these blueprints to reveal them in objective forms. This includes both dense forms (e.g., our physical body) and subjective or immaterial forms (e.g., our emotional responses and mental programming). The magnetic desire energy creates the electromagnetic pull that attracts the appropriate grades of matter needed to produce the objective forms that allow us to experience what we're thinking and feeling.

What we think and feel is very important to the creative process; after all, everything is energy, and energy follows thought. The divine Thinker (the Monad) is the architect, the soul is the builder, and the bodies are the temples we produce. The personality is the sum total of the consciousness working within the temples—the vehicles of expression. It emerges out of the creative process as a self-conscious entity or unit of self-directing, sentient, creative activity.

Chakras, or energy centers, are the means through which thought is translated into form. They are the energetic avenues through which energy or force is directed by the Spirit into the lower material worlds. The rotational movement of these energy centers creates the necessary magnetic pull to attract matter and produce manifestation.

The next thing we need to know is that there are various grades of matter in the physical plane of the universe. They

76

aren't just the dense physical matter we're all familiar with—the atom of science. Rather, there are also more subtle forms of atomic matter that traditional science has not yet been able to detect. For our purposes here, we need to understand that in addition to dense matter, there is etheric, astral, and mental matter—all are progressively more subtle than dense matter. The various bodies or forms we use in the physical world to experience our life here on Earth are composed of these various types of matter.

The etheric body is the underlying energy body of the dense physical body and is composed of a certain grade of etheric matter called the Fourth Cosmic Ether. As the energetic counterpart of the dense physical body, the etheric body substands the dense body and provides the scaffolding on which the dense form is precipitated. It is the conduit of life energy that animates the body. Without it, there can be no life in the dense body.

Our emotional-sentient body is called the astral body and is composed of a subtler form of astral matter. The mental body—both the lower concrete mind and the higher abstract mind—is composed of even subtler mental matter. Now, the mental body is not to be confused with the brain, which is the dense physical counterpart of the mind. There are even higher and more subtle types of matter in our physical universe, but we'll limit our discussion to these three types for now. The chakra system is composed of these three types of subtle matter. Each body of consciousness has a corresponding chakra system, and these chakras are all interdependent and interpenetrating.

Once again, it is not the body that is the *source* of expression but rather the Spirit. And the chakra system is generated by the activity of the Spirit as it merges with matter.[35] The level of organization and integration of the chakra system in any

---

[35] Bailey. *Esoteric Psychology II*, p. 64.

given person gives us insight into the evolutionary stage—or relative spiritual age, if you will—of that person. Through the evolutionary process, mankind is learning how to reveal its innate subjective divinity in objective form. The coordination and eventual mastery of the relationship or interplay between the consciousness of spirit and the consciousness of matter is the creative process of the human kingdom. We are the bridge between the spiritual and material aspects of divinity.

I think the most important points to understand from our discussion of the interplay of spirit, consciousness, and matter are the following:

- We are not our bodies or even our emotions and ideas.
- What we are thinking and feeling directly affects not only the quality of our experience but also the quality of the forms we dwell within.
- We are learning from this process how to become enlightened creators.
- We learn from both what goes well and what doesn't.
- We are up-stepping the responsive quality of matter by working with it. And working with matter is helping us develop and improve the quality of our contact with the greater field of Life both in terms of consciousness and in terms of the forms we can build. Matter and consciousness are both learning how to reveal love— the second divine aspect of God.

We will explore these points in greater detail in Part II when we take a look at the rise of the ego in human consciousness. So, stay tuned!

Involution and Evolution

Over many eons, the Earth plane was created. A range of spiritual teachings such as Christianity, Judaism, Theosophy, and *The Urantia Book* (to name a few) all teach that creation happened in stages. In truth, it continues to happen in stages. From our human standpoint, these stages are so long that it's impossible for us to observe them as they're happening. Clearly, the history of our planetary development is too long and involved for me recount it here (even if I knew it). But it can help us arrive at a better understanding of our current situation if we have at least some broad idea of the larger process we're a part of. Thus, we're going to take a brief look at three broad developmental phases: involution, evolution, and ascension.

OK, let's start with the form side of things. Remember that the Infinite Spirit (also known as the Third Logos and Active Intelligence) is the aspect of the Trinity that manipulates energy into the creative playgrounds (or fields of expression) within which the Monads can fulfill their evolutionary purpose. Both Theosophy and *The Urantia Book* teach us that in our part of the universe within the physical plane (the lowest or most dense plane of the Cosmos), the first creative task was to create a system that contained the necessary building blocks for evolving and sustaining intelligent life. This is a vast and complicated topic, and many books have been written on the subject. To keep things as simple as possible, let me say that the material development of life on Earth may have gone roughly something like this: God, in the aspect of the Third Logos, stimulated the preexistent building blocks of the universe and initiated the properties called inertia, mobility, and rhythm. These building blocks are a manifestation of the Third Logos, and they are stimulated and "enlivened" by this same aspect of deity. This infusion caused matter to move out of a stable equilibrium of rest into an unstable disequilibrium of continual motion. This motion set the energy of matter into play and caused the various parts within the system to begin to interact with one another. This first creative outpouring entered into the solar system as Fohat, or electricity, and enlivened the pregenetic primordial substance of the universe, giving Life to the atomic matter of our solar system.

Once intelligent matter came into manifestation, a second creative wave poured out from the Second Logos, the Son of God. Energetically, this quality of deity shows up as magnetism. It is that which draws to together opposite poles. Spirit, the formless aspect of God, holds the positive charge, and matter holds the negative charge. The love aspect of deity establishes the magnetic pull between the two charges. Once these two charges are brought close to one another, a magnetic phenomenon is induced, producing heat and light and resulting in the manifestation of the objective solar system. In this way, the solar system is an outward expression of the Son. Alice Bailey writes the following in *A Treatise on Cosmic Fire*:

> *When the two electric poles are brought into definite relationship we have...both heat and light. This relationship is brought about and perfected during the evolutionary process. This heat and light are produced by the union of the two poles, or by the occult marriage of male and female, of Spirit (father) and matter (mother). In terms of the physical, this union produces the objective solar system, the Son of the Father and the Mother.*[36]

In phase one, deity bestows a basic level of organization on matter in the form of inertia, mobility, and rhythm. These same building blocks have the latent ability to respond. In phase two, deity establishes the next organizing principle of magnetism, causing the moving bits of matter to move into specific patterns yielding light, heat, and ultimately a variety of forms.

On our planet, the evolutionary process proceeded in the following order. First, atomic matter was formed into the elemental or mineral kingdom. Then, the plant kingdom was developed; after that, the animal kingdom. Theosophy teaches us that all this activity and development first happened in

---

[36] Bailey. *ATCF*, p.228

a solar system previous to our current system (the first and second creative outpourings). The creative mandate for that system was to imbue matter with an innate intelligence or level of consciousness that could sustain Life and respond to the creative demands of spirit. The involutionary process of merging spirit with matter, and the evolutionary process of developing it over eons, yielded a tremendous amount of diversification and differentiation as streams of Life descended and moved into the various kingdoms, dividing and subdividing, developing into successively more complex life-forms.[37] This process continued until an animal form emerged that was sophisticated enough to express an individualized self-awareness. In this way, over an enormously long period, the human *form* eventually emerged out of the animal kingdom, and a vehicle of expression through which Spirit could manifest as a *self-aware personality* became possible.

---

[37] Involution: A period devoted to carrying the Life impulse of the Monads lower and deeper into denser matter until material forms are finally possible. The creative goal of the involutionary phase is the development of forms (or vehicles of expression) that can attain self-consciousness.

Evolution: A period devoted to the development of consciousness and form culminating in a balancing of the energies of consciousness and form within the creative unit.

Ascension (also called Initiation): A period consisting of large expansions of consciousness whereby spirit is liberated from the limitations of form.

| The First Creative Outpouring stems from the *Third* Logos ||
Form Side	Consciousness Side
Motion *Rotational Spin* Results in the activation of the material building blocks needed to build the bodies of all forms. This wave of creativity infuses atomic substance with a capacity for basic intelligent activity and puts matter into motion.	*Mind. Intelligence. Activity.* Our ability to adapt physically, emotionally, and mentally. Human intelligence as seen in the development of the rational and abstract mind.
The Second Outpouring stems from the *Second* Logos	
Magnetism *Spiral-cyclical Movement* Creates the avenue through which matter is ensouled and woven into different kingdoms and countless forms. Energetically, it is the source of Prana or Vitality, which animates the dense physical body. At the phenomenal level it is seen in the activity of magnetic attraction and repulsion. Spirit draws to itself the atomic matter it needs to create the vehicles of expression. The Monad is the architect. The Soul is the builder. And the incarnated personality is adapter.	*Love-Wisdom, or intelligent love.* Manifests as the Christ Principle in the higher mind of man, and as aspiration in our astral-emotional nature. This quality of deity ultimately gives us the ability to experience at-one-ment. It is the quality (latent at first) that precipitates the comprehension of expanding *Wholenesses*. For instance, the personality is *greater* than the sum of its physical, emotional, and mental parts. It is something in and of itself, which contains and is informed by these lesser parts.
The Third Outpouring stems from the *First* Logos	
Synthesis and Revelation *Forward movement, momentum* The impulse to express Life – to create, destroy, and reveal. The ability to form a material entity by combining parts or elements into a single or unified whole.	*Will. Power. Force.* The impulse to express Life – to create and reveal. The ability to synthesize.

Figure 12: Creative Outpourings

Once we had a high-enough animal form to work with—one with the latent potential to comprehend the presence of a self-conscious being within—the third great outpouring or wave of creativity took place.[38] This outpouring allowed the soul to individuate within a human being, and a distinct sense of "self" arose within the human consciousness. Theosophists refer to this stage in the evolutionary process as "individuation." At this point, the human experience began. Powell writes the following:

> *The process of subdivision continues until, at the end of the first great stage of evolution, it is finally divided into individualities, i.e., into men, each being a separate and distinct soul, though at first, of course, an undeveloped soul.*[39]

The Sons of God now have a life-sustaining environment into which they can incarnate or move from subjective experience to objective. As they clothe themselves in matter, the causal (or soul) body begins to develop. So, the third organizing principle is human consciousness as it moves through its developmental phases. The etheric body correlates with the first creative outpouring. It is the organization of energy into a life-generating pattern from which the dense body is precipitated. The astral-emotional body correlates with the second outpouring. It is the desire body. Energetically, it is the generator of the drawing power that precipitates forms. It is the *pulling force* that draws substance into a particular pattern to reveal the desire-thoughts of spirit in some tangible manner. The mental body corresponds to the third outpouring that resulted in individualization. The mind is that which

---

[38] This process occurred over many millions of years and happened in waves. For instance, our current mineral kingdom is the manifestation of a newer wave of incoming divine Life relative to ours. The current plant kingdom is a more-evolved wave than the current mineral kingdom but emerged from the *previous* mineral kingdom. The animal kingdom is a higher evolution of a previous plant kingdom, and our human kingdom is a higher evolution of a previous animal kingdom. Keep in mind we are talking about only the matter side of things right now, not the consciousness side of things.

[39] Powell. *The Causal Body*, p. 12.

divides, discerns, discriminates, learns, and knows. Self-awareness is anchored in the mind. Figure 12 on page 82 provides a quick outline of the three creative outpourings in terms of form and consciousness.

Why is this process necessary?

The Monadic level of consciousness exists in a pre-personal state of unity or at-one-ment with the entire Creation. It does not know separation or individuality per se. But through this involutionary and evolutionary process, Monads are able to create an experience of differentiation or separation in the lower planes of expression for the purposes of experiencing, activating, and actuating their divine qualities in response to their experience. The involutionary phase encompasses the descent of spirit into matter. The evolutionary phase encompasses the development of self-awareness and the evolution of consciousness. Ascension—or the Path of Return—is the point where the personality as the prodigal son turns back toward the Father and slowly expands out of the limitations of form identification. Desire for life in the lower worlds declines, and a rising aspiration to reunite with God develops. The moment conscious contact with the indwelling soul is experienced, the aspiration to return is stimulated, and entry to the Path becomes eminent. Reunification is achieved through a series of great expansions of consciousness and happens in a stepwise manner.

Building the Forms

The spirits involved in creating physical reality didn't individually embody the physical forms they were developing as incarnated personalities or self-aware individual units of consciousness until the human form was ready. Instead, they worked within their larger Monadic groups, slowly building and differentiating the group souls that formed the lower kingdoms (elemental, mineral, plant, and animal). Individualized incarnation began with the human experience.

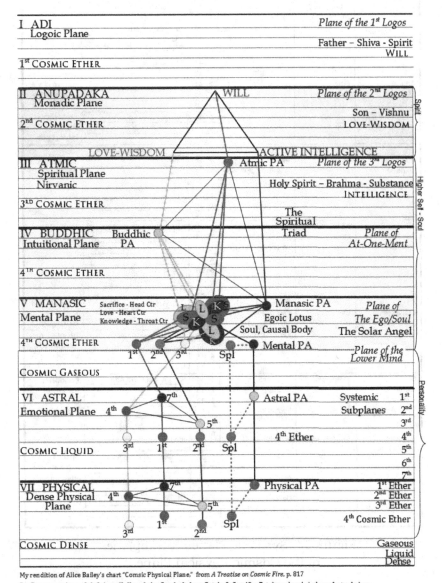

My rendition of Alice Bailey's chart "Comsic Physical Plane," from *A Treatise on Cosmic Fire*, p. 817

PA=Permanent Atom; Spl=Spleen; K=Knowledge Petals; L=Love Petals; S=Sacrifice Petals ; colored circles refer to chakras

Figure 13: The Cosmic Physical Plane

Cosmic Physical Plane	Cosmic Energy	Aspect or Quality	Sub-plane	Qualitative Aspect & Type of Energy Expressing	Aspect Emanating
1st Adi	1st Cosmic Ether Atomic	1ST LOGOS Deity Father Pure Spirit	1 49	Adi|Atomic|1st Ether	
			2 48	Monadic|Sub-atomic|2nd E	
			3 47	Atmic|3rd Ether	
			4 46	Buddhic|4th Ether	
			5 45	Manasic|Gaseous	
			6 44	Astral|Liquid	
			7 43	Physical|Dense	
2nd Anupadaka Monadic	2nd Cosmic Ether Sub-Atomic	2ND LOGOS Son, Vishnu, Spirit	1 42		The Monad on its own plane as pure spirit a Trinity of will, love-wisdom, active intelligence
			2 41		
			3 40		
			4 39		
			5 38		
			6 37		
			7 36		
3rd Atmic Spiritual Nirvanic	3rd Cosmic Ether	3RD LOGOS Infinite Spirit, Brahma, Substance Active Intelligence	1 35	Atmic Perm Atom	Spiritual Triad: Will
			2 34		
			3 33		
			4 32		
			5 31		
			6 30		
			7 29		
4th Buddhic Intuitional	4th Cosmic Ether	Central At-one-ment	1 28	Buddhic Perm Atom	Spiritual Triad: Love-wisdom
			2 27		
			3 26		
			4 25		
			5 24		
			6 23		
			7 22		
5th Manasic (Mental)	Cosmic Gaseous	Soul Causal Body Higher Mind Personality Lower Mind	1 21	Manasic Perm Atom	Spiritual Triad: Active Intelligence
			2 20		
			3 19		
			4 18	Mental Unit	Personality Mental Body or unit
			5 17		
			6 16		
			7 15		
6th Astral (Emotional)	Cosmic Liquid	Emotions Desire Sentience	1 14	Astral Perm Atom	Personality Astral-emotional Body
			2 13		
			3 12		
			4 11		
			5 10		
			6 09		
			7 08		
7th Dense Physical	Cosmic Dense	Etheric Activity Dense	1 07	Physical Perm Atom	Personality Physical-etheric body
			2 06		
			3 05		
			4 04		
			5 03		
			6 02		
			7 01		

Figure 14: Systemic Planes & Subplanes
of the Cosmic Physical Plane

For the human Monads, the first order of differentiation happened in the superconscious levels of our minds on what the Theosophists call the Atmic, Buddhic, and Manasic planes of existence. These three planes (or dimensions of time and space) are the home of the Spiritual Triad. The Triad is the first order of creative activity of the Monad as it begins to "involve" itself with matter. The Monad dwells on the Monadic plane (also called the Anupadaka plane), which is a type of deity-level existence.[40] (See Figure 14 p. 86) The Atmic, Buddhic, and upper Manasic planes comprise the fields of higher consciousness where our divine Self is actively creating for the duration of our sojourn through the Cosmic Physical Plane of the Cosmos. It is on these levels the Monad initiates the process of building vehicles of expression.

The Manasic (or mental) plane is the meeting ground between the Monad and the incarnating personality and is the dwelling place of the soul. It is the highest of the three lower planes of human consciousness. (The other two are the Astral and Dense planes.) As you can see, the Spiritual Triad actually dips into the field of human endeavor through the mind (at the higher abstract levels of the soul).

The Monad produces an energy center on the Atmic, Buddhic, and Manasic planes to form the Spiritual Triad (also called the upper triad) from which a lower triad is eventually built to produce the lower bodies of man.[41]

---

[40] Wikipedia definitions: *Adi*: Sanskrit (Skt.) word meaning "first." First cause; unity; the unchanging reality. In the Paradise Trinity, it is the Infinite Father or that aspect of God that extends beyond the physical plane of the Cosmos and ensouls the Grand Universe of All That Is. *Anupadaka* (Skt.) means "self-existing." In Theosophy, it has to do with the first effect of the first cause. For me, this translates as the "Son of God"-level of consciousness or the purely divine Self. *Atma* (Skt.) means "inner self" or "soul." The true Self of an individual beyond identification with phenomena. In Theosophical terms, I interpret this as the first level of activity or the initial turning outward of consciousness toward expression.

[41] Theosophists refer to these energy centers as Ultimate Physical Atoms, or seed atoms. It is interesting to note that they use the word *atom* to refer to any specific unit of energy. For instance, our solar system is an "atom" in the larger body of a greater Cosmic being.

Janet Myatt

- The Atmic atom (a center of energy, or seed atom) is the first order of manifestation of the divine will of the Monad.
- The Buddhic atom is the first order of manifestation of intuition or love-wisdom.
- The Manasic atom is the first order of manifestation of the mind or pure reason.

Building the Upper Triad

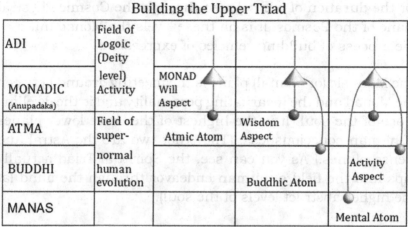

ADI	Field of Logoic (Deity level) Activity			
MONADIC (Anupadaka)		MONAD Will Aspect		
ATMA	Field of super-	Atmic Atom	Wisdom Aspect	
BUDDHI	normal human evolution		Buddhic Atom	Activity Aspect
MANAS				Mental Atom

Note: This chart was inspired by a chart published by A.E. Powell in his book *The Causal Body and the Ego*, p. 24.

Powell uses the sanskrit term *Anupadaka* for the 2ⁿᵈ level. Alice Bailey uses the term *Monadic*. Both refer to *causation* – the relationship between an event (cause) and the resulting event (effect).

Figure 15: Building the Spiritual Triad

Building the Lower Triad

The energy and information contained in the Triadal permanent atoms flow into the first four subplanes of the Mental (Manasic) plane forming the causal body of the soul. If we use the image of the lotus to picture the causal body, we can trace the progression of energy from the Triad into the causal body of the soul and from there down into the incarnating personality. Each Triadal permanent atom forms three "petals" of energy in the causal body. (See Figure 13 p. 85)

88

- The will/sacrifice petals are formed by the will permanent atom (located on the highest subplane of the Atmic plane).
- The love/wisdom petals are formed by the love/wisdom permanent atom (located on the highest subplane of the Buddhic plane).
- The intelligence petals are formed by the intelligence permanent atom (located on the highest subplane of the Mental plane).

Life energy flows from the petals into the lower three worlds forming the lower three permanent atoms from which the lower vehicles of expression are formed.

So, the permanent atoms have to do with how *life* energy flows from the monad into the incarnating personality via the causal body. This energy flows into the personality via the crown chakra and anchors in the heart. *Consciousness* flows from the soul through the crown chakra into the mind and anchors into the brain.

Divine Life flows from the Monad through the Atmic energy center (permanent atom) into the lower triad to form the etheric body. The etheric body is the energetic scaffolding that informs and vivifies the dense physical body. Without an etheric body, there can be no Life in the physical body; however, there can be an etheric body without the dense form, at least while there is still a conscious entity flowing Life energy though it. Physical "death" occurs when

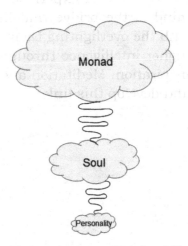

Figure 16: Flow of Divine Life

the soul extending Life energy into the etheric body severs its connection with the dense physical body. We'll explore

Janet Myatt

the etheric body in more depth when we examine the lower vehicles.

The Buddhic energy center of intelligent love and intuition is the center through which desire or love energy flows into the lower triad to form the astral-emotional body. This lower vehicle allows us to be sentient—to feel, register, and respond to impacts from the external world and to express and experience our internal desires. It is the intermediary communicative link between the body and the mind. It is the vehicle that enables us to perceive and be aware of stimuli originating outside or inside the physical body through our senses. And it allows us to experience affective states of consciousness—our feelings or emotions.

Divine intelligence flows through the Manasic energy center into the lower triad to form the mental body or mental "unit." This body is twofold, consisting of the higher abstract mind and the lower concrete mind. The mental body is the vehicle through which the incarnating personality is able to express and experience the world of ideas. The abstract mind is the bridge that links the mind of the personality with the overlighting Divine Mind of the soul. We access this higher intelligence through our intuition, illumination, and inspiration. Meditation and quiet reflection help us open up and develop this link.

Building the Lower Triad

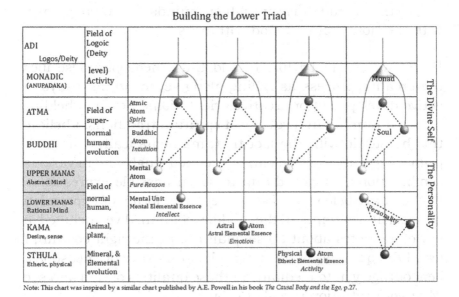

ADI Logos/Deity	Field of Logoic (Deity				
MONADIC (ANUPADAKA)	level) Activity				Monad
ATMA	Field of super-	Atmic Atom *Spirit*			
BUDDHI	normal human evolution	Buddhic Atom *Intuition*			Soul
UPPER MANAS Abstract Mind	Field of	Mental Atom *Pure Reason*			
LOWER MANAS Rational Mind	normal human,	Mental Unit Mental Elemental Essence *Intellect*			
KAMA Desire, sense	Animal, plant,		Astral Atom Astral Elemental Essence *Emotion*		Personality
STHULA Etheric, physical	Mineral, & Elemental evolution		Physical Atom Etheric Elemental Essence *Activity*		

The Divine Self / *The Personality*

Note: This chart was inspired by a similar chart published by A.E. Powell in his book *The Causal Body and the Ego*, p.27.

Figure 17: Building the Lower Triad

Once the upper and lower triads are formed and the lower vehicles of expression are built, the Monad has three levels of self-expression. It exists as follows:

1. As pure Spirit, the Mighty "I Am" Presence, the God-self in the upper worlds on the Anupadaka/Monadic plane and extending into the Triadal planes.
2. As a Higher Self (Triad + soul) on the Atmic, Buddhic, and upper Manasic/Mental planes. The Monad has begun the evolutionary journey of merging with matter for the purpose of revealing God in active, objective form.
3. As a personality in the lower worlds on the physical, astral, and lower Mental planes. The soul is taking on material forms and is actively expressing its creativity.

It's helpful to note that the mind provides the point of connection between the personality and the soul and is the

link to the Monad. It is through our minds that we reconnect
with the Holy Spirit, or God-within-us.

Before we go on, I'd like to add that Theosophy describes
the creative process as falling along seven primary rays of
active development or creative orientations. Seven is held as
a sacred number in a variety of spiritual traditions. I believe
this has to do with the fact that, mathematically, the three
primary qualities of God can be grouped singly and in various
combinations, which add up to seven possible expressions.
In the chart below, I've listed the seven forms of expression
in the left column. In the middle column, I've included a
few of my notes about these qualities. In the right column, I
listed the qualities of the seven planetary rays of Theosophy.
I encourage you to meditate on these qualities of God and see
what your intuition reveals to you.

Seven Expressions of God	My Notes	Seven Rays of Theosophy
Father	Will or creative force – the impulse to create and express. The power to create and destroy.	Ray 1: Will or Power
Son	Love-wisdom – the impulse to attract, connect, extend, relate.	Ray 2: Love-Wisdom, or intelligent love. Magnetic Impulse. Law of Attraction & Repulsion
Infinite Spirit	Active intelligence or divine mind – the impulse to know, organize, reveal, respond, prepare, minister.	Ray 3: Active Intelligence, Adaptability, Mind
Father + Son	Will + Love-wisdom. Cocreativity, the desire to express and extend love.	Ray 4: Harmony through Conflict Love of Beauty & Harmony
Father + Spirit	Will + Active Intelligence. The impulse to create forms of expression.	Ray 5: Concrete Knowledge Science
Son + Spirit	Love-Wisdom + Active Intelligence. The ability to reveal love actively and intelligently in objective form.	Ray 6: Devotion or Abstract Idealism
Father + Son + Infinite Spirit	The Trinity – the full revelation of God	Ray 7: Ceremonial Magic, Ritual and Order, Alchemy. God fully revealed in objective form

Figure 18: Seven Expressions of God

To summarize what we've talked about so far in terms of our discussion of the descent into matter, the Monads created these very high-level centers of energy on the subtle planes; from these centers, the life force of the Monad was able to differentiate along its ray type and begin the process of merging with matter. As this happened, the soul level of experience was developed—first through the process of group-souls in the initial kingdoms of nature and then as individual souls in the human kingdom. We've been looking at the flow of divine life into the physical plane, the development of the four vehicles (causal, mental, astral, etheric), and the dawning of conscious self-awareness in the human kingdom.

Several things happened at the point where we began to ensoul human bodies as individual personalities. The

Seth teachings tell us that in order to incarnate into such dense and individualized life forms, we had to spiral down increasingly distinct (and thus relatively smaller) parts of our consciousness into lower and more differentiated energetic frequencies. This affected us greatly at the personality level, as it eventually resulted in a loss of conscious connection with the vast majority of our originating consciousness, which remained outside our awareness at higher frequencies on the higher planes.

As we descended, we actually had to learn how to anchor our consciousness into the lower energy centers of the body and establish a strong will to live in physical form. Once this lower polarization of our consciousness took place, the demands of our physical bodies and physical reality began to consume our attention and eventually changed the way we came to identify ourselves. We began to identify with the forms we created rather than with our spirit. We came to believe that we existed because we had a body rather than knowing that the body existed because it had a soul that chose to create it. Thus, we became body identified rather than spirit identified, and this fundamental misperception formed a primal belief that we are bodies first and consciousness second. Because all forms pass away, this overidentification with our bodies conspired to create a situation ripe with fear as we lost awareness of our immortal Self. Our consciousness split into a vertical pair of opposing states of mind.

The consciousness of the soul remained anchored in the upper mental plane. The mind of the personality became anchored in the next plane down—the astral-emotional plane—where it is still the locus of identity for the majority of human beings to this day. The lower half of the mental body (the intellect) has slowly been developed in this particular age, and the majority of people have at least developed the lower concrete mind.

The lower self focused exclusively on its experiences in physical reality, while the rest our mind remained cosmically connected and unified with the greater whole at the soul and monadic levels of consciousness. This condition is sometimes referred to as the "Fall from Grace" or the perceived state of separation from God. Seth teaches us:

> *Using your free will, you have made physical reality something quite different than what was intended... you were always to be aware of your own inner reality, and of your nonphysical existence. To a large extent you have lost contact with this. You have focused so strongly upon physical reality that it becomes the only reality that you know.*[42]

Today, our task is to awaken from the state of spiritual amnesia we have been in for so very long. It has been suggested by some spiritual teachings (The Urantia Book and in the esoteric writings of Alice Bailey, for example) that this forgetfulness does not happen in the majority of other evolving planets and systems. If this is the case, then it was not the body per se that led to the amnesia but the process of getting so fully entrenched into the body in the way that we did.

Let's review what we've discussed so far. As our attention was drawn away from the higher planes of existence by the demands and sensations of our animal body and nature, the egotistical, separated state of mind emerged. The human ego[43] is a set of beliefs and thought patterns built on our perceptions in the phenomenal world. It arose out of our need to understand and organize our experiences in physical reality without the benefit of the larger point of view of our divinity and interconnectedness with God. I have come to understand that the development of our spiritual amnesia didn't happen overnight or the minute we incarnated into bodies but instead slowly over time. There are conflicting teachings about this time in our evolution, and I believe this

---

[42] Roberts. *The Seth Material*, Kindle edition, Location 4234
[43] Not to be confused with Theosophy's use of the word *Ego* (with a capital *E*), which they use to refer to the soul.

Janet Myatt

has to do with the angle of vision one is looking through. From the spiritual level, it appears we fell and forgot. The psyche of the Spirit moved from unity and at-one-ment with God into separation from one another and God. From the animal level, it appears we rose up out of a pre-personal or unselfconscious state into a self-conscious state that we have been evolving ever since individuation took place. Either way, it is in the human kingdom that delusional thinking arose, but it is also the human kingdom that links the lower kingdoms in nature with the higher. The mind is the connecting link between the lower self and the higher.

On the consciousness side of things, Theosophy teaches us that three broad types of delusion arose in our minds over the course of our experiences in the lower worlds:

1. Maya: the belief that we exist only if we have forms or bodies—development of a physically based identity. "I am my body."
2. Glamour: the belief that we are our emotions—development of an emotionally based identity. "I am my feelings and emotions."
3. Illusion: the belief that we are our thoughts—development of an idea-based identity. "I am my thoughts and ideas."

According to the writings of Alice Bailey and many other esoteric writers, maya developed during the first age of human development—the Lemurian age—as the incarnating souls were focusing their attention on learning how to inhabit their material forms. This polarization of their attention into the physical body and powerful awareness of the instinctual and sensual drives of the animal body eventually swamped the mind and led to the first perception of separation from the divine Self. Emotionally, a primal need for acceptance from the tribe first arose during the Lemurian age to ensure one's safety.

Glamour developed during the second great age—the Atlantean age—as the astral body was developed. Once humans believed they were their bodies, fear entered into their minds because all bodies die. Experiences in the physical world took on even more heightened and fearful proportions. In the Atlantean age, competition for resources and rampant acquisitiveness took over the mind. The emotions in general became the central defining experience as humans fell under the alluring spell of their feelings and perceptions.

Illusion has developed in our current Aryan age[44] as humans develop their rational and abstract thinking and move into a mental orientation and identification. In this age, we have endeavored to understand ourselves and our emotional nature better. We have sought to unravel the secrets of the universe we live in and overcome our emotional nature. This is all to the good; however, we still have the proclivity to misidentify ourselves. We take our ideas very seriously and become identified with them. We idealize our ideas. We think, "My idea is the best idea." "My idea is the right idea." "I am my ideas." The good news is we become highly motivated to try these ideas on for size. We work very hard to manifest them. But the bad news is they also become mental prisons from which we cannot escape. How can we change our minds about ourselves, others, or the world around us if our very identity is tied up in our ideas?

All these distortions—maya, glamour, and illusion—are still present to varying degrees in our minds to this day. The job of the incarnated personality is first to gain a sufficient level

---

[44] In Theosophy, *Aryan* is the term for the fifth root race. Each root race has seven subraces that branch off the root. The Lemurains were the third root race. The Atlanteans were the fourth root race. Our current human race is the Aryan race. Theosophy says there are still remnants of the fourth race on the planet, but most of the humans on the planet at this time are of the fifth root race. There will be two more root races before this round of human evolution is complete, but those races won't be seen on the planet for thousands of years to come.

of mental, emotional, and physical integration to become an integrated personality. This is the person who is effective in his life. He is able to set goals and manifest them, and he is able to make an impact on the world around him. Once integration is well established, the ascension phase opens up, and the incarnated personality begins to work its way out of these various degrees of distortion as it merges with increasingly higher states of awareness.

Division into Genders

Another aspect of our descent into matter has to do with our division into male and female genders. In our discussion so far, I hope we have begun to discern the difference between matter and consciousness. The former is activated energetic substance that has an impersonal type of intelligence or an ability to respond to the intention of the

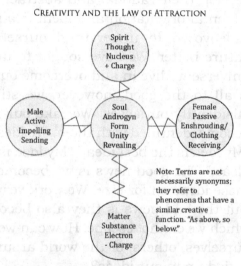

CREATIVITY AND THE LAW OF ATTRACTION

Figure 19: Pairs of Opposites

Spirit directing it. The latter refers to personal, self-aware intelligence. The material building blocks of an active system consist of electrical units with positive, negative, and neutral charges. For example, atoms are made up of electrical components that contain a negative charge (electrons, female) a positive charge (protons, male), and a neutral charge (neutrons, androgyne). Opposite charges attract, and like charges repulse. These differing electrical charges create a polarized field that generates and facilitates movement. Particles are attracted and repulsed as the two poles seek to create a balanced whole. In a similar fashion, as the souls on our planet extend their consciousness into physical bodies, consciousness moves from a state of balanced androgyny at the soul level into gender identities at the personality level. This gender identity creates a polarized field where the male corresponds to the positive charge, and the female corresponds to the negative charge. These opposing charges create a magnetic field of attraction that draw the two types together. If you want to explore this topic in greater detail, I suggest you take a look at Rudolf Steiner's hypothesis on why and how this happened. For our purposes, let me state that I believe the division into genders served the following evolutionary purposes:

- It sets us into motion seeking out one another in an effort to find balance and restore wholeness.
- It gives us the opportunity to explore both sides of the creative process. We start out in a state of imbalance as we delve deeply into one side or the other. Over the course of many lives, we develop both our feminine and masculine traits and abilities until we can bring them once again into balanced wholeness.

So, the whole process of incarnation has to do with the principles we see displayed in the phenomenon of electricity. All forms in the physical plane of the universe have positive and negative charges that are magnetically drawn together. Be it the dense atom of science and all that we can see and touch, or the invisible thought-form, all forms correspond to this phenomenon. This is such an important concept to understand because it is the fundamental mechanism of creativity. This will become clearer as we get into our exploration of the rise of the ego and the way we create our reality. When we understand the process, we are able to use it consciously. Conscious understanding leads to mastery and transformation. The healing of our world begins when each human being learns to understand what he or she is doing and how and why it affects not only him- or herself but the Whole. One day, when enough of us have awoken to our creative potential and greater purpose, the long-sought kingdom of God will be revealed. Initially, we will do this one by one, but we will ultimately achieve our divine purpose together.

The Law of Attraction

Applies to all types of form building from
thought-forms to body types to gender identification

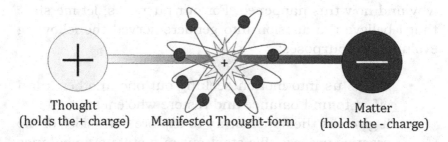

Thought
(holds the + charge)   Manifested Thought-form   Matter
(holds the - charge)

Analogous Polarization of Energy

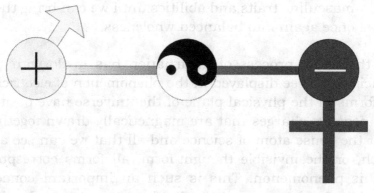

Figure 20: The Law of Attraction & Form Building

100

Chapter 3 Exercises

1. Involution
   - What lights up in your mind when you ponder this part of the creative process? Do any soul memories get stirred up?
   - Pay attention to the sensations in your body when you think about involution and the descent of consciousness into matter. Does your energy go up and get lighter, or does it seem heavy or dragging, or is there no change?
2. The evolution of consciousness
   - What do you notice about how the consciousness of mankind has shifted over the course of our history?
3. What happens to your perception of yourself and the world when you consider the mechanics of the creative process?
4. Self-assessment tool: How balanced are your male and female qualities? What needs development, and what needs to be toned down or counterbalanced?
5. "It is our loss of contact with our higher consciousness and with God that causes us pain. It is our body oriented way of thinking that gives rise to the perception of death." What comes up for you as you consider this idea?

CHAPTER 4 ~ THE LOWER VEHICLES OF EXPRESSION

The Eternal Law of Life is that "Whatever you think and feel you bring into form; where your thought is there you are for you are your consciousness; and whatever you meditate upon you become."[45]

A body, whether composed of objectively visible substance (e.g., the dense physical body) or subjectively subtle energy, is a specific creative *vehicle of expression* used by the evolving soul to experience and grow within.[46] Here in the lower worlds of physical reality, we use three energy-bodies to express through:

- The etheric-physical
- The astral-emotional (also called the desire body, the sentient body)
- The mental body

Each body works cocreatively and interdependently with the others; therefore, each is affected by the other. The way we run our creative energy through these various bodies affects our overall health, well-being, state of integration (or lack thereof), and overall power to create.

Let's examine these three vehicles more closely.

---

[45] King, Godfrey Ray. *Unveiled Mysteries*. Kindle edition, Locations 294–295.

[46] Please note that the word *body* refers to a collection or pattern something.

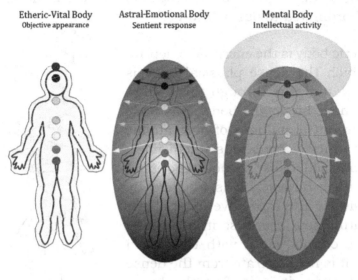

Etheric-Vital Body
Objective appearance

Astral-Emotional Body
Sentient response

Mental Body
Intellectual activity

Figure 21: Three Lower Vehicles

The Etheric Body

It has only a diffused consciousness belonging to its parts, and has no mentality, nor does it readily serve as a medium of mentality, when disjoined from the dense counterpart.[47]

As we discussed earlier, to function on the physical plane, the soul extends a magnetic thread or current of life energy into the body. This soul-thread is divided into two streams: 1) the life aspect, which animates every atom of the body, flows into the heart and is anchored there, and 2) the consciousness aspect flows into the brain and is anchored near the pineal gland. From these two points, the soul is able to build the mechanisms necessary for incarnation. The consciousness aspect makes us intelligent, self-conscious, rational entities that are self-directing. The life principle enables us to be self-determined and provides us with the means of holding all the

---

[47]   Powell. *The Etheric Double.*

atoms that make up our bodies together in their right place and subordinated to our will-to-be.[48]

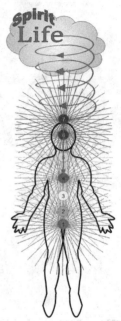

The etheric body is the energetic blueprint from which the dense physical body is animated, and it is through this vehicle that we have life in the body. This body is formed out of millions of little atomic lives or units of conscious intelligence. This consciousness is not emotional or cognitive; however, it is intelligently responsive to the attractive force of the incarnating soul. Because it is a subtle body, we cannot see it with the naked eye, but it is not separate from the dense physical body—it is in fact the living intelligent consciousness of the body. However, it is not a "self-aware" level of consciousness; it cannot perceive or comprehend meaning. It serves two primary functions. First, it keeps the dense physical body alive through the

Figure 22: Etheric-Energy Body

absorption and distribution of life force energy known as *prana*, or vitality. Second, it picks up the impulses and impressions coming into the body via the physical senses and communicates these impressions via the brain to the mind. The etheric body and the dense body work together. If we damage our etheric body, we create illness in the physical body. When we leave the physical body at "death," the etheric body rapidly dissolves.

48   Bailey. *A Treatise on White Magic*, p. 495.

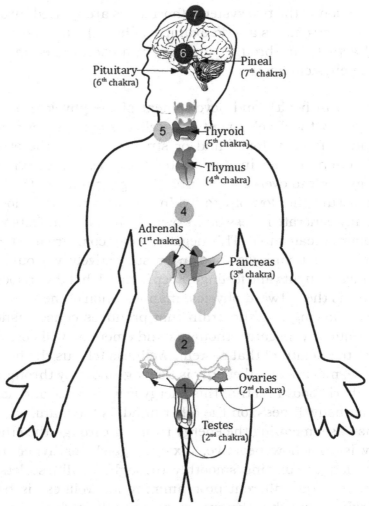

Figure 23: Glands

Within the etheric body are lines of energy (called *nadis*) and energy centers (called chakras) through which vitality or life force energy flows. These lines of force and the places where they intersect to form the centers (minor and major) are the avenues through which the etheric body carries out its functions. The nadis are the subtle lines of force that give rise to the nervous system. The chakras give rise to the glands and endocrine system. The life principle anchored in the heart uses the bloodstream as its mode of expression, while the consciousness principle uses the endocrine. The interaction of the two systems (hormones are carried through the bloodstream) is a good example of how the two aspects of soul activity are brought together in a coordinated manner in the physical body.

The overall health and development of the physical body is affected by the development and wellness of the etheric body. Negative, foreign, toxic, and/or stuck energy in the etheric body often results in illness and disease. These types of energy work to override the innate programming of the body and disrupt the flow of vitality. In this way, the body doesn't actually generate illness on its own; rather, it manifests what is communicated to it. This negativity can come from external sources via toxins we take in or subjectively via our own negative thoughts and feelings. Keep in mind that the endocrine system is the outward physical manifestation of the stream of energy flowing into the brain that produces consciousness. Consequently, negative thoughts and emotions will certainly affect the health of that system. Wellness tells us the body is at ease, meaning vital energy is flowing smoothly throughout the etheric body and that this energy is in balance and native to that body. Illness, on the other hand, is the manifestation of dis-ease, meaning the energy running through the etheric body is somehow negative, toxic, sluggish, or hyper and/or no longer running smoothly throughout. Illness lets us know that the inherent programming for wellness is being overridden and that the energy running through the etheric body is out of balance, stuck, or toxic. In short, illness is a reflection of the information we are using and the choices we have made either consciously or unconsciously, overtly or covertly.

As a quick aside, let me point out that even the toxic external agents loose in the world today are the result of choices we have made collectively as the human kingdom. These choices have created imbalance in the ecosystem. On a macrolevel, then, the imbalance in our ecosystem collectively mirrors the imbalances in our collective and individual consciousness, with the same poor results. I'm not suggesting that as a race we knew how to do better, but I am suggesting that the phenomenon is consistent whether looking at it individually or systemically. Thus, as we gain mastery over our vehicles, the whole ecosystem and the lower kingdoms will equally benefit.

Physical bodies were originally intended to be used only as forms through which we could express our creative intention in physical reality. Originally, our consciousness remained in an awakened state of awareness of God-within-us and operated only in present time. We created directly from our present intention and held the form(s) in place for as long as we held our attention in them. Then, when the forms had served their purpose, we destroyed our creations by moving our attention out of them so that we could experience something new. This process still underlies all that we do, but we're no longer consciously aware of it. This amnesia has resulted in confusion; ultimately, it is the underlying cause of our aging process and most of our illness and unhappiness. The amnesia, coupled with our identity crisis, has caused us to become overly attached to our forms. This includes our attachment to our dense forms, emotional patterns, and thoughtforms — all our experiences, beliefs, and ideas. Once we build it, we're afraid to destroy it for fear of no longer existing. Consequently, we loop our creative energy through everything we've manifested over the course of our life. Unconscious looping is helpful when we're running the energy through a healthy blueprint. For instance, we don't want to have to focus our attention on our hearts or lungs throughout our day in order to keep them in manifestation. Instead, the necessary attention is held "below the threshold" in our subconscious mind, and the form persists until we're ready to vacate the dense body at the end of an incarnational phase of creativity. However, this subconscious control of the body eventually becomes compromised as we accumulate thought patterns that undermine and counteract its original form. The physical blueprint gets overlaid by the emotional and mental blueprints we create over time, and states of disorganization and conflict arise.

Before the rise of our amnesia, we could materialize a healthy body for as long as we chose to. The etheric body, then, was in a constant state of Grace. This means that vitality was not distorted by fearful, "dark" thoughts or emotions because none of our consciousness sat in those states of mind. Thus, the body did not age or become ill or suffer. This is what has been described as life in the Garden of Eden. Once we chose to operate independently of this awareness, we moved out of Grace into a world of our own design. Thus, the consciousness of the body became subject to the toxicity of the fearful and conflicting thoughts and emotions of the personality sitting in a paradigm of separation. In this way, we moved out of materializing our consciousness through bodies in accordance with the divine blueprint (or Plan). Instead, we filtered our consciousness through beliefs and thoughtforms that cause us to be born through pain, to age, and ultimately to die as we create an increasingly toxic etheric body over the course of our lifespan. In short, this fundamental change in the way we run our consciousness into physical reality led to bodies that age, become ill, and die.

I remember how baffled and incredulous I always felt when I read the accounts in Genesis of people living for hundreds of years. I couldn't understand how the "book of truth" could be so blatantly wrong. Now, I've come to realize that these accounts—be they historical accounts of actual people or mythological allegories—are speaking about this deeper mystical truth. When we live fully in present time expressing only God-within-us, our physical bodies remain completely vital and healthy. That that is where we're headed as we expand our consciousness and ascend.

How does all this pertain to the here and now? It points us in the right direction of understanding, once again, that the world we experience is the world we create with our thoughts and feelings. This is true for all our vehicles of expression. Right now we're discussing the physical vehicle, and it's important to understand that our current job is to regain dominion over the physical body once again. How do we do such a thing?

We first come to understand that the original divine blueprint or plan for inhabiting a physical body enabled us to have bodies that are well. The mechanics of running our consciousness through spiritual vehicles that subsequently take shape is still true today. Thus, when the physical body is unwell, the root cause is generally not with the body but with the consciousness in charge of it. The divine blueprint for etheric bodies is in alignment with cosmic intelligence. And etheric bodies *are the consciousness*, the *animating force*, of physical bodies. Thus, the physical body was divinely planned to be perfect. The human blueprints we form in our separated minds are subject to error. Currently, the consciousness assigned to the body is primarily wrapped up in the ego, which sits in a belief in separation and is full of fear and conflicting ideas. This fear and conflict runs through the etheric body, creating conflict in the body consciousness.

I want to include an important side note on this subject of blueprints. In Alice Bailey's book *Glamour: A World Problem*,[49] the Tibetan Master Djwal Khul teaches that at this point in our evolution there is a certain amount of "inherited evil." We began to develop problematic human blueprints after the idea of separation occurred in the mass consciousness, and we are working those out as we gain mastery of our vehicles. (Note we have not altered the original divine blueprints, however.) He explains this is worth noting because it's overly simplistic to assume that *all diseases* can be overcome simply through the application of mind over matter *at this time in our evolution*. Much can be done, and is being done, at this point to overcome

---

[49]   Bailey. *Glamour: A World Problem*

these patterns, but there are still mass agreements that affect the race as a whole. For instance, an amputee cannot regrow a limb at this time.

Returning to our examination of how our thoughts and feelings can affect the health and integrity of the etheric body, let's consider a common example. In a body, cancer cells were originally normal cells that worked in harmony with the body as a whole. However, some kind of negative agent caused the cells to turn from their original harmonious state to an inharmonious state. As cancer cells, they no longer work in cohesive communication with the rest of the body; they operate in conflict with the whole. This reflects perfectly how the ego works within cosmic reality. The consciousness wrapped up in the idea of separation sets itself apart from its God consciousness and no longer works in cohesive communication with the rest of the cosmos. Cancer is a perfect mirror of this state of mind; it is an outward manifestation of an inward state of mind—*as is all reality*. The root cause of this shift from harmonious, healthy cell to inharmonious, unhealthy cell can always be traced to consciousness and how it's working in the body. I am not in any way suggesting that people who develop cancer *deserve* it, no more than any of us deserve to have bad things happen to us. I'm simply pointing out that the physical condition accurately mirrors the effect of what happens when consciousness is working at cross-purposes and out of alignment with the greater whole. It is one highly charged example of how cause and effect works in physical reality: conscious sitting in conflict with the whole (the cause) manifests as cancer (the effect).

Chances are that when we look at where the cancer manifests in the body, we will be able to discern the nature of the thoughts and beliefs that are sitting in opposition to God consciousness. Louise Hay's book *You Can Heal Your Life* is an excellent resource for diagnosing the thought patterns that underlie various illnesses. For example, she suggests that cancer stems from "Deep hurt. Longstanding resentment.

A deep secret or grief eating away at the self,"[50] and breast issues have to do with "mothering and nurturing" and "overmothering, overprotection, overbearing attitudes, cutting off nourishment."[51] When breast cancer manifests in the body, it may be tied to painful thought patterns deep in the consciousness around mothering and nurturing. For me, I see that cancer (wherever it is in the body) is a perfect reflection of how the conflicting thoughts we hold in our mind create conflict in the consciousness of the body. When the mind is fragmented, it inevitably works at cross-purposes creating confusion, a disjointed reality, and loss of power.

Because the health of the body is dependent on the health of the etheric body, it is vitally important to take excellent care of it. This is why the Ascended Master teachings tell us the first "initiation" or step in returning to a state of wholeness is to master the physical body. Once we understand just how much our thoughts and emotions affect our physical wellness, we understand how important it is to bring those thoughts and emotions back under the control of Spirit. This can be done only by employing our intellect and developing our willpower, insight, and intuition to illuminate our minds to the greater truth resting in our God consciousness. In short, we must change our minds and act according to the greater truth living deep within our inner wisdom.

The Astral Body

The astral body is a subtle body that connects the mind to the physical body, resulting in a sentient being. Sentience is the power to perceive—to become aware of, know, or identify things by means of the senses. The astral body is the vehicle of expression that enables human beings to perceive and

---

[50] Hay, Louse. *You Can Heal Your Life*, p. 159.
[51] Ibid, p. 157.

interpret both their internal desires and external contacts. It establishes an experiential connection between the mind and the brain. It is a separate vehicle of consciousness from the physical body. Because this is the case, we do not need a physical body to have an astral body. (Remember that this is not the case for the etheric body.) For instance, after a human being withdraws from the physical body at "death," the consciousness persists in the astral body for a period. Every night when we go to sleep, we withdraw our consciousness out of the etheric-physical body and move into our astral body. The difference between sleep and death is that the life cord is not withdrawn during sleep as it is when we decide to withdraw from dense physical life.

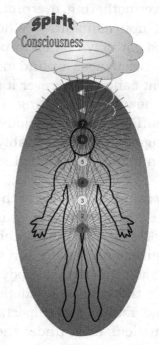

Figure 24: The Astral Body

The astral body is of a higher vibration than the etheric body and is vivified by the magnetizing energy of desire. In terms of consciousness, the astral state is the motivating quality of intention that makes us want to do something, experience something, and express something. In terms of energy, it is magnetic force. The astral plane is the lower reflection of the Buddhic plane—the plane of at-one-ment. It is that quality of God that draws things together and puts things into relationship. Desire is the lower reflection of love. Powell defines desire as "divine Will turned outward interacting with the surrounding environment."[52]

---

[52]   Powell. *The Astral Body*, p. 24.

The astral body is formed by our desire to materially experience ourselves physically and emotionally. It is consciousness taking an interest in external things and is the vehicle where our emotions can be expressed and experienced.

In short, the astral body serves three main functions:

1. To make sensation possible
2. To serve as a bridge between mind and physical matter
3. To act as an independent vehicle of consciousness and action[53]

The astral body is extremely sensitive to impacts from both inner and outer impulses. It receives these impulses and transmits them to the brain. Externally, the vibrations picked up in the etheric body by the five physical senses are received by the astral body and translated into sensations. Internally, the vibrations of our thoughts are also received by the astral body and translated into emotions. Thus, pleasure and pain do not arise in consciousness until the astral body is reached.

Like the physical body, the astral body and our emotional nature must be mastered in order for one to ascend. This takes us to the third function listed above. As we evolve, we are learning how to develop and utilize the astral-emotional body as a vehicle of conscious expression both in daily life and on the astral plane during sleep and after death. Through the emotional-desire body, we can experience anything from the lowest levels of "hell" to the highest levels of "heaven" and everything in between. For instance, in the lowest levels of our consciousness, we experience extreme fear without the reasoning power of the intellect; in the highest, we experience connection, love, and joy. All these experiences precipitate astral forms—animated pictures—that we believe are real. And they are *temporarily* real. In other words, what we are experiencing is real for the moment. Our perceptions are

---

[53]   Ibid, p. 23.

real for as long as we hold our attention in the thought or sensation. So, in the worlds of time and space, an astral form (an emotional experience) persists until we destroy it. However, we're reluctant to do this because we think we are our emotional experiences and that our very existence is dependent on them.

So, we end up with a pretty junky emotional space over time. For instance, what we call hell is really the sum total of animated fearful thoughtforms that the human race has experienced over the course of our evolution. It is populated with fearsome ideas that are animated by our attention. (And this attention can be conscious or subconscious.) These "demons" and "devils" persist because we have not moved our thinking out of these things. On the high end, astral heaven is the collection of ideas or ideals that reflect our highest aspirations and our experiences of love and of God. These high-level thoughtforms are also animated by our attention; they inspire us and increase our desire to create these experiences tangibly.

The astral body and the entire astral plane are meant to be instructive. The astral body teaches us about the quality of our thinking and our resulting experiences. When we begin to awaken to the stirring of the soul, we are led out of our astral polarization. This journey requires us to develop dominion over our lower passions and allow our soul to direct our emotional nature, thus bringing it back into alignment with divine love. Saint Germain teaches us:

> The feeling activity of Life is the most unguarded point of human consciousness. It is the accumulative energy by which thoughts are propelled into the atomic substance, and thus do thoughts become things. I tell you the need of guarding the feeling cannot be emphasized too strongly, for control of the emotions plays the most important part of anything in Life in maintaining balance in the mind health, in the body-success, and accomplishment

> *in the affairs and world of the personal self of every*
> *individual.*[54]

Moving this vehicle of expression out from under the control of our animal passions and lower sensibilities offers us the opportunity to experience our creativity as directed from our soul's will rather than through the pleasure-and-pain principle of the physical body. In short, in order to fulfill our divine potential, we will have to gain dominion over our emotions and reunite our desire with the desire of God-within-us.

This quest applies not only to our waking life but to our sleeping life. During an integrative spirituality workshop I attended several years ago, writer Ken Wilbur spoke briefly about becoming aware of and directing our dream-space in order to master the astral body. This made a lot of sense to me, as I have found that dreams tell us a tremendous amount about where significant amounts of our attention are focused. In addition, paying attention to our astral explorations reminds us that we are immortal beings creating various forms of expression to experience ourselves through rather than purely physical beings.

Let me clarify something to avoid confusion. Day and night, human beings are interacting and "living" on the astral plane. The astral-emotional body is the lowest-possible body of *personal* awareness; thus, even when we're awake, we are operating on this plane of activity. During the day, we're consciously including the physical body directly in our emotional world; at night, we are not. We move our consciousness out of it enough to allow it to rest while we carry on with our mental-emotional life. When people talk about having an "astral experience," they are typically referring to the dream state we experience at night. However, the only difference between the sleeping dream state and the waking is that the astral body is no longer *in* the dense body during

---

[54]   King. Locations 304–307.

sleep. This gives us the advantage of traveling through time and space in a way that the dense form cannot, and we simply continue our mental-emotional experience on this subtler plane. Without the limitations of the dense body, we are able to locate our consciousness in different places and even different bodies, and we can move in and out of experiences more fluidly. This flexibility gives us a place where we can work things out, try things on for size, and express our desire body more fully without tangible consequences to the dense bodies involved in the experiences.

As we awaken, we have before us the task of becoming conscious on the astral plane at all times whether awake or asleep. Through meditation, quiet reflection, and energy work, I have been steadily shifting large blocks of consciousness from the lower levels of this plane up to higher levels both during sleep and while I'm awake. As I raise my consciousness in my daily life, my dream life reflects these shifts more and more. Shifting our identity out of our emotional thoughtforms and knee-jerk reactivity is the primary goal of anyone traveling on the path of return. We have the opportunity to learn how to stop experiencing our lives through the vast ocean of old emotional patterns—both personal and collective—that color our perception.

Theosophy and other traditions encourage us to take charge of both our awake state and our sleep state so that we can manifest dominion over our desires and realign our small will with our greater divine will.

The Mental Body

The mental body consists of the both the lower mind and the higher mind. The lower mind is the seat of our intellect and rational thought. It is here that the individual learns to use reason, judgment, and concrete thought processes, where problem solving is accomplished in a concrete, systematic fashion based on what is perceived. The lower mind is externally focused, and logic and linear analysis predominate the thinking. The higher mind is situated in the causal body and is the seat of our abstract thought (illumination,) intuition, and inspiration. The higher mind has access to divine Knowledge and is holistic in its understanding. It is able to perceive the greater truth of a situation, including what is hidden from the externalized self, and is able to see the past, present, and future with ease. The upper mental body moves us from the externalized mind to the internal consciousness of soul. It is here that we begin to see holographically and intuitively and develop a working relationship with our inner wisdom and the greater field of life. We see God-within-us and God-within-others and begin to live from that understanding. Because true clairvoyance is now possible, we are able to see and to know beyond the surface of things. The ability to move into the soul's point of view and understand spiritual concepts and laws is accessed here. The mental body gives us the ability to apply our will in specific ways and to harness the emotional body for higher purposes. This moves us off the emotional roller coaster of conflicting and quixotic emotional states and gives us the ability to respond to Life rather than merely react to the world around us.

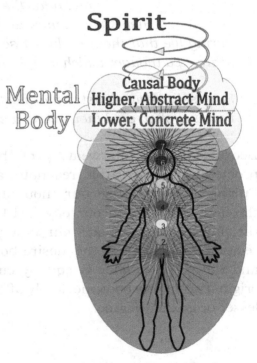

Figure 25: Mental Body

Kama-Manas

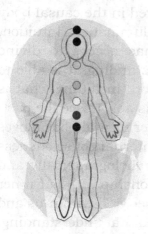

Figure 26: Kama Manasic Body

Most of the time, the astral body and the lower mental body work primarily as one body, and the Theosophists call this intermingled body the Kama-Manas or the Desire-Mind. Powell writes:

During earth-life, kama [Desire] and lower manas [lower mind, or intellect] are joined together, and are often spoken of as Kama-Manas. Kama supplies...the animal and passional elements; lower manas rationalizes these, and adds the intellectual faculties.

The two together, Kama-Manas, are so closely interwoven during life that they rarely act separately, for there is scarcely a thought which in uninfluenced by desire.[55]

So closely are men's astral and mental bodies intertwined that it is often said they act as a single body. [56]

Because of this interweaving of thoughts and emotions, problems in one area resonate and affect the other. Furthermore, because our thoughts and emotions affect the flow of vitality in our physical body, and the health of the physical body affects our thoughts and emotions, the relationship between the desire-body (the Kama-Manas) and the physical body is equally circular. Thus, problems originating in one body inevitably affect the other bodies to a lesser or greater degree.

---

[55] Powell. *The Mental Body*, p. 34.
[56] Ibid, p. 35.

For example, major depressive disorder is most commonly rooted in emotional pain caused by distorted thinking, which then results in a significant decrease in the levels of certain key neurotransmitters in the brain. Thus, there are problems in all three bodies, and these issues exacerbate one another.

- Mental body: Increased negative thoughts
- Astral body: Increased negative emotions
- Physical body: Decreased neurotransmitters important for controlling pain perception

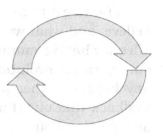

Let's pursue our example a bit further. Healing work must address all three bodies in order to be effective, liberate the consciousness from the depressive state, and gain mastery over all three vehicles. Modern psychiatry currently focuses primarily on the physical aspect first and advises a recovery plan built on medications that raise the neurotransmitter levels in the brain. However, this approach alone does not address the actual underlying cause of the depression, as it fails to address the imbalances in the emotional and mental planes of consciousness where the trouble began. Thus, medication alone typically results in limited success over time and often fails in the end. A holistic approach that addresses the emotional, mental, and spiritual levels of consciousness wrapped up in fear and distortion has a far greater potential to create the transformational shift in consciousness necessary for a lasting recovery. Furthermore, this type of healing approach provides the sufferers with the opportunity to discover new ways of understanding themselves and the world around them. A holistic approach offers an avenue through which we can rediscover our God consciousness and activate our divine potential. This, in turn, makes the experience useful to the evolving soul; in this way, a silver lining may be uncovered.

What is important to understand is that challenges will continue to come our way in life so long as we have portions of our consciousness sitting in opposition to God. Thus, every challenge offers us an opportunity to heal and activate this consciousness into the Light. It is the choices we make when dealing with the challenges in our life that are important and of interest to the evolving soul. What we think, what we believe, and what we have our attention focused on not only affects what we manifest but also either enhances or delays our spiritual evolution. Illness, disease, and deficiency of any kind—whether it is physical, emotional, or mental—is feedback that our thinking, beliefs, and attention are out of divine order. *How we return to divine order is the creative work of the evolving soul.*

Each vehicle of expression, then, must be brought back into communication with our inner God consciousness. This requires us to be willing to change the way we think and feel about ourselves, others, and the world around us. We have to stop rationalizing the pain and imbalance we experience in our bodies, hearts, and minds and commit to a full recovery. This means we cannot continually give in to destructive ways of living and being. When we realize something isn't working in our lives, it's important for us to leave no stone unturned in our commitment to correct it. We can find truly successful answers to all our dilemmas, challenges, and failures within our God consciousness. And we will increase our successes with any goal we are envisioning if we align and take direction from our indwelling soul along the way. The divine within us will always find a way to communicate to us in a form we can recognize and understand if we ask and are willing to receive.

Mastering the Lower Vehicles

While the lower vehicles all work together, and while progress gained in one area helps us progress in others, a basic order or progression is involved. The first order of business is to gain mastery over the physical body. For us currently, this involves looking at and gaining mastery over where the demands of the physical body and the primal drive for survival rule the consciousness and control one's behavior. Once mastery over the physical body has reached a high level, the next step is to gain mastery over the emotional body. The lower nature must be brought under control, and the higher emotional states of love, devotion, and a sense of joy through service to others must be brought forward. According to spiritual teacher Joshua David Stone, the first two stages are the hardest and can take many lifetimes to master. But once the emotional body is brought under control, the next two levels (mental and integrated personality[57]) can be mastered relatively quickly.[58] Not coincidentally, it is through our intelligence (an extension of the Infinite Spirit) that we are able to master the lower two bodies—the physical and emotional.

This brings us to the mental body. Mastering the mind involves becoming aware of the mental paradigms we sit in and take for granted. All of us have a set of ideas and working assumptions that provide us with a framework for understanding our experience. This framework establishes a certain level of security, and we use these assumptions to comprehend and make sense of our world. The problem we face is that all these mental paradigms are limiting; they all cause bias. When we understand this, we can more easily move out of a paradigm we've outgrown into a larger or different viewpoint that better serves us in present time. If, however, our very sense of reality and of ourselves is dependent on the current framework, we heavily resist anything that challenges it and consequently become imprisoned in it. This is an unnatural creative state and produces tremendous tension in the evolving consciousness. We are hardwired for a return

---

[57] The lower quaternary is composed of the three lower vehicles plus the integrated personality. The personality is a fourth entity—it is that which is greater than the sum of its parts (physical, emotional, and mental).

[58] Stone, Joshua David. *The Complete Ascension Manual*, Location 453.

to wholeness, and anything that prevents that return will eventually become intolerable.

God is creative, and so are we. The creative process is twofold: create and destroy. We create forms—be they physical or psychological—and use them to experience life. Once a form has served its purpose, it must be destroyed. When it is not, it becomes a prison, and the life force and consciousness trapped within it can no longer evolve.

Recall, if you will, that during our descent into the lower three worlds we moved into smaller and smaller points of view. This enabled us to experience a limited range of creative activity in great detail. On the path of return, we must move back up into increasingly larger points of view. These expanding states of consciousness exist beyond our current mental paradigms; therefore, they will necessarily have to be abandoned. This process is spiral-cyclical. We move out of an old set of beliefs and understandings into a new set and experience them for whatever length of time is necessary. Then, when we have learned what we need to learn, we move out again into the next larger state of awareness. Thus, we must learn the art of detachment and decentralization. Taking our ego out of our ideas and beliefs gives us the freedom to move into new states of awareness and identification.

Mastery over the mental body moves us out of our illusions. Instead of working through old, outdated ideas and ideals, we move into present-time creativity (rather than looping our creativity through past thoughtforms) as we open up to our intuition, which always exists in present time. Inspiration and illumination take over our mind, and we begin to live spontaneously and in sync within the greater field of life. The will of the personality is aligned and responding to the directing will of the Spirit, which is a living arm of God's will working in alignment with His purpose.

The awakening personality is committed to using their physical, emotional, and mental bodies as expressions of their inner God consciousness. This means, for example, when we have a physical, emotional, or mental problem, we go within and seek the guidance and direction of our soul to resolve it. Saint Germain explains that whenever we finally comprehend that we have miscreated, we must immediately stop, seek the council of our inner God consciousness, and ask for instruction on how to proceed with our creativity properly. This is how we come to master the lower vehicles—namely, by surrendering our creativity to God-within-us and pursuing our divine abilities rather than continuing to invest in the habitual thought patterns and misperceptions of the separated self.

When we have mastered and coordinated the lower vehicles into an integrated personality *whole* and then merged the personality with the soul (which exists on the upper mental plane), becoming the soul-identified personality, we are able to extend our God consciousness all the way through the body into the physical world. In the fullness of time, as God's plan is worked out, humanity will one day reveal the divinity of God in material form. During this evolutionary process, each person who does this work changes not only his or her own reality but also the reality of the whole.

A Destructive and Constructive Process

Ascension is both a destructive and constructive process that profoundly changes our understanding of who we are and why we are here. I found the following quote the other day:

> *Make no mistake about it—enlightenment is a destructive process. It has nothing to do with becoming better or being happier. Enlightenment is the crumbling away of untruth. It's seeing*

*through the facade of pretense. It's the complete
eradication of everything WE imagined to be true.*

—Adyashanti

This is an interesting quote and speaks to heart of the matter.
The second line may be hard to understand because it refers
to something few us fully understand. Ascension is not about
fixing the world at the physical, emotional, and mental levels
of being. It is about moving out of those limiting states and
seeing them for what they are—temporary experiences that
teach us about the quality of our creative activity. This is
such an important and oft-missed point. What we think of
as "reality" is really just an "ideality"—a massive collection
of ideas and experiences that we have generated over time.
It is actually much closer to a dream state than we'd like to
admit. It serves as a training world designed to teach us the
art, science, and ethics of creative activity.

As I mentioned above, initiation into higher states of being
is quite necessarily a destructive process as we break away
from the delusions of separation and the myopia of our
limited range of awareness. In essence, we progressively
"destroy" the ideality we believe in as we divest ourselves
of our misinterpretations and illusions. But it is also a
constructive process that brings us into affinity with the
larger interconnectivity of our planetary and cosmic reality.
This initiation process opens the door to higher states of
consciousness and creativity. When the soul begins to overlight
the consciousness of the personality, spiritual goals begin to
supersede lower personality desires. This work is not easy,
for it requires an enormous reorientation of the heart and
mind out of our excessively individualistic, acquisitional, and
selfish orientation into a group orientation and a concern for
the welfare of all. It requires an understanding of the Oneness
of Life. The Christians refer to this shift as the manifestation
of "Heaven on Earth," and it is esoterically known as the
"return of the Christ" throughout the brotherhood of man.

In this way, the goal of the ascender is not happiness (emotional satisfaction) but joy (a spiritual state of being). Alice Bailey explains that happiness is seated in our emotions and is a pursuit of the personality and the "goal of the separated self." We experience it when one of our personality desires has been met, such as when we experience physical well-being, contentment with our environment or with the people around us, or satisfaction with our mental endeavors. Joy, she explains, is a "quality of the soul and is realized in the mind when alignment takes place."[59] *It is the result of the realization of the oneness of all beings.* That's an important statement to ponder. When we are able to experience *the oneness*, we are out of the clutches of the individualistic personality and operating at a planetary level of consciousness that recognizes the interconnectivity of all Life. When we operate from here, we live our lives in concert with the greater field of Life. This brings us into alignment with the divine Plan, and we begin to live in sync within a much larger creative process.

Personally, I have found that it does have quite a bit to do with "becoming better" if we define *better* in terms of experiencing freedom from delusion and from the struggles and strife that stem from fearfulness. In other words, we do not arrive at this betterment through repression of the mind or emotions but through liberation from illusion and glamour.

Also, I find that we do have higher states of "happiness" that approach the joyfulness Bailey describes as we free ourselves from the shackles in our minds. Every time we successfully gain more control over our lower instinctual nature, emotional reactions, and fearful thought patterns, we satisfy our aspiration to move beyond our limitations. We en*joy* those moments of clarity and insight that release us from suffering, fear, and pain. However, we also develop a heightened awareness of our imprisonment within our limitations, and this causes us increased frustration and

---

[59]   Bailey, *A Treatise on White Magic*, p. 370

pain. This heightened awareness serves a divine purpose when it impels us to do something about it. Thus, both the joyful and the painful experiences can serve to inspire the mighty explorer within us who fearlessly seeks out the "new land" of higher consciousness.

For those on the path of return, an acceptance of a heightened sense of duality is necessary. We must accept that, for now, we have a higher self and a lower self, and the agenda of these two "selves" is not always the same. And we benefit greatly when we understand that all change is dependent on this dynamic combination of creating and destroying and the associated states of equilibrium and disequilibrium that this process demonstrates. Without both, divine Life would become static and unchangeable. The more we open ourselves with gratitude to *both* aspects of the process, the greater our capacity becomes to awaken and experience joyfulness throughout our journey. Author Brené Brown is noted for teaching us that when we lose our capacity to be vulnerable, we lose our capacity to feel joy.

In the end, a pursuit of happiness will not provide us with sufficient motivation to tread the path of return. Instead an undying and laser-like commitment to *discovering and manifesting our God consciousness* despite any temporary unhappiness this entails is in order. When we become willing to lose the little self we think we are in order to discover the True Self we really are, we grow. In the process, we will be discarding, dismantling, and destroying what we have made out of ignorance and learning how to construct a new reality that is in accordance with Divine knowledge and wisdom. What we gain along this path is well beyond value to anything we lose along the way.

Creating a Bridge to Our Higher Mind

How do move out of our mental and emotional prisons? How do we make contact with the soul and stimulate our intuition? Well, it has to do with building a bridge from the lower mind into the higher. Theosophists call this bridge the *antahkarana*.

As we saw in our description earlier, the mental body is composed of two levels:

1. The lower mental body is the domain of the personality and the seat of our rational, concrete mind.
2. The upper mental body is the domain of the soul and the seat of our abstract mind. It in turn links us to our intuition, which is the domain of our Spirit or Monad.

The lower mind is focused on external reality and concrete thought. It uses reason—that is, inductive and deductive thinking to gain understanding. It is reliant on tangible facts and experiences that are visible and/or observable. The higher mind is focused on the inner planes. It employs abstract thinking and accesses the intuition to gain understanding. Abstract thinking is conceptual and not reliant on tangible facts or observable phenomena. It is reflective, meditative, nonlinear, and holistic. It is the vehicle through which the personality can make contact with spirit through opening the intuition. Intuition is the ability to acquire knowledge without reliance on previously accepted premises or assumptions. Esoterically, it is known as "pure reason," or ideas that are not colored or distorted by preexisting ideas or beliefs.

The antahkarana is built over time as we awaken the heart center and cultivate our intelligence to employ right thinking.[60] Jesus defines right-mindedness as thoughts and emotions that foster and promote love rather than fear.[61] Master Djwal

---

[60] Bailey. *The Light of the soul*
[61] *ACIM*

Khul refers to this process as learning to keep the mind steady in the light, where light is the great revealer. It shows us our nakedness and inspires us to discover the hidden truth. We build this bridge through the internal practices of meditation, quiet reflection, abstract thinking, and intuition, as well as the external practice of being of service to others. The internal practices take our focus off the busy, externalized world and turn our attention inward toward the soul and with the greater field of Life. The soul in turn connects us with the Triadal levels of the Monad. In this way, we learn to work with multiple levels of reality simultaneously. We are continually swinging back and forth between the point of view of the ego-bound personality and the point of view of the soul. At first, the agendas of these two aspects are difficult to align. For example, the personality typically feels it has to earn or acquire love. It comes from a position of lack and wishes to bring love into itself from outside itself. The soul's desire, however, is to express the inherent love within it. It seeks to connect from the fullness of love it knows itself to be and that it knows exists at the center of all things real. The common ground is the experience of love, but the approaches are in opposition, as are the underlying motivating principles. The goal of the ascender is to connect these two states and bring the lower into the higher so that both agendas are fulfilled. Thus, we are challenged with the task of moving

- Out of a lower state of unity where only the personality's reality is known,
- Into a state of duality where both the reality of the personality and the reality of the Spirit are experienced, and
- Back to a higher state of unity where only the reality of the Spirit is known.

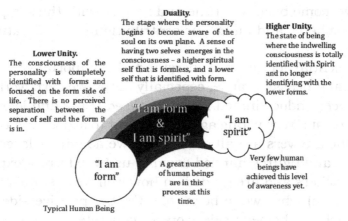

Duality.
The stage where the personality begins to become aware of the soul on its own plane. A sense of having two selves emerges in the consciousness – a higher spiritual self that is formless, and a lower self that is identified with form.

Higher Unity.
The state of being where the indwelling consciousness is totally identified with Spirit and no longer identifying with the lower forms.

Lower Unity.
The consciousness of the personality is completely identified with forms and focused on the form side of life. There is no perceived separation between the sense of self and the form it is in.

"I am form & I am spirit"

"I am spirit"

"I am form"

A great number of human beings are in this process at this time.

Very few human beings have achieved this level of awareness yet.

Typical Human Being

Figure 27: Unity-Duality-Unity

It is in this second phase that the bridge is created between the lower form-identified self and the higher spiritual Self. And because even the lower self has a level of free will, *it* has to be the one to take the initiative and reach out to the soul on its own plane. Once that direction has been established in the consciousness, the soul can respond. The soul on its own plane enters into "deep meditation" and does not cease until connection and reabsorption are realized in the due course of time.[62]

For the purposes of building this bridge, I cannot stress the meditation aspect enough. Spiritual studies are also important, and quiet reflection is necessary. Prayer is a state of mind where we are able to make our heartfelt requests for guidance, and meditation is how we get our answers. The meditative process of bringing the brain, mind, and soul into energetic alignment allows us to connect our lower mind with our higher. It puts the mind and brain of the personality into a quiet, receptive state that allows the presence of the soul to come forward in our awareness. Now, the soul can communicate and become the active director of the receptive personality. This is how we intuit our answers and discover our part of the larger Plan we are operating within. This is

---

[62]   Bailey. *A Treatise on White Magic.*

how we come back into tune and in sync with the symphony of the spheres and make our contribution to the Creation.

It's essential for us to understand the importance of this internal process because, especially in the Western world, we have been indoctrinated in *externalized* living and learning. Starting at a very young age, we are sent to school and taught that the answers are all outside us. We acquire a large pool of facts and figures handed down to us by external "experts" and teachers and are graded on how well we assimilate (and agree with) what we've been told. On the positive side, this approach has helped us develop our concrete, rational minds. We have been well trained in the art of concrete thinking. With such things as the introduction of advanced mathematics and quantum physics, we have even made strong inroads into abstract thinking. This has all served to stimulate the initial development of our mental body. The negative is that is has taught us to distrust our own intuition and others', too. We've been programmed into thinking that someone else needs to approve or sanction our inner knowing before we can trust it. This is especially so if our intuition is leading us to question the status quo or introduce new and "foreign" concepts.

Now, however, we are ready as a human race to activate and employ our abstract mind by developing what I call holographic thinking—the ability to see connection, pattern, or relationship between seemingly disparate parts. This ability is reliant on intuition, visualization, and neutrality, which are all divine qualities. Intuition is direct one-to-one communication with Spirit unfiltered by preconceived notions. Visualization is the ability to receive an idea being transmitted to us from a higher plane and to imagine its expression. Neutrality is freedom from fear and judgment, and this freedom opens us up to infinite possibilities; it enables us to think outside the boxes we've created in our minds. Intuition, visualization, abstract thinking, and neutrality have underpinned every invention and every major advancement made in the course of mankind's evolution. Martin Luther had to question the status quo and invest in his inner vision of direct one-to-one communication with God to usher in a new era of spiritual inquiry and expression. The founding fathers of America had to envision a radically different form of government and pursue that vision with unwavering perseverance, sparing neither life nor limb to realize their dream. Edison had to imagine the lightbulb was possible and follow his intuition in order to bring it to fruition. He had to remain neutral to failure and ridicule and persist with his work until he succeeded. The Wright brothers had to dream of flying and think outside the box to bring us the airplane. These are just a few examples of people who moved out of what was known and established in order to tap a deep well of inner wisdom that enabled them to bring something new into manifestation.

Meditation allows all the lower bodies to let go and make room for new ideas and experiences that are in greater alignment with our divine purpose. Each higher body provides us with what is necessary to master the body below. Mastery of the mental body stems from the causal body—the body of the soul—and it is the seat of our intuitive mind. Our intuition gives us new ideas, a new point of view, and a new plan. From there, we can use the rational mind to help us execute the new plan. As we strengthen our minds, we are able to master our emotions. As we learn to be still, to detach from emotional upheaval, and to let go of the past, we arrive at a level of discernment that allows us to choose to invest in thoughts and emotions that foster love rather than constantly being pushed around by the tides of our emotions. As we master the emotional body, we increase the wellness and energetic coordination of our etheric-physical body. It is in the work of interconnected alignment and the development of discernment and intuitive living that we build the bridge and provide the means for mastery of our lower vehicles of expression.

Janet Myatt

In Sum

In Part I, we have taken a look at the following points:

- We exist within God, and everything in the Creation is in God and of God.
- There is a descending and ascending hierarchy of beingness within which deity expresses, creates, and evolves as the experiential aspect of God.
- Deity experience exists in various degrees of evolutionary progress.
- There are interconnecting playgrounds of creative activity within this hierarchy, each with various degrees of scope and specificity and in various stages of the evolutionary process.
- There is a downward journey from unity into individuation and an upward journey from individuation back into unity.
- The triple qualities of will, love, and intelligence are the basis of all creative activity, but the process of manifesting is dual:
  o Spirit and matter
  o Thought and energy
  o Positive charge and negative charge
  o The activity between the two poles precipitates a third state, quality or form (e.g., consciousness, form, attraction)
- We use three vehicles of expression during an incarnation, and they are interconnected and interdependent but serve different functions.
- Individuation took place in the human kingdom once the human animal form was sophisticated enough to support self-awareness.
- During the individuation phase of evolution, human beings mistakenly identified themselves with their vehicles of expression rather than with their true identity as spirit.

- This led to various types of delusion that we are still in process of recovering from to this day:
  - o Maya—thinking we are our bodies
  - o Glamour—thinking we are our emotions
  - o Illusion—thinking we are our ideas and ideals
- Misidentification gave rise to a fearful state of mind, which colors the experience of the ego and distorts our perceptions of ourselves, others, and the world around us. (We will be exploring this stage in depth in Part II.)
- We have before us the task of mastering our bodies, emotions, and thoughts and coordinating them into one integrated whole that enables us to be impactful and effective in the world.
- The integrated personality then has the task of making contact with and merging with the soul and entering the path of return.
- This starts the initiation or ascension process.
- This gives rise to a heightened sense of duality and of having two "selves"—a higher and a lower.
- These two aspects of self have conflicting agendas until the personality learns to understand and trust the soul and to identify with it.
  - o This shift moves us out of a focus on the fulfillment of purely selfish or self-oriented desires and into a focus on serving the highest good of the whole. We move from a focus on *me* to *we*.
- The mind is the gateway to the soul and the means by which we master the physical and emotional bodies and integrate our personality. It is the avenue of approach into higher levels of consciousness and states of being.
- Ascension is a creative and destructive process that involves large expansions of consciousness and movement into new ways of identifying ourselves that lead us out of our delusional "ideality" and into the greater reality of God.
- Meditation, spiritual study, quiet reflection, and being of service to others are the avenues of approach that

Janet Myatt

enable us to build the bridge between the lower self
and the higher self.

In Part II, we're going to explore the rise of the ego or the
consciousness side of things from the perspective of the lower
self because this is where we all start, and because this phase
of our journey is the toughest. Understanding how fear colors
our experience and how the wounded ego works gives us the
information we need to begin to move out of that state of
mind. In Part III, we'll explore the integration process—again
from the perspective of the lower self as it seeks to make
contact with and understand the higher. This gives us specific
strategies to employ to aid us on our journey.

Chapter 4 Exercises

The Eternal Law of Life is that "Whatever you think and feel you bring into form; where your thought is there you are for you are your consciousness; and whatever you meditate upon you become."[63]

1. Take a few moments now to sit in quiet reflection, still your body and mind, and go within to that neutral place where you can act as a witness reviewing your personality in everyday life.
   - What kind of thoughts are running through your mind throughout your day? Are they mostly positive and loving or negative and defensive?
   - What are you teaching yourself about life with these thoughts? What kind of reality are you bringing into existence?
2. Over the next week, tune in periodically throughout your day and become aware of the quality of your thoughts, both those in the foreground and those running in the background almost at a subconscious level. At the end of the week, make an honest assessment of the percentage of thoughts that are positive, supportive, and kind (toward yourself and others) and that carry a vibration of harmlessness compared with the percentage that are negative, judgmental, fearful, competitive, worried, stressed, and so forth.
3. In meditation, tune in to your body and pay attention to what happens to it when you run positive thoughts and emotions through your system and what happens when you run negative thoughts and emotions. For example:
   - Place your mind in a negative frame and see where the energy clenches in your body.
     o What does this tell you about your health or any chronic issues you may experience?

---

[63] King. Locations 294–295.

- o What is your body trying to show you about the quality of your energy?
- Place your mind in a positive frame and see how the body responds energetically.
- Place your mind in a neutral frame and put your attention on the areas in your body you noticed in the first step. Imagine using your "God-hand" to direct that energy out of your space. Use a grounding cord (a line of energy you envision extending from the base of your spine into the center of the planet) and guide that energy right down the drain.
  - o To help you do this, imagine a color for the stuck or painful energy and watch that color flow out of your space.
  - o Now, replace the energy with what you want in there instead. Again, imagine a color for the new quality you're bringing in. Ask your Higher Self to send that energy to you in a huge golden ball of energy above your head, reach up, and pull that energy right in. Imagine it filling all the places that just released.

4. In our discussion of creating and destroying, we talked about the difference between the pursuit of happiness and the pursuit of joy. What is your spiritual goal for this lifetime?
   - It's important to be honest when working with ourselves, and we are typically working on several things simultaneously—at least in the beginning. The point of this question is to give you the opportunity to check in with your soul, access your inner wisdom, and see if the creative goals you hold at the personality level are aligned or in conflict with the goals of your soul. If the latter, ask your soul for clarification and guidance on your incarnational purpose.
     - o What needs to be destroyed in your life?
     - o What needs to be created?

- Revisit this question after you've completed the book. The answers you uncover may change, deepen, or become clearer.
- This is a good daily practice to include in your meditation and quiet reflection space. Each day, check in with your soul and ask what needs to happen that day.

Part II: Rise of the Ego

Your ego is so focused upon physical reality and survival within it that you do not hear the inner voice. You must realize that what you are cannot be seen in a mirror.

—Janet Roberts, *The Seth Material*[64]

Ego is no more than this:...complete identification with form—physical forms, thought forms, emotional forms. This results in a total unawareness of your connectedness with the whole...This forgetfulness is original sin, suffering, delusion.

—Eckhart Tolle, *A New Earth*[65]

The ego is a wrong-minded attempt to perceive yourself as you wish to be, rather than as you are...It is capable of asking questions but not of perceiving meaningful answers, because these would involve knowledge and cannot be perceived.

—Jesus, *A Course in Miracles*[66]

---

[64]   Roberts. *The Seth Material*. Kindle edition, Location 3597.

[65]   Tolle, Eckhart. *A New Earth*, p. 22.

[66]   *ACIM*, p. 42.

Chapter 5 ~ Misidentification

The development of maya, glamour, and illusion during our early evolutionary stages put us in a position where we became misidentified with our forms of expression. The ego of the lower self is a state of mind that hinges on our overidentification with our forms, emotions, and thoughts. It's a state of mind that's built on our sense of separation and isolation from one another and the universe we dwell within.

The Ageless Wisdom teachings point out that all three lower bodies are material. They are all forms made up of bits of charged matter—dense or subtle—and are distinguishable by the particular manner or definite patterns they display. These patterns reveal the particular condition and quality of the body being used. *Life* energy flows into the patterns we call "bodies," animates them, and reveals the patterns in tangible form. The ego, however, does not see it this way. In simple terms, the ego identity believes the *body* gives us life and that our experiences define who we are. But this is actually a reversal of the truth. We are the indwelling spirit that gives Life to the body. We are the sentient being who has desires and the thinker who has thoughts. As such, our experiences teach us about the quality of our thinking and feeling in the lower three worlds but in no way change the fundamental fact of *who* we actually are, which is divine Spirit in action.

Reversing Cause and Effect

Through our overidentification with the form side of life, we have reversed cause and effect in our minds. We think that

141

the world is the cause of our misery, and we all spend a great deal of time trying to get the world around us to change so we can be happy. We want others to love us so we can feel safe and good about ourselves. We want the world to stop being so hard so we can enjoy our lives more. We want our bodies to stop hurting so we can enjoy them. But, try as we might, we cannot get life to conform to our wishes. We cannot change the world, we cannot change others, and we often feel betrayed by our own bodies when they get sick or don't work the way we want them to. This is because we are going about it backward. We are trying to change the effect rather than the cause.

Believe it or not, we are each the causal force of our own lives, and the world we create is the result of our creative activity. The creative process works much like a slide projector: Divine Life energy is like the light that shines through a projector. It is neutral and flows into the lower mind, which is full of our thoughts and beliefs. Thoughts and beliefs form blueprints or "pictures," which work like the slides in the projector. The chakra system works like the projector. It converts the pictures into a tangible form just as a projector throws an image out on a screen. Perception—what we become aware of—is our "screen."

Figure 28: Our Thoughts Create Our Reality

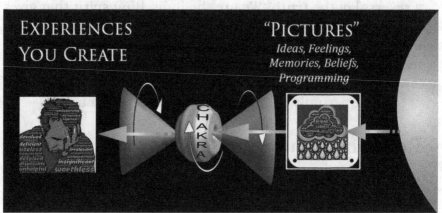

External reality is our mirror. It reflects back to us what we're projecting. Most of us repeatedly try to change or manipulate the refection, but it's merely the effect (the picture on the screen) rather than the cause (our thoughts and beliefs). It cannot be done. We must change the picture the light is shining through; we must change the thoughts and beliefs we are focused on and perceiving life through.

We know this from our own experience. When we're in a bad mood, we have bad day. When we're in a good mood, we have a good day. When we're happy, we see the good in others. When we're unhappy, we see the bad. And what determines our mood? We often think it's the external world, but it's really our reaction to the external world. We're always saying, "You did this to me." But in reality, we feel the way we do about the other person's behavior because of our own internal thoughts about their behavior. And these thoughts are based on our own needs and beliefs. In the end, this is actually good news and shows us just how much power we actually have.

This does not mean that we are responsible for other people's bad behavior or for all that is happening in the world around us. It means that the way we're experiencing it is dependent on our perceptions, and our perceptions are dependent on our beliefs and judgements. We cannot change our external reality from the outside in; we can change it only from the inside out.

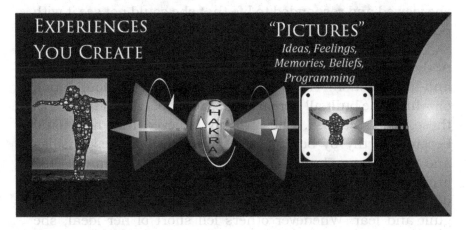

Change the thought or belief that we are projecting, and we change our experience. Let me give an example.

Rickie's Story

Rickie came to me after a painful crisis at work. She was devastated over an incident where one of her employees had accused her of creating a hostile work environment. The company took this charge seriously and opened up a monthlong investigation. Rickie wholeheartedly believed the charge was completely unfounded and felt deeply betrayed by both the employee and the company. She was also afraid she might unjustly lose her job.

Even though Rickie was eventually exonerated, our work together revealed that she did have anger issues that would occasionally show up in her tone of voice and her attitude, despite the fact that she was generally a friendly, loving, warm person overall. The tense tone and angry vibe stemmed out of an overwhelming need to be viewed as perfect, capable, and responsible; these in turn stemmed out of a deep need to feel accepted, safe, and in control of her environment. She had no idea that she was communicating her irritation and judgment in her meetings with others because she also worked very hard at "being nice." Her perfectionism and need to control everything was such a major lens through which she viewed and responded to life that she could not see it with perspective. It worked as a "given" in her life.

At the root of it all was a deep, abiding sense of worthlessness and imperfection. These core beliefs created the foundation on which she built all her strategies for coping with the stress these beliefs caused. She strongly believed that she could become worthy by being perfect, efficient, and responsible, and these things looked a particular way in her mind. This premise also became the foundation for judging the worth of others. Whenever she fell short of her ideal, she suffered guilt and fear. Whenever others fell short of her ideal, she felt anger and resentment. Surprisingly, she had no idea that these emotions and judgments were showing up in her communication because she was focusing on making sure the job was done right rather than on the quality of the communication involved in getting the job done. She also assumed she was right and they were wrong.

Over time, Rickie came to understand that these subconscious fears and beliefs about herself (her pictures) were causing repeating patterns of miscommunication and invalidation in her life. With this realization, she began to make a huge shift in the way she valued herself (she began to change her pictures). This caused a change for the better in the way she communicated with others. Her external reality (the effect) began to change as a result of the internal change she was making about her worth and value. She continues to struggle with her perfectionism, but with her new awareness she is able to have insight into situations when they go astray and make constructive changes that enable her to be much more successful in her communication with others she finds challenging.

Rickie's story is a great example of how cause and effect works. She unconsciously believed she was worthless and imperfect; as a result, that was reflected back to her in her experiences at work. Rickie came to understand that the rejection she experienced in the external world was an outward manifestation, or projection, of her internal rejected state of mind. As she learned to move her identity out of feelings of worthlessness and imperfection, her need to control her environment decreased, along with her anger and hostility toward the imperfection of others.

Rickie's story is everyone's story. At the heart of all our suffering is a core belief or set of beliefs rooted in fear about our safety and our worth.

How does this happen, and why?

Janet Myatt

We have created a reality that is distorted by the delusions we have about who we are. When we first started experimenting with material reality, we understood ourselves to be the Formless One creating forms (such as human bodies) to express through. Over time, however, we began to believe that the forms we live in were the basis of our existence. We slowly forgot that we were That which made the forms. We sank our consciousness deeply into the body and its animal drives, sensations, and responses.

Overidentifying with our bodies led to the next level of delusion, which emerged as a result of our sentient, emotional responses to the physical world. We began to believe that we are what we feel rather than That which feels and experiences. This physical sense-centered existence gave rise to countless conflicting emotions and feelings that in turn created a conflicting external reality. As our human consciousness continued to evolve, we sought to understand what we were experiencing, and this led us into a third type of delusion, which formed around our ideas. We eventually came to think of ourselves as being our bodies, our emotions, and our thoughts and beliefs rather than That which thinks and experiences.

Imagine you are a playwright, and you write a story you find so fascinating and love so much that you decide to play the leading role day and night. You literally want to *become* this character and viscerally experience his or her world. Over time, though, your conscious awareness attaches so deeply and exclusively with the character and his or her experiences that you eventually forget you are the originating author, not the character.

Having bodies, emotions, and ideas is not delusional. However, believing that we exist only within these forms is. The minute we came to believe that we exist only when we have a body, physical survival took center stage in our minds. We lost touch with our immortal divine Self and became filled with a fear of dying. Out of this fear, the lower ego is born, and it colors what we experience for as long as we believe in it.

Birth of the Ego

In childhood, the bond with our primary caregivers is of vital importance and has an incredible impact on our developing identity. We intuitively know ourselves to be utterly dependent on our "mother" (whoever takes on that role) and instinctively strive to remain connected with that source of food, comfort, and safety. In this way, connecting with external reality and an external source of care replaces the disrupted connection with our divine Source and our internal Spirit.

In *The Shadow Effect*, spiritual teacher Marianne Williamson remembers coming into the world at birth full of love and light. But the delivery doctor's slap jolted her consciousness and threw her into an unexpected frame of mind. She lost her connection with her spiritual Self and was flooded with pain and resistance:

> So just as I felt this extraordinary love beaming out of me to all living things, in the very next moment I felt myself slapped. The doctor, whom I already loved, had hit me. I remember being absolutely and totally confused, hurt, and traumatized. Why would he do that? I just could not believe that this had happened. And then my mind went blank.[67]

As soon as her mind went blank, a new reality began to form.

When the connection with our God-self is lost, the resulting void must be filled. This new reality is the spawning ground

---

[67] Chopra, Deepak; Ford, Debbie; Williamson, Marianne. *The Shadow Effect: Illuminating the Hidden Power of Your True Self.* Kindle edition, p. 152.

of the lower ego. Because we are utterly dependent on others outside ourselves for our physical survival, we are indeed forced turn our attention outward. And it is "out there" that we try to get our needs met. In infancy, our instinctive primary need is to be loved and cared for by the people we belong to in order to ensure our survival. Consequently, we instinctively look externally for love, care, protection, acceptance, safety, and security, and these external experiences color our internal world and form the initial pictures we have about ourselves, others, and the world around us.

When I looked at my own birth psychically, I was puzzled by my lack of any sense of "I" or "me." As I watched myself being born, I was aware that I was not in the infant body. I existed as a nonphysical, loving, intelligent Presence in the room, watching the body as it was being born. I observed all that was going on, but there was no "me," no ego. My sense of myself was not yet connected to the infant body or physical reality. I still identified myself as a nonphysical being—a spirit. I hadn't experienced this particular life in the body and had not yet formed an ego identity with body-based ideas about myself or the world.

Over time, I began to develop an identity around my body-based experiences. I eventually learned to identify myself as Janet, as a girl, as a daughter, as a sister, and so forth. These are just labels and don't mean much in and of themselves. It was *how I experienced being* Janet, being a girl, and so forth that created the central core of my ego. From there, I learned my family's beliefs and values and internalized them as my own. As my focus became more external, my sense of myself and my value quickly became dependent on what I experienced in my body and my physical environment, especially in relationship to others.

This is key: our relationship with others outside ourselves replaces or usurps our internal relationship with our God-self, which is now perceived as something separate from us or nonexistent.

This is what the lower ego is really all about. It is an identity that emerges from a sense of separation from the eternal Self, rooted in an overattachment to the body and formed in response to our perceptions of our relationships with others and with our environment—perceptions that form our beliefs.

Primal Drive for Acceptance and Love

Medical intuitive Caroline Myss explains in her book *Anatomy of the Spirit*[68] that our dependence on our caregivers creates a strong emotional need for acceptance, security, and stability. In the basic animal level of our consciousness, we know that without a strong connection to at least one primary caregiver, we will die. Any experience that we perceive as a threat to that connection will carry a huge charge because it is so closely tied to our survival. And because cause and effect are reversed in the ego, we believe the world around us causes our reality and what we experience is the effect. As a result, our dependency on others for our basic survival puts persistent stress on our psyche.

The foundational beliefs of the ego develop during this early experience of dependency. As young children, not only are we dependent on others, but we are also unable to understand the larger context of our experiences, and we take everything personally. We do not have the cognitive ability, life experience, or larger perspective to interpret our experiences fully.

Imagine waking up on a strange planet, with absolutely no memory of how you got there or who you are. You don't speak the language, you don't know where anything is, everyone and everything is a stranger, it's getting cold and dark, and you're hungry. What do you do? Step 1: You look around for

---

[68] Myss, Caroline. *Anatomy of the Spirit*

help. You try to communicate with whomever you find nearby, and you try to build some kind of connection with that person because you need food and shelter now. Step 2: Once your immediate needs are met and you know you will survive, you try to fit in and belong. You learn to speak the language. You learn the customs. You learn what's expected of you in order to feel accepted, safe, and so forth. As children, this is how we go about surviving in the external world; we look for external resources and adapt to them. The younger we are in the above scenario, the more dependent we are on others. In response to our pressing needs, we come up with our own unique strategies for coping with the stress of our survival. How we experience this process deeply affects our feelings about ourselves, others, and the world around us.

Let's look at the stressful environment of a temper tantrum. A screaming, crying child is angry and frustrated because she cannot have her way. Different parents respond in different ways. Some will attempt to reason with the child. Another may ignore her and wait it out. Another parent may scold, belittle, or even spank the child to get her to stop. And some will give in and give the child what she wants even if it's not in her best interest (candy, for example). No matter what the response from the parent is, the child will arrive at certain conclusions about herself, others, and the world as a result.

At the same time, those conclusions will not account for other factors, such as the parent's mood or stresses that have nothing to do with the child. For example, if her parent kindly but firmly denies her the candy, the child will not appreciate that her parent is actually acting in her best interest. If her parent ignores her and leaves her to calm down on her own, the child may well conclude that she's not very important and that her parent doesn't care about her. (This is not a given conclusion but a possible response, for the sake of our example.) If her parent gives her the candy, she will not understand that her behavior is negative.

If the parent spanks her, the scenario gets even more intense because the child feels the spanking emotionally *and* physically. This adds to her original distress. From her point of view, she is simply behaving from an emotionally authentic place and not getting her immediate need met. With spanking, she is experiencing physical pain and emotional rejection, too. In all these examples, the child doesn't have the ability to understand that it is her behavior and not her "self" that is not OK. This is of fundamental importance. Feel the difference in the following two statements:

- "I am not OK."
- "My behavior is not OK."

The former works as a label. It is definitive—fixed, static, and final. There is little room for change; it works as an identity. The latter describes an action or reaction, and it can be changed.

Feeling "not OK" adds to our fear of death. On an instinctual level, it threatens our inclusion in the group, which in childhood is absolutely necessary for our survival. We instinctively develop strategies to ensure our survival, and these become the subconscious rules we live by. They form the early mental/emotional blueprints (the pictures in our slide projector) that create repeating patterns in our lives. For instance, in the example of the temper tantrum, the child may conclude any of the following:

- "It's not safe for me to ask for what I want."
- "It's not OK for me to be angry or show my feelings."
- "The world is unfair, and I can never have what I want."
- "I am a bad person, and I don't deserve love."

How we respond to stress is unique to us. Three different children in the same home facing the same types of stress will arrive at three different assumptions and three different strategies for coping. Adding to the complexity, many of these assumptions and strategies often stem from past-life experiences that are carried over into the current life for resolution.

Other more neutral situations affect our developing sense of self, too. We are constantly taking in what is happening to us and trying to make sense of it. For example, a child may be hungry and want food, but the parent has not cooked dinner yet. The child will have to wait. One child may learn to ignore his hunger and distract himself with his toys. Over time, this fairly positive adaptive behavior may develop into more widespread avoidance behavior in adolescence and adulthood. For instance, he may develop the habit of mentally and/or emotionally "checking out" when stressed. He may begin to ignore his problems by diverting his attention into playing video games, watching TV, or continually looking the other way instead of dealing with stressful situations head on. Another child may not be content to wait and will become fussy and demanding. If that behavior gets him the results he's looking for, he may develop into a rather demanding person when stressed.

The point is that within the ego, everything seems personal. In early childhood, our experiences carry an additional emotional charge because they are so closely tied to our need to survive. What happens within these primary relationships establishes deep-seated patterns or blueprints that repeat throughout our lives until we finally stop and question them in adulthood.

When we are conscientious parents, becoming aware of this process can often fill us with confusion. How do we discipline our children and teach them right from wrong, knowing they will experience their reactions in this immature way? I can share with you only my evolving understanding. I have learned that it is indeed our job to set limits and provide reasonable consequences. However, I have found that we must also allow our children to work things out for themselves. The trick is to find a healthy balance between these two things. We have the opportunity to encourage them to discover their own answers and to guide them with a steady, loving hand that slowly releases the reigns over to them as they mature and grow in experience. We have to accept that aspects of our children's lives will be difficult. If we send them the message that they are OK and we know they'll figure it out, we help them feel confident and able. If we send them the message that they are not OK and we're afraid they will fail, we undermine them.

The Dalai Lama says we should teach all children how to meditate when they're eight years old and start directing them inward for their answers. I sure wish I'd done that with my children. I have learned repeatedly with each of my children that each of us has his or her own road to travel in life. When we choose to incarnate, we set the stage for certain lessons to take place, and we all arrive with certain predispositions, which we have to work out in our own way. At the soul level, parent and child choose one another, and we know ahead of time that certain issues will have a high probability of occurring. We are here to learn from our experiences—the positive and the negative—and in so doing activate our divine potential.

Initial Supercharged Experience of Loss

I discovered in my own process as an adult that it is not just the needs of the body that urge us to connect with others. Rather, connection is the inherent truth of the universe, and it's in our nature to want to connect. Even after birth, when we have forgotten our spiritual origins, we have a vague memory of the interconnectedness of all things and seek it out, however unconsciously.

In fact, we have to learn to believe in separation. Psychologists have pointed out that newborns and infants don't initially experience themselves as separate from their mother (or primary caregiver) or from their environment. The experience of being an individual separate from "mother" slowly emerges in our minds at around age two, and this developmental phase is usually fraught with anxiety; we've all heard the phrase "the terrible twos." Once we experience ourselves as something separate and apart from everything else, we begin to feel vulnerable and afraid. From birth forward, we instinctively feel safe when we feel connected and loved, and we feel unsafe when we feel alone, isolated, or unloved.

I believe our primary disconnection with the true nature of the Universe actually creates our first supercharged blueprint of loss. We feel cut off, cast out. Our emerging identities arise amid this monumental sense of loss and rejection, regardless of the positive or negative circumstances of the external environment. Our egos can explain this feeling of deep loss only by concluding that we were rejected by *something* because the ego itself is unable to question our misidentification. It is the very orientation of the ego that creates the experience of separation. It cannot have a conscious understanding of a Self that it cannot conceive of.

For example, one of my core beliefs is that I'm not good enough, so I wanted to get to the bottom of this belief. How did I arrive at this conclusion? The first memory that came up for me was of being bullied when I was in middle school. This was something I had processed many times over the years. Yet I felt certain that there was something deeper at play, something that had already been in place before that experience. I began tracking a familiar coping strategy of mine: striving to please others, even at my own expense. My question was, "When did I first decide that I needed to please others in order to be safe?" I didn't come up with a specific memory. Instead, a symbolic "movie" emerged in my mind's eye. I saw an image of my two-year-old self standing with her arms outstretched. She was feeling confused and forlorn because she wanted her mother to pick her up, but her mother couldn't do that because she had a baby in her arms.

I was very surprised by this revelation from my inner child, but it's true that my brother was born when I was almost two. I went from being an only child with my mother's undivided attention to a sibling who had to share her mother. It became clear to me that because I was so young, I simply wasn't able to understand why my mother couldn't pick me up every time I cried or needed a cuddle anymore. Baby Janet felt that something vitally important was somehow in jeopardy. My baby interpretation of this external experience was a projection of my internal, primary, supercharged blueprint of loss—the one formed shortly after birth when I moved from my identity as a divine Self experiencing connection with God into a self who identified with the human body experiencing separation. My mother served as a replacement for God, and that two-year-old experience of disconnection from my mother mirrored my original experience of loss of connection with God.

I believe we all deeply long for the total connection we had with the Divine before we were born. Just about every client I've ever worked with has felt some level of sadness or disappointment—and, in many cases, deep anger—over the quality of the connection they had with one or both of their parents. We all arrived with a recollection of our divine connection. But as soon as we identified with our bodies, the connection was lost. The moment that happened, our initial blueprint of loss was established. What is important about this is the fact that in a very real way the sadness, disappointment, or anger we feel toward our parents was inevitable. It was a projection of this initial blueprint of loss or rejection. As we saw earlier, what we feel colors our experiences. Everything we experienced after birth was already flowing through that initial blueprint of loss.

In my case, the two-year-old Janet experienced a loss of attention (stressor) that was beyond her understanding. From her childish point of view, she concluded that she needed to be pleasing in order to be loved (adaptive response). The underlying belief of "I'm not good enough" was already in play. It was the effect caused by my loss of connection with the Divine within me and all around me. Obviously, the feeling that I might somehow be less valuable to my mother because she now had another child makes sense only from the point of view of my two-year-old self. From the larger lens of my adult self, my childish impression is clearly not true and doesn't make sense. But what is key here is that from the even larger lens of my divine Self, external love can never replace internal love. All that drama exists only within the lower ego, and the ego exists only in the part of our consciousness that believes it is cut off from our divinity.

It's true that in the world of the ego, we also have positive perceptions of our experiences that temporarily help offset the negative perceptions. However, both perceptions are experienced within the separated ego, and thus they add to the storm of conflicting ideas and beliefs we have about ourselves. Both the positive and negative perceptions are conditional and passing and do not include the possibility of a divine Self.

For example, the developing ego may conclude, "I'm okay because my parents love me." This is quite different from the divine Self's understanding of, "I am a creative expression of God and worthy simply because I exist as such." The child feels "OK" when he is pleasing his parent and "not OK" when he is displeasing his parent. Either way, his internal state depends on something or someone outside himself. It is conditional; certain conditions must be met. Emotionally, any behavior that is rejected by the parent (or others) will create some level of anxiety that the parent's love (or love in general) may go away.

Children come to their own conclusions about their experience, and degrees of anxiety will vary from person to person. But either way, in the end, children's self-worth is dependent on what they believe about themselves, others, and the world around them. This creates a distortion because we are not what others believe we are; we are not even what we believe we are. We are the children of God, and this truth sits outside any ego-created beliefs. In this way, then, our most potent beliefs, opinions, and assumptions about ourselves and the world around us (stemming as they do from this formative time when we had no way of understanding the greater context of our experiences) are inherently immature and biased toward self-protection. Furthermore, even though our adult mind can certainly take into consideration the larger context of any given situation, it is still stuck in the false paradigm of separation from our divine identity, and this continues to pose a problem for us. Our sense of self-worth becomes relative to our experience rather than a given. Thus, it is always in a state of flux, and this increases our fearfulness. The soul on its own plane uses experience not to determine self-worth but to activate our creative potential. We are meant to learn about the quality of our thinking and the quality of our desires. Do our thoughts and beliefs result in a feeling of connection with others and with God, or do they result in feelings of separation from others and from the greater field of life?

As children of God, we are worthy simply because we exist. In any given situation, what we do with our creativity may be spiritually valuable or a waste of time, but what we do does not change *who* we are. When we get this straight, we can stop wasting time trying to fill ourselves up from the outside in, and we can begin to shine our light from the inside out. This understanding frees us to use our creativity as God had in mind.

It is very important when coming to terms with our ego that we understand that every thought, idea, and belief we hold ultimately comes from a choice we made consciously or unconsciously, actively or passively, to accept it as truth. When we really begin to understand this, we finally have the opportunity to get out of a victim mentality and start to rediscover our power.

Repeating Patterns

One of the very first things I do with clients is help them identify the root cause of repeating patterns of loss or limitation in their lives. This invariably leads us back to early childhood and their relationship with one or both of their parents. I have found that no matter how attentive or ideal one's childhood might have been, no parent can replace God. No parent—no other person outside ourselves—can possibly fill all our needs all the time or be who we need them to be to feel completely safe, worthy, and good about ourselves.

Sarah's Story

Sarah's mother wasn't really interested in being a mother. She spent most of her time talking on the phone with her friends, going out to lunch, shopping, and generally ignoring her children. She let them fend for themselves. Sarah's father was a nice but ineffective man. He made sure dinner was on the table and that Sarah had lunch money, but he never confronted his wife about her neglect of the children. He was passive as a husband and father. As a result, Sarah grew up feeling unimportant and unloved. She resented her mother greatly and wondered why she even had children in the first place if she wasn't going to nurture them. Sarah loved her father and felt he cared about her, but she was frustrated by his inability to form a deeper emotional connection with her.

Sarah came to me because her love relationship was confusing and dissatisfying. Her married lover was in an open relationship—somewhat available but not fully available— and was sending her mixed signals. She felt as if she needed to end the relationship but couldn't bring herself to do so. Her lover had showered her with attention and thoughtful gifts for several months and then backed off as soon as Sarah became deeply attached. Sarah wanted to please her lover and tried to honor a request for more space, but the lover continued to text her daily and remain involved in her day-to-day life. This was very confusing and hurtful. One moment, her deep-seated need to be loved was being fulfilled; the next moment, she was being rejected again.

Sarah's situation was a perfect reflection of the painful belief she had formed in early childhood: "I desperately want love and attention, but I can't have it." Rejection was a repeating pattern in her life. Her first marriage also reflected this pattern when her spouse suddenly decided to leave her shortly after their daughter was born. The current relationship found her once again wanting but not having.

By the time Sarah came to me, she was ready to make a transformational shift in her life but didn't know how. She had done some previous work with a therapist and was already aware of her lingering resentment toward her mother. In our work together, she allowed herself to access her inner wounded child and open up to new levels of compassion, forgiveness, and self-validation for herself and her mother. Once she understood the larger context of her reality, she allowed her divine Self to take over the role of primary caregiver in her life and let go of her resentment toward her mother. These powerful experiences helped Sarah begin to dissolve her early blueprints, and she began to give herself the acceptance, attention, and unconditional love she craved. She came to see the situation with her lover within the larger context of this repeating blueprint, and this freed her to think in new ways and make new choices.

As a result of this work, she began to have a better relationship with her mother and ultimately found she had the strength to end the relationship with the hot-and-cold lover. No sooner had she done this than a new love relationship based on mutual giving and receiving appeared in her life. Her journey taught her the importance of forgiving her parents for being less than she needed. This enabled her to release the pain of the early neglect and rejection she experienced, and it showed her how to give and receive love from the divine Source that had been within her all along. From the soul's perspective, this was a successful experience. It caused Sarah to activate and actuate the powers of forgiveness, compassion, and self-care. Once activated, she was able to create her life in a way that reflected these divine qualities.

Life Theme

The core pictures we form in early childhood set up the unconscious theme for our life. This theme persists until we uncover and move out of the core belief. Our coping behavior gives us an important clue about our core fears and our deepest needs.

Here are a few examples to give you an idea of how you can uncover your life theme.

Coping Behavior	Underlying Need	Core Belief	Theme
People pleasing	Acceptance/ love	I'm not good enough.	Attracting and focusing on situations where one feels rejected and unloved
Bullying	Power/ control	I'm powerless.	Attracting people and situations that involve power struggles; chronic feelings of anger and disempowerment

Withdrawing emotionally	Safety/ connection	Emotions are bad. I'm unsafe, I'm unloved.	Continually overwhelmed by life
Hiding	To be seen	It's not safe to be me.	Afraid of others, afraid of life, afraid to take risks
Drama queen/king	Attention	I am not important.	Focuses on problems and on the self

This short list gives you an idea of how you can go about uncovering your core belief(s).

1. What is the recurring theme in your life?
2. How do you react—what is your coping strategy?
3. What do you really want/need?
4. What is your underlying belief?

Once we figure out the honest answers to these questions, we can start to make corrective changes and ask directly for what we want and need. We can begin to reach out to our inner wise Self and discover the divine qualities that need to be activated to move out of this repeating story. As we do that, we find the silver lining and serve the higher purpose of the soul.

Chapter 5 Exercises

Am I My Body?

Shifting your awareness from the body to the Spirit is an important step in realizing who you really are. Do you believe you are your body? Do you believe you are your actions? Do you believe you are your possessions, your accomplishments, or even your thoughts? Are you ready to question those beliefs? Let us begin with the body. Can you imagine for a moment that you are not your body?

Find a comfortable chair and sit quietly for a moment. Close your eyes and pay attention to your breathing. Allow your body to rest. Now, ask yourself, "Am I my body? Am I my big toe? Am I my fingernails? Am I my skin? Am I my hair, my eyes, my heart?" Go through all the parts of your body and ask if this part is you. Be aware of which parts cause you to laugh and realize, "Of course I'm not _____." Be aware of which parts of your body that you're really attached to—parts that have defined you in your own mind.

What answers came up for you? What questions? It might be helpful to write them down. Keeping a journal of your experiences can be quite validating. You can do this exercise with any number of beliefs you have about who you are. But the essence of what is intended here is for you to discover that the part of you that is observing you asking the question is you. The consciousness that is watching you go through the parts of your body is you. You are a spirit. You have a body. You are a spirit having a physical experience. Your body and your possessions are things that you have, but they are not you. Your actions come from your thoughts, but they are not you. Even your thoughts are not you. You are a spirit. You have thoughts and you act, but you are neither your thoughts nor your actions. They belong to you, but they are not who you are.

Personal Exploration

I have outlined six powerful topics for contemplative self-exploration below. I recommend you work with these one at a time and spread this work out over time.

1. Cause and Effect
   - What came up for you in our discussion about cause and effect?
2. Birth
   - What role do you play in your family? (e.g., the peacekeeper, the motivator, the achiever, etc.)How does this role define your sense of yourself?
   - What have you learned or developed from taking on that role?
   - What limitations does this role place on you?
3. Family
   - What values and beliefs did you learn from your family?
   - How do they serve you?
   - How might they limit you?
4. Self-worth
   - How did you feel about yourself as a young child?
   - How did you feel about others and the world around you?
   - How do you feel about those things today?
   - If there is a difference, what changed for you?
5. Core Issues
   - Think back to your childhood. What conclusions did you come to about yourself, others, or the world as a result of that situation?
   - What coping strategies did you come up with at that time? How did you deal with stress?
   - How do those coping strategies work in your life today?
   - When you think of doing the opposite of whatever your strategy is, what happens?

Janet Myatt

- Can you imagine that there might be a middle ground that includes the leeway to choose the best-possible response?
6. Repeating Patterns
   - What patterns do you see in your life today that seem related to these early experiences?

164

CHAPTER 6 ~ HOW WE USE THE MIND

The Creative Process

Let's take a deeper look at the concept that our reality is dependent on our state of mind.

First, we must understand that the lower ego is not the entirety of our mind; it is just a portion of it. Recall from Part I that the soul (higher intuitional mind) and the intellect of the personality (lower concrete mind) dwell on the same plane—the Mental (Manasic Plane). The soul resides on the upper four subplanes, and the intellect of the personality resides on the bottom three. (The fourth subplane is the meeting ground of the two aspects of self.)

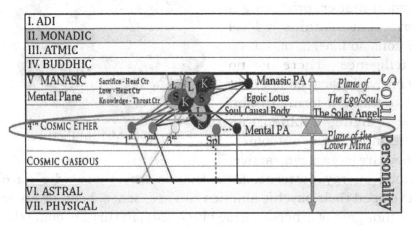

Figure 29: Fourth Mental Subplane

Janet Myatt

Next, we must truly come to understand for ourselves the power of the mind and how it works in the creative process. Theosophy teaches that the entire objective universe is formed by the merger of two types of energy, which produces a third: Life energy (or spirit) combined with atomic energy (or matter) produces some form of consciousness (soul). Everything in the physical universe contains some form of consciousness, or some expression of "soul" energy (intelligence, adaptability, purpose, responsiveness). Furthermore, consciousness is a blend of all three aspects of God (purpose/will, love/wisdom, and activity/intelligence). However, this triple nature shows up differently in different forms. In humans, it shows up as self-awareness and the power to think, act, direct, respond, and decide. In matter, it shows up as the ability to respond, organize, adapt, and cohere to the needs of the creative entity merging with it. Innate intelligence refers to the phenomenon wherein an organism has the ability to respond, learn, adapt, organize, and establish order. So, both matter and man have an innate intelligence.

Thoughtforms are made from the merger of the attracting energy of desire or love with mental matter, producing a form that contains a level of consciousness, or innate intelligence. There is no densely physical component to a thought-form; rather, the living blueprints determine the outcomes. They are organized, active,

Figure 30: Mental Pictures

subtle energy patterns. (And that is why those who have developed their psychic abilities can see, sense, hear, or know the thoughts of others.) These blueprints, in turn, become the positive nuclei that attract the required type of atomic matter to produce more forms.

166

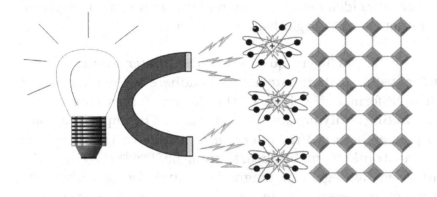

Ideas energized by love or desire attract corresponding grades of matter which adhere and cohere to the pattern producing forms

Figure 31: Desire/Love is Magnetic

Let's break this down a bit more and look at the energy of desire. As human beings, we are impelled into creative activity by our desire to experience something. Whether that "thing" is a physical urge, an emotional want, an intellectual idea, or an intuitively held ideal, it is our desire to experience it that propels us into creative activity. So, desire is of the Spirit; it is generated within the formless aspect of ourselves and drives outward into the sea of matter to produce results. Desire is the lower reflection of love. It is the rudimentary, or primordial, creative energy that over time is transmuted by the power of mind into the higher form that we recognize as love. When the energy of desire or love is focused in the mind as a tangible thought, a blueprint is formed. The desire/love component is attractive and operates on the astral or Buddhic planes; the thought component is patterning and works on the mental plane. Desire-love energy is the force that literally pulls together the types of matter it needs to fulfill the requirements of the blueprint. And, as we just discussed, the atomic building blocks on all the various planes have an inherent ability to respond and adhere to the pattern. Hence, the original idea becomes a living form vivified with a type of consciousness or organization of its own.

One of the intelligent qualities in the matter we use in this solar system is its innate ability to adhere to the magnetized thought-form and cohere to the pattern for as long as the originating entity has its attention there. The important point to ponder here is that *attention is magnetic*; therefore, "As a man thinketh in his heart, so is he."Proverbs 23:7 Thus, the amassed aggregate of magnetic thoughtforms within the mind of the personality becomes quite substantial over time. Collectively, these various thoughtforms create a whole that is greater than the sum of its parts, and we call the entity the ego. *The ego shares the same innate tendency to persist, and it is imbued with a natural tendency to resist change, as that would lead to its destruction.* Remember that if the attention is withdrawn from the thought-form, it will eventually lose coherency and break apart. But we are innately resistant to moving our attention out of it because we think we *are* our ego. This is worth thinking about for a moment, because the point I am making here is that we are not our ego at all. We are *That* which thought the ego into existence! As such, we can choose to think otherwise. When we start to figure this out, we begin to liberate ourselves from our mental-emotional prisons.

We can understand this phenomenon on a smaller scale from our own life experience. Take establishing a new habit as an example. It takes time to break an old habit and establish a new one. We have to painstakingly choose to move our attention out of an old pattern and deliberately move it into a new one. And we have to do this over and over again for several weeks or months before it begins to come naturally to us. But once we have sufficiently abandoned the old pattern and invested in the new pattern for a long-enough period, the new pattern seemingly takes on a life of its own. The same principle can be applied to the way we choose to identify ourselves. Right now, the tendency to identify with the thoughtforms of the ego typically supersedes the intuition flowing in from the soul because the ego contains the largest proportion of our attention. If we withdraw our attention from those thoughtforms in meditation and quiet contemplation, they will eventually break apart.

This gives us a *huge clue* on how to overcome the ego without attacking it. The ego *exists only within thoughtforms*. This is quite different from the Spirit, which exists independently of thoughtforms and independently of matter altogether. The ego is not real outside the thought-form. The spirit is real with or without form. It is important to realize that the force that produces self–awareness within the human psyche is *spiritual* and not material. The thoughts generated by the incarnated personality (an extension of spirit into the lower three worlds) impregnate mental substance and give rise to a form (the ego) that stays intact until the impregnating consciousness is withdrawn. Thus, the key to moving out of the ego is not to attack it or make an enemy of it, for that would simply be a case of generating *more* thoughtforms about the ego and adding more fuel to the flame. The key to awakening is to move the attention out the ego and into the soul. As this happens, the mental forms that house the ego lose the attractive force previously supplied by the personality, and they break apart. In sum, it's not about pounding the ego into something perfect, for this keeps the consciousness fixated on the form. Instead, it's about focusing on the indwelling soul and allowing that energy to transmutate the form. The soul teaches us to produce different types of form because it is rooted in love and focused on the larger unit or ensouling entity in which all humanity is a part.

OK, let's return to our larger topic of fragmentation and the separated mind. How did the personality come to believe in this idea of separation in the first place? How did it come to pass that all the human beings here on Earth developed this fragmented mind-set? ACIM teaches us that once the Child of God began to wonder who it was (rather than simply *know* who it was), doubt crept in and began to divide the mind. *The Urantia Book* explains that this doubt was the result of a mysterious narcissism that arose in the mighty cosmic entity—whom they call Lucifer—who ensouled our system.[69] The way they describe it, Lucifer (who was one of the very brightest of the galactic-level Sons of God) began to doubt that he was created by God the Father and eventually decided that he was the source of his own being. In this manner, the idea of separation took hold in his consciousness. He moved his consciousness into the belief that he created himself. Even though he later acknowledged that God did in fact create him, he then asserted that because he was made in God's image, he was in fact a God *unto himself* and didn't have to answer to his Father. Furthermore, that answering to the Father undermined his inherent godliness. Lucifer's rationale was that if he was cocreating with the Father, then he, Lucifer, was not directly asserting himself and thus not acting as the god he assumed himself to be. (Sound like any teenagers we know?) This story perfectly reflects the position the ego is in regarding the Spirit (or the Monad). The personality level of consciousness believes itself to be independently real, even though this is an impossible idea. Therefore, its identity is nothing more than a huge thought-form sitting in a mental quarantine.

ACIM teaches us that this premise of Lucifer's—that he could experience his "godliness" only in separation from the Father—is an *inherently insane idea*. God creates by *extending Himself into all His creations*. In the physical plane of the universe, He

---

[69] The *Urantia Book* names this cosmic being Lucifer, but I'd like to point out that the Theosophists adamantly disagree with this identification. Theosophists do not give a name for this narcissistic entity and claim that Lucifer is in fact the name of the Mighty Cosmic Being of Light and Love who volunteered to come into this system to save it by surrendering His high place to come into a system fallen into chaos in order to restore divine order. For me, the name is not the important factor but rather the role of narcissism, which appears to be some aberrant side effect of individuation + desire + thought.

reveals Himself in His Sons as loving and wise self-awareness. He reveals Himself in matter as intelligent activity. All Sons are creative expressions of His love. All Sons are *of* God, *within* God, and in eternal relationship *with* God. Like the Father, the Son (Spirit, Monad) creates by extending the love within him into matter to create forms. That love comes from the Father and *is* the Father. Again, Jesus speaks of this great truth several times in the Bible:

*"I and the Father are one."*John 10:30

*"Believe me when I say that I am in the Father and the Father is in me."*John 14:11

Thus, Lucifer (who is at the very least symbolic of the condition of the human ego) cannot create anything real on his own, because he is not real on his own. His idea of being a separate creator is an impossible idea. He exits within God, and the power to create flows through him from his Source. If a son uses his mind in such a way that he cuts off communication with his Source, he is only out of communication but not actually disconnected. Clearly, he can succeed in mentally quarantining himself, but he cannot make himself *independently and creatively real.* He can only ever manage to be deluded. Thus, anything he *believes* he creates in that separated state of mind is not real; it is only a dream, a thought-form, because it does not flow from God. Only God is real. This is worth pondering until we can really grasp this important point.

Once that original thought of separation occurred, we moved into a whole-new ballgame experientially. Now the incarnated human being (also called a son of man) who thinks he is separate must find ways to make himself feel real. And so, he turns to the forms he has made and places his identity in those forms. When consciousness gets fractured like this, it loses power and integrity, meaning it loses its ability to be consistent and coherent. It is isolated and out of rhythm with the greater whole. Think of the violin section of an orchestra turning their back on the conductor and away from one another. Meanwhile, each person continues to play his or her own song in a unique key and unique tempo. Ugh! Creativity begins to work at cross-purposes.

Now, imagine the same fragmentation happening within yourself. You have some thoughtforms that are playing beautiful music and other thoughtforms that are making ugly noises, all carrying on at the same time. We know what this is like: one moment, we're running our creative energy through a positive thought ("I'm OK"); the next moment, we're running it through a conflicting thought ("I'm not OK"). When this happens, we experience powerlessness and creative confusion. Because our consciousness is scattered into a million different conflicting ideas about who we are, we create in a fragmented and limited way. The more we create this way, the more we experience being limited and powerless. This reinforces our belief that we are just physical beings without divine power.

Fluctuating Reality

The lower ego experiences this fluctuating ideality all the time. You wake up one morning, and the birds are singing, the sun is shining, and you're well rested and feeling great. You look in the mirror and like what you see. You dress nicely and head out the door with enthusiasm for the day. At work, you smile and exude warm, friendly vibes. People smile back. You open your e-mail and find twenty messages. This pleases you, for you've been waiting for information from a variety of sources. You happily go through your mail, looking for what you need. It's a positive day.

On another day, you wake up, and it's cloudy and cold outside. You didn't sleep well because of a headache. You don't like what you see in the mirror, so you immediately start criticizing yourself. Grumpy, you throw on some clothes and head out the door. The usual morning traffic disgusts you, and you arrive at work exasperated and full of anger and frustration. As you walk to your office, negative thoughts wash over you, and you fail to connect with anyone. This time, the twenty e-mails are overwhelming. Feeling overworked, you're having a negative day.

Because our perception of ourselves changes so easily based on our thinking, our relationship with ourselves and consequently with the world around us is in a constant state of adjustment, variation, and fluctuation, and this is quite taxing. In the example above, we saw how one's thoughts about oneself changed one's experience, but this applies to one's thoughts about others, too. Jesus says in ACIM that *just thinking* about another person can cause our perception of that person to change *without even having to interact* with that person. This is how unstable and unreliable the mindset of the ego is. This is the problem with relying on the perception of the ego rather than the higher knowing of spirit.

> *Everyone makes an ego or a self for himself, which is subject to enormous variation because of its instability. He also makes an ego for everyone else he perceives, which is equally variable. Their interaction is a process that alters both, because they were not made by or with the Unalterable. It is important to realize that this alteration can and does occur as readily when the interaction takes place in the mind as when it involves physical proximity. Thinking about another ego is as effective in changing relative perception as is physical interaction. There could be no better example that the ego is only an idea and not a fact.*[70]

I've experienced this myself. Many years ago, I was in a choir, and the woman who stood behind me seemed unfriendly one

---

[70]   *ACIM,* p.56

day. I thought, "She doesn't like me." My whole perception of her changed in that moment as I thought, "She never liked me." Suddenly, I felt really stupid and uncomfortable around her. I didn't want to talk to her anymore. I actually *believed* this for a few minutes before I allowed my higher consciousness to intervene and assure me that this thought pattern was not based on the truth. And just as quickly, my perception of her changed again, as I thought, "Oh, she's probably having a bad day. I'll ask her how she's doing after rehearsal."

This was a classic ego projection. I felt her grumpiness and *assumed it had to do with me personally.* Yikes! Egos are inherently narcissistic. The degree to which we are able to hide this is called coping. I projected *my own internal feelings of invalidation on her* and created a mirror of my feelings about myself as they were momentarily personified by her *in my own mind*. The subconscious pattern of reversing cause and effect looped in my mind and was experienced as, *"I'm* not rejecting me, *she's* rejecting me." Then I began to "cope" with this rejection by emotionally distancing myself from that person. All this activity took place *in my own head.*

Luckily, it was only a momentary lapse of sanity, and I allowed myself to be receptive to the prodding of my higher mind and keep my friend. The point is that this is how fragile and unstable the ego mind is. No words were actually spoken, no interaction actually took place, and my world changed from one "reality" to another in a matter of moments. What a confusing way to live!

These are two rather straightforward examples of how our thoughts and emotions affect our reality. Where it gets more complicated is when we have a combination of contradictory thoughts and emotions underlying our experience all happening simultaneously in different levels of our awareness. For instance, we might consciously be focusing on a positive thought, such as "I want to go exercise today because it makes me feel good," but we find we're being sabotaged by a stronger subconscious belief of "I'm powerless. I can't change anything, so what's the point?" This conflicting use of our creativity makes it much harder to get to the gym.

In another example, we may have a great desire to experience a loving romantic relationship in our conscious mind but have an unconscious belief that we're not good enough, or that love always disappoints, or that the cost of love is too high. Thus, we may find ourselves yearning for a love relationship but never actually manifesting one because

- The subconscious fearful beliefs hold a stronger charge (because they are more closely tied to survival),
- The fearful beliefs rest just beyond our daily awareness and therefore remain unresolved, or
- The coping strategies we've employed for so long have become automatic and continue to block us. For example, we break off the relationship when things get serious or sabotage the relationship with jealous or insecure behavior.

Competition and Control

The ego is always asking "Who am I?" in relationship to something or someone outside itself. It asks, "Who am I in relationship to my family? Who am I in relationship to my race or tribe? Who am I in relationship to my society? Who am I in relationship to this person or that person?" It defines itself *through comparison*, which inevitably leads to competition. The soul on its own plane knows we are all part of One soul, One humanity.

Competition is an inevitable by-product of the ego because the egoic state of mind seeks to assert that it is "real." But it is not and never can be. Only God is real, and God is immortal. Therefore, any "thing" that can pass away is a *form*, an effect, something that was built, but not *the Source* which made it. So, bear with me here, and remember that the ego is an identity that is dependent on its thoughtforms in order to exist. And we've just seen that forms are effects and that all forms eventually pass when their usefulness expires. Consequently, the ego exists only temporarily in time and space—only for as long as the Thinker holds his attention in it—and can never be immortal. We intuitively sense that it is not real, and yet we work very hard to justify its reality because it's the identity we're in. How does the ego make itself feel real? It accomplishes this by getting others outside itself to agree with it, to think the same things, to feel the same way, and to approve of it. Anyone who doesn't go along with it is perceived as a threat. Therefore, if someone disagrees with us, we experience it either as a negation of self or a negation of the other person. This creates a situation where comparison and competition are inevitable. The ego feels OK if there is agreement or if it feels that it has won in a disagreement. Where there is no agreement, the ego goes into judgment to justify its position and negates the reality of the other person. In this way, we are constantly competing with other peoples' truth in order to validate our own truth. When we assess our value, our very worth, by comparing ourselves to others, everything becomes relative or conditional.

For instance, the ego believes "I'm more (or less) valuable than others' depending on how much of some given parameter I possess in comparison to others"—namely, money, beauty, influence, power, love, etc. Our sense of self-worth is always in flux as we make these comparisons because invariably someone else has more and another has less. The ego mind is always *reacting* to its perceptions at any given moment. Without fail, something always comes along to rock the boat, tip the scales, and destabilize any temporary sense of self-esteem. Even the wealthiest, most beautiful, most powerful people in the world suffer from feelings of lack in some other area of their life, or they live in fear of the day they will lose everything they have that makes them so "valuable." Look at how many "beautiful" stars have subjected themselves to extensive plastic surgery in an effort to "maintain their value." Look at the "successful" stars who have killed themselves because of overwhelming feelings of misery and worthlessness. We intuitively know that the ego is false and live in constant fear of being exposed. We are constantly trying to assess our value by comparing ourselves to others and competing to have more of what we feel we lack. This, in turn, makes us very controlling. We want to make other people see things the way we see them, do it the way we want it done, believe what we believe, and so on and so forth. When we are trying to control others, we are competing with them on some level. We are seeking to assert our point of view over theirs rather than make room for all points of view to come together and work cocreatively with one another.

The mind of the Higher Self works very differently. It knows itself to be a part of the whole intelligent, loving activity of God and works as a point of view within the unified mind of the Creator. At that level, everything works in sync and holistically. We are connected to the plan and working within God's purpose. When the incarnated personality learns to align with this loving intelligence, it begins to perceive God's ideas and can actively begin to create its part of the plan to the best of its ability in the given moment. In the world we have created with our egos, everyone is afraid and trying to fill themselves up with a feeling of importance and validity by making the world conform to their own ideas. But the soul does not feel this need to justify or defend anything because in that unconditionally loving state of mind everything is working together as a greater whole.

When I was in the teachers' program at the awareness center I was a part of, I experienced tremendous competition and control from a couple of the other senior teachers. I had a certain style, and I was very confident of my ability to teach the classes and to attract the students who wanted to learn from me without having to work in the way the other teachers thought was best. This challenged the beliefs of these other teachers, and they were in a position of authority over me. It was not OK for me to think differently, and they wanted to force me to do things their way. There was no room for differing truths. The energy of competition was very high until I capitulated and did things their way, even if I didn't believe it was right. On the flip side, I have done this, too. I have felt certain that my children should do things a certain way. When they wanted to do things in their own way, I would feel exasperated and try to get them to do it my way. This is an issue that continues to be my teacher.

When we get into these tugs-of-war with others, we are ensnared in the conflicting energy produced by the pairs of opposites that dominate the egotistical mind—right/wrong, good/bad, powerful/powerless. But if we take a moment to stop, go within, and seek the guidance of our higher Self, we have the opportunity to navigate our way through the pairs of opposites to the higher ground of the soul. The soul is able to help us discern the point of harmony, which is invariably love intelligently understood and practiced. At the personality level, our job in any given situation is to determine what steps we need to take in that moment to work toward that result. This will always have to be determined in the present moment. Other than seeking what serves the highest good of all concerned, there is no single answer or pathway through the pairs of opposites.

For example, sometimes we may find we need to yield or see things differently to find the point of harmony. At other times, we may be led to stand steadfast in what we know while maintaining an attitude of loving kindness and harmlessness toward the other person. Imagine a great warrior who finally grows tired of incessant fighting. In his weariness, he sits down between the opposing armies to meditate on the situation. Suddenly, in the stillness of his mind, he realizes that both sides are essentially fighting for the same thing. What puts them at odds is that each side is fundamentally stuck in their own stubborn ways of thinking about it. From that point of stillness in the middle, he sees the *point of unity* between the opposing parts and no longer sees the value in battling. Instead, he becomes interested in finding a way to manifest the unified whole at the essence.

Law of Attraction and Repulsion in the Ego

Let's look at how the Law of Attraction works psychologically in the ego. Currently, the vast majority of human consciousness is polarized positively in our desire-astral body. That is the vehicle through which we pour our consciousness and experience our "reality." Thus, the mind is open (receptive +) to desire and closed (not receptive –) to the higher states of mind. Additionally, we are focused on the world of form. This means that our emotionally charged thoughts (which form the positive nucleus) radiate out and seek to merge with matter (which is negatively charged). Activated thoughtforms likewise attract other thoughtforms that conform to them and repulse those that do not.

Let's work with the thought-form "I'm ugly." Consciously, this idea is not energetically neutral; it is skewed to the qualitatively negative end of the beautiful-ugly dichotomy. And because the ego works to prove it's right, it is receptive to experiences that match its blueprint and closed to those that do not. Why? Because experiences that conform to the thought *validate* the belief, and those that contradict the thought negate it. The conforming experience feeds the belief, and the belief grows. In *A Treatise on Cosmic Fire*, Alice Bailey explains that under the Law of Economy (a subdivision of the Law of Attraction), energy follows the path of least resistance at the form level.[71] Following this law, negative emotions attract and radiate negative experiences, calling in more of the same, while positive emotions extend and attract positive experiences.

---

[71]   Bailey, *ATIF*

All mental-emotional energy is highly magnetic and contagious. We experience this all the time. When we find ourselves around a negative person, it can be quite difficult to stay positive. When we find ourselves around positive energy, it is much easier to be positive. Why? First, we don't yet know how to keep our own mind steady in our own intention, and we allow our consciousness to match the energetic vibrations emanating from those around us. Second, once this happens, we begin to manufacture the same qualitative experience.

So, continuing with our example here, an experience that might be contrary to the "I'm ugly" idea, such as "I'm beautiful,"

1. Isn't being attracted, and
2. Is actually being resisted, as it would functionally negate or invalidate the ugly belief.

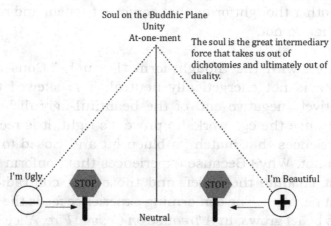

Soul on the Buddhic Plane
Unity
At-one-ment

The soul is the great intermediary force that takes us out of dichotomies and ultimately out of duality.

I'm Ugly

STOP

STOP

I'm Beautiful

Neutral

Activated thought-forms resist being neutralized by the opposing force. In order to break free of the thought-form, the Thinker has to destabilize it by withdrawing the activating thought. The ego resists this because it is identified with the form – it believes that the loss of form is loss of self. The Buddhic plane where the soul resides is the place of unity or at-one-ment. Dichotomies are irrelevant – one is either both beautiful and ugly or neither and so the distinction is no longer of interest.

Figure 32: Polarization

The qualitatively positive thought (if accepted by the thinker) would negate the qualitatively negative thought. *But once a thought-form is formed, it will adhere to the original pattern unless and until the Thinker withdraws his or her attention from it.* Only then will there be room for a new experience to manifest. This works with qualitatively positive beliefs, too. If we believe we're special, and our ego is tied up in that idea, we will be very intolerant of any experience that challenges that notion. Thus, we tend to get into emotional trouble when our identity is tied up in our thoughtforms. When this is the case, as it is with any of our core beliefs, our tolerance for moving out of those thoughtforms is very low. For if we change our fundamental beliefs about ourselves and the world, how will we know who we are and how the world works? We'd have to have a tolerance for entering into an interim state of not knowing. This is the primary reason why experiences that don't conform to our beliefs tend to be discounted or ignored.

One reason so many self-help books advocate the use of positive affirmations is that the positive belief has the potential to destabilize and break apart the negative thought pattern, ultimately freeing us from that thought-form. One reason this technique often fails is that the thinker has trouble believing it, and so it fails to generate enough charge to attract the new form. The soul, however, is the level of consciousness that can lead us out of the pairs of opposites altogether. The Buddhic plane, where the love-wisdom aspect of the higher Self has its place, is the plane of unity or at-one-ment. Dichotomies are irrelevant; one is either both ugly *and* beautiful or neither, and so the distinction is no longer of interest. Using positive affirmations does hold the potential for helping us gain control over how we're using our minds. But our ultimate goal is to turn away from the astral world of desire and live as soul.

Janet Myatt

Pole Shift

In electrical magnetism, like poles do not attract because the lines of force are flowing in the opposite direction. Unlike poles attract and thus create unity because the lines of force are flowing in the same direction. So, why do we say that "like attracts like" if the laws of electromagnetism appear to contradict this? There actually is no contradiction. We're simply focusing on the result (the effects) of the creative process rather than on the process. This statement comes from the observation that negative thoughts attract negative results. And vice versa, positive thoughts attract positive results. What we're observing is that whether or not a thought is qualitatively positive or negative, it is the medium that forms the electrically positive nucleus of a thought-form and attracts to it the matter that will give it form. It is the attention, intention, or thought of the thinker that produces the electrically positive nucleus around which negatively charged matter adheres, producing a manifested thought-form.

Moving on to an even deeper understanding of how the Law of Attraction works in the awakening process, let's consider the following. When the personality is invested in the lower desire nature, the mind energy of the personality is the directing positive agent (+). This energy is directed down toward the lower planes attracting the matter (−) needed to manifest the desire. The mind is not receptive to the higher planes of consciousness, which remain beyond the threshold of awareness. The individual who is "on the Path" is endeavoring to learn how to use the mind differently. There are two aspects that change as a result of this aspiration:

1. The ego mind learns to stop being the sole directing agent and becomes receptive (−) to the soul, which over time becomes the directing agent (+) of creative activity.
2. Eventually, the mind of the personality merges with the higher mind of the soul. The matter of the lower three worlds is then used to reveal higher thoughtforms that

foster and promote that which serves the highest good of the whole.

During this transition, the aspirant struggles with the apparent conflict in agendas ("What's in it for me?" versus "What's in it for us all?"). As I've mentioned before, he or she becomes more aware of these two "selves," and this creates confusion and frustration for a certain period until the merger is complete (which can take up to several lifetimes).

Why is it important to understand the creative process? We want to understand the actual power we have to transform our reality by

1. Changing our thoughts and
2. Changing where our consciousness is polarized.

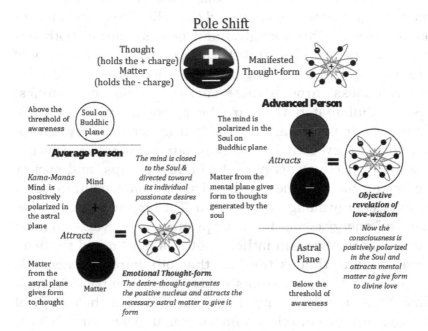

Figure 33: Pole Shift

Knowledge gives us the opportunity to figure out what's motivating our creativity. Are we being driven by our lower fearful self or directed by our higher wise and loving Self? Is our mind busy generating millions of conflicting desire-thoughts of varying degrees of quality, or is it able to be still and become receptive to the intuition, illumination, and inspiration of our inner divine wisdom and love, which can see a larger picture?

Individual and Collective Blueprints

Everything is energy. All consciousness is energy. On an energetic level, our consciousness is interwoven with the consciousness of the people around us. Just as smoke mingles and joins with the air, our individual consciousness does not exist in a vacuum; it does not exist in isolation. We have our individual identity, but we are also a part of the tribal mind-set of the groups we belong to and the collective consciousness on the planet. Our thoughts and beliefs contain both our personal point of view and the internalized point of view of those around us to varying degrees. Once again, we run our consciousness through these various beliefs and manifest results that match them in the physical world. Because many of our beliefs are a part of a larger belief system or paradigm, they contain not only our personal energy but also the collective energy of the family, groups, and society we belong to. This means the ideas we have contain other peoples' energy along with our own. The biggest source of this "foreign" energy comes from our primary caregivers—in most cases, our mother and father—but it is not limited to them. Compounding that is the fact that our parents' energy is enmeshed with their parents' energy and so on back through time. Thus, family energy is very enmeshed in the energy of the ego. Our egos are closely interwoven into our family's "ego" because they are developed in concert with them.

Family identities are enmeshed in progressively larger group identities such as ethnic, racial, cultural and religious identities, and national identities. Finally, all these group identities are enmeshed in our human identity. Thus, our beliefs are greatly influenced by the family, social, ethnic, religious, national, racial, and human beliefs we are exposed to. And these beliefs contain a huge amalgamation of the energy of all the people in the group. Thus, the programming and beliefs that reside in these mass agreements have a tremendous amount of energy and charge on them, making them some of the most difficult to change. As our individual and group blueprints develop over time, those with the most charge will manifest the most readily. Likewise, those that contain the largest agreement collectively will be the hardest to change.

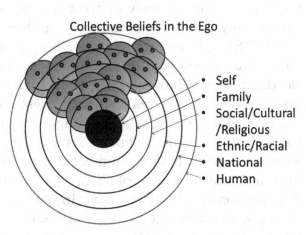

Figure 34: Collective Beliefs

An example of a changing national ego can be seen in our own history here in the United States. In the eighteenth and nineteenth centuries, the collective consciousness in America was in agreement with slavery. Individually, many people began to resist this notion and slowly began to fight for change. Once enough people within the group agreement held a dissenting opinion, the agreement began to break down. But this took several hundred years. In some ways, we are still recovering as a group from the toxic side effects of that agreement as it slowly dissipates out of the collective consciousness. This same phenomenon exists within smaller group agreements with the same type of effect. Family, racial, ethnic, religious, national, and global patterns repeat through the generations, locking individuals in group patterns of behavior that perpetuate until enough individuals gather together a significant-enough counterforce for the patterns to break down.

Many lightworkers (souls intent on awakening to the divine Self and anchoring divine light on the planet) are here to break down these repeating patterns. They are here to help break down group agreements that are out of sync with the divine and make way for a new way of living and being. Some people are actively and consciously doing this within their family line. For example, my mother was raised in the South. Through her family, she was exposed to a type of fear-based evangelism that promoted concepts of sinfulness and worthlessness that caused her to feel intense pain and finally anger. One day, she realized with crystal-clear clarity that she could not participate in that agreement, and she walked away from her family's church. As a result, my brother and I were not exposed to that mind-set. A good friend of mine came from a family where alcoholism was the norm and passed from one generation to the next. In her twenties, she decided to break the chain, joined AA, and endeavored to raise her family outside that pattern. A client of mine grew up in a family where bullying was an acceptable way to relate to one another. Somehow, she survived this mental-emotional abuse with a loving heart, moved away from her family of origin, and worked very hard to create a loving, nurturing environment for her husband and children.

On a larger scale, we are beginning to see some significant shifts in the mass-conscious attitude toward homosexuality. The tide is turning; one by one, more individuals are embracing the idea of equality for all people regardless of sexual preference. At the same time, we are also experiencing a heightened polarization in our political system. This often presages the collapse of the stagnant ideas and ideals sitting at odds with one another. The vast energetic structure involved is ultimately de-energized through this exploration of the extremes. Over time, individuals and groups begin to see that we cannot have one side without the other and eventually begin to look once again for a new way that embraces a greater understanding of the whole.

Because the aggregate quantity and magnetic quality of the energy involved in group beliefs is so great, it takes a considerable amount of effort to get out from under them. This is one of the things we continually have to face in the process of recovering our spiritual point of view. It takes great insight, honesty, and courage to face our fears—both individual and collective. On the positive side, though, the soul on its own plane is participating in a divine collective consciousness that vastly outweighs humanity's collective consciousness in the lower three worlds. So, we will get there in the end. Each person who links up with this greater collective makes it that much easier for everyone else to do the same.

At-one-ment

At-one-ment is the state of mind of God and therefore the only real state of mind. Everything else is only an "ideality"—a temporary substitute for that which is real. At-one-ment is a state of mind that is unified or holistic. The ego lives in the ideality, and the Spirit lives in reality. Theosophy introduces us to the concept of "isolated unity," which is another approach to understanding the reality of at-one-ment.

> Isolated Unity is that stage of consciousness which sees the whole as one and regards itself, not theoretically but as a realised fact, as identified with that whole. It is a whole which is "isolated" in the consciousness of the man, and not the man himself who regards himself as isolated. [72]

---

[72] Bailey. *Esoteric Psychology II*, p. 392

Janet Myatt

In the above quote, Bailey is referring to a state of mind where one's identity is no longer localized in one of the parts within the whole but rather in the larger encapsulating whole that is an entity in and of itself. The word *isolated* refers to the fact that the mind of this ensouling entity is focused *on the whole* as *one living organism*, even as it knows that it lives within all its parts. It is undivided. For instance, the Supreme Being is an Entity that is *greater* than the sum of Its parts. The Supreme Being is not just a *collective* consciousness; it is a *personal* consciousness that contains the collective. By way of analogy, the integrated personality is something more than just the sum of the mental, astral, and physical levels of consciousness. It is a fourth entity in and of itself.

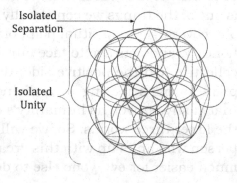

Figure 35: Isolated Unity

The emerging personality encompasses all these lower levels and is greater than the sum of these levels of consciousness.

This marks a certain evolutionary milestone. It reveals that a sufficient level of mental, emotional, and physical organization, coordination, and synthesis has taken place in the mind to enable the incarnated human to decentralize out of the lower points of view into a new higher synthesized "identity." This expanded identity works as a centralized, unified field of creative activity—an isolated unity, or an undivided unity. It is actively coordinating all that is contained within it but is focusing on the whole experience—in this case, the experience of the personality.

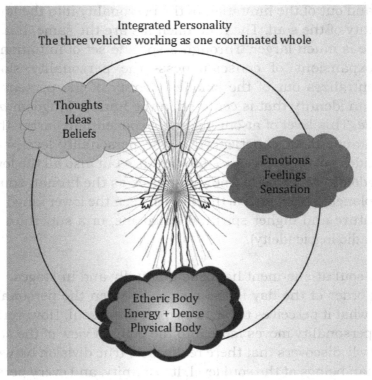

Figure 36: Integrated Personality

Here's an analogy I like to use. Let's say you think you are a heart. You look around at the spleen, stomach, and liver, and you think, "I'm not that. I'm a heart." Of course, all the while you're really part of a larger whole. And you're completely interconnected and interdependent with everything in that larger whole, whether you think you are or not. Eventually, after many experiences and expansions of awareness, you finally realize, "Ah-ha! I am a body! I was never just a heart. But the heart is a part of me. We are indivisible. Furthermore, I am *more* than the sum of all my parts. This excellent combination of things has yielded something greater than just a bag of parts."

So, the integrated personality is one of these larger states of awareness. It is the isolated unity or at-one-ment that takes place within the individualized being. The next step is to expand out of the limitation of the personality into the larger identity of the soul. The fundamentals are the same, but the scope is much larger. Through a specific set of initiations—or expansions of consciousness—the personality slowly decentralizes out of the smaller identity of the personality into an identity that is centered in the human kingdom *as a whole*. This level of at-one-ment is exponentially larger than the at-one-ment experienced at the personality level, as it includes not only the entire human race but also all the lower kingdoms. We come to know ourselves as the human soul of the planet—that which is the link between the lower kingdoms of nature and higher spiritual kingdoms, or a superhuman, monadic logoic (deity).

This soul at-one-ment happens gradually and in stages. The first order of the day is the merger between the personality and what it perceives to be its own personal soul. However, as the personality moves more into the point of view of the soul, it slowly discovers that there really is no true division between human beings at the soul level. It is a unity, and every person is seen as part of this larger whole. Now, that does not mean that the soul doesn't recognize the differentiation happening at the personality level. Rather, the soul understands that all the "different parts" are interdependent parts of a whole. Just as all the cells in the body are unique points of creative activity, they are all a part of the larger whole we call the body.

In our analogy, the heart would start out by gaining a sense of the body and think of it as "my body." It would think, "I am a heart, and I have a body." As the spleen awakens, it thinks, "I am a spleen, and I have a body." These two identities still see themselves as separate from one another, and each has a proprietary relationship with what they believe is "their" body. It isn't until much later, when the identity moves fully into the body whole, that all the parts are seen as belonging to the same whole.

How does one move out of the smaller identity into the larger? Mostly, this is done out of necessity. We eventually begin to feel the squeeze of our limiting ideas and our painful experiences and begin to seek a way out of our confinement. This is done through gradually building a bridge of conscious awareness from the lower to the higher. As we liberate the bits of our consciousness tied up in the ego and align with the intuitive mind of the soul, we gradually awaken. This is internal work, and it happens spontaneously at first. A moment of deep intuitive knowing—a revelation, an epiphany—occurs in the mind, and the initial tentative link is made. This experience fires up our internal "homing device." Our divine blueprint includes a deep innate longing to know God and to return home. Once the desire nature has been satiated and we can no longer adequately explain our purpose, we begin to turn our attention away from the astral plane. The mind begins to turn inward and upward toward the mental plane and the reality of the soul. The Prodigal begins his journey home.

I think it's helpful to understand that God does have a plan and that the evolution of our consciousness is proceeding along proscribed lines of development. In the initial stages of human development, our mind is used to experience a separate, individual identity and to learn how to manifest our personal desires. This is as God intended. We learn about the creative process in the Earth's school of cause and effect, and our creativity is limited to our personal realm of activity. We do not yet have access to broader levels of creative activity, and this is a good thing. Our consciousness is focused uniformly on the lower self—that is, on our desires, thoughts, and experiences in the lower three worlds. Even our more altruistic emotional states such as sympathy and love are experienced or understood only in terms of our own *personal* experience and not from an experience of at-one-ment.

Janet Myatt

Later on in our human development, however, we begin to recognize another aspect of ourselves. At first, this mysterious aspect seems to be "other" than us, or separate from us. But, eventually, we come to realize it is our own soul or indwelling Spirit. The discriminating power of the evolving mind begins to recognize that it has been trapped in thoughtforms that aren't real. It begins to comprehend the illogic and inconsistency of its thinking and begins to seek a higher perspective from which to contextualize its experience. Once this turning point occurs, the evolving mind works to synthesize its experience into a meaningful whole. The "ascender" sees that the differentiating mind of the personality and the unifying mind of the soul are two aspects of one whole "thing," which is divine awareness. This person now uses his or her discriminative faculties of mind to discern what is actually true and learns to move away from that which is not true and not real. The aspirant begins to understand that That which is real in himself is also That which is real in his brother and in all that exists. Now the mind is used both to unify and to separate. Slowly, our creativity is directed toward building what is perceived as unifying rather than toward purely selfish ambitions as the aspirant trains his or her mind to align with God's thoughts rather than with the ego's and with God's desire rather than the lower self's. The aspirant uses personal will to carry out the larger plan of God's will. Creativity is now focused on revealing this larger unified reality.

> The consciousness (released from all material pettiness and self-centeredness) sees not only the periphery of the Whole but the beauty and purpose of every aspect of the inner structure. [73]

The mind is a powerful thing. It can be used to create an experience of separation and to unify. Jesus takes great pains to point out in *ACIM* that when we use our mind to foster and promote fear, we move into isolation and away from

---

[73]   Bailey. *Esoteric Psychology II,* p. 395

at-one-ment. When we use it to foster and promote love, we move into connection and unity. Bailey points out that both the discriminating and unifying qualities of mind are a part of the creative process. At first, we use our mind to create a separate experience and unify our private experience into some kind of self-contained whole. Later, we use these same qualities to extrapolate ourselves from our delusions and unify with the increasingly larger states of aware being. As we talked about earlier, during this bridge-building stage we experience a heightened sense of duality as we become aware of being both the lower separate self and the higher unified Self. This is a difficult phase of our growth and leads to much confusion and struggle as we strive to reconcile these two different points of view and seemingly opposite agendas.

Chapter 6 Exercises

1. Think about how your reality changes depending on the mood you're in. How do you feel about investing in a reality that shifts in this way? How do you explain it?

2. Have your beliefs changed over time?
   - What happened to your experience of yourself, others, and the world around you as a result of the change?

3. Think of a time when you wanted to change a particularly hard habit to break.
   - What did you have to do to break the hold of that pattern?
   - What did you have to do to create the new pattern?
   - What does this tell you about the power of thought?

4. "Thinking about another ego is as effective in changing relative perception as is physical interaction. There could be no better example that the ego is only an idea and not a fact."
   - Have you ever made an assumption about someone that effected how you felt about them, only later to discover your assumption was wrong? How did your experience of this person change?
   - What does this tell you about the unreality of the ego?

5. Think about a time when you felt angry with someone because he or she did not agree with your point of view.
   - Why was it so important to you that the other person agree with you? What need were you trying to fill? What was at stake for you?

6. Imagine sitting down in the middle of opposing points of view (yours and the other person's). Detach from the outcome and ask yourself:
   - What is each person trying to establish or experience for him- or herself?
   - What is the common ground? Keep going until you find the thing that both sides have in common.
   - What happens when you find the common ground?

7. If you have worked with positive affirmations before, what results did you experience?
8. What collective blueprints have colored your experience of yourself, others, and the world around you?
9. Can you imagine a state of at-one-ment? What comes up as you open yourself up to this idea?

CHAPTER 7 ~ FEAR

And the light shines on in the darkness, and the darkness has never put it out.^{John 1:5}

What is needed, rather than running away or controlling or suppressing [it], or any other [form of] resistance, is understanding fear; that means, watch it, learn about it, come directly into contact with it. We are to learn about fear, not how to escape from it. [74]

As we are liberated from our own fear, our presence actually liberates others. [75]

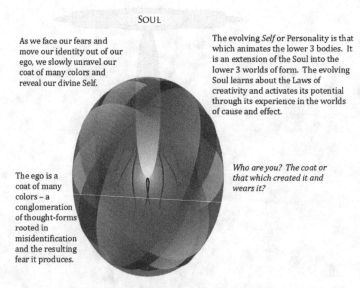

SOUL

As we face our fears and move our identity out of our ego, we slowly unravel our coat of many colors and reveal our divine Self.

The evolving *Self* or Personality is that which animates the lower 3 bodies. It is an extension of the Soul into the lower 3 worlds of form. The evolving Soul learns about the Laws of creativity and activates its potential through its experience in the worlds of cause and effect.

The ego is a coat of many colors – a conglomeration of thought-forms rooted in misidentification and the resulting fear it produces.

Who are you? The coat or that which created it and wears it?

Figure 37: Ego's Coat of Many Colors

[74] Krishnamurti, Jiddu
[75] Williamson, Marianne. *A Return to Love.*

Psychologically, the greatest limiting factor in our lives is fear. Understanding the mechanics of fear can help create a level of neutrality that will enable us to work with our emotions and the blockages we've created as a result of our fearful thinking. The true Self lies hidden behind multiple energetic veils containing all the pictures, programming, and beliefs we've built up in our minds. It is only through looking directly at those veils and learning how to let them go that we can become fully conscious souls. There are no shortcuts in the Earth plane. If we were already dwelling in our divine consciousness, the ego would not exist. If we were already reunited with the one-mindedness of creation, we wouldn't be experiencing dual-mindedness in a fearful way. So, how do we engage our divine consciousness if we don't remember it and cannot access it because it is enshrouded in layers of fear energy? The only way I personally know we can find our divine Self is to do the work of facing our fears and dropping the veils repeatedly until we are able to find our authentic self on an experiential level.

The Mechanics of Fear

Let's take a look first at the mechanics of fear and see how it works energetically.

> *Fear is a distressing negative sensation induced by a perceived threat. It is a basic survival mechanism occurring in response to a specific stimulus, such as pain or the threat of danger. In short, fear is the ability to recognize danger leading to an urge to confront it or flee from it (also known as the fight-or-flight response) but in extreme cases of fear (terror) a freeze or paralysis response is possible.*[76]

When we are afraid of something or someone, our attention focuses intensely on the perceived threat, whether it is external

---

[76] Wikipedia.org. Fear

in the form of a person or activity or internal in the form of a thought or memory. The body's reaction to fear is biologically sound. When one is physically threatened, it is imperative to remain focused on the source of the threat and be prepared to fight or flee.

From a consciousness perspective, it is important to understand that fear creates a contracted state of awareness. If you were to imagine Divine Mind comprising 360 degrees of awareness, fear produces the exact opposite. It creates tunnel vision. In juxtaposition, the emotional quality of love is expansive and attracting, while fear is contracting and repulsing.

Imagine standing at the top of a mountain on a clear day and being able see the surrounding countryside for a full 360 degrees. The view is spectacular, and you are filled with a sense of well-being. The air is fresh; you are warm and relaxed and feel in tune with nature. You feel expansive. Now, imagine you hear the rattle of rattlesnake! Suddenly, all your attention is on finding a way to either kill the snake or get away from it. *Nothing else matters.* The spectacular view, the bounty of the surrounding countryside, the warmth of the sun on your skin, the fresh air—poof! They no longer concern you. All you are aware of is the snake, and all you are thinking about is how to kill it or flee from it.

This is the power that fear has. It makes perfect sense when we are in a life-or-death situation.

Now, imagine you return to the top of the mountain on another gorgeous, clear day. Instead of noticing the beauty around you, all you can think about is the rattlesnake you encountered the last time you were here. You are terrified that you will stumble across another one, and you remain highly alert and agitated, focused on scanning the ground nearby for snakes. Your awareness is not expansive, you are not experiencing a sense of well-being, and you are missing out on an opportunity to appreciate the full 360 degrees of beauty you are in the midst of. If you never turn this contracted fearful state of mind around, you will soon stop going up that mountain. The fear will control your life at that point. And this is how the fearful thoughts, beliefs, and memories stored in the ego work in our lives. To varying degrees, depending on how invested we are in them, fear controls our life. It prevents us from gaining the full 360 degrees of awareness that our divine potential holds.

Part of what's tricky about coming out from under the control of the fear in our mind is recognizing it. For example, prejudice is rooted in fear. Discrimination, competition, jealousy, and just about any other negative emotion we can name are all rooted in fear. But so is people-pleasing, codependency, manipulation, overachieving, arrogance, bullying, following the crowd, and so on and so forth. When we really get good at examining our underlying motivation, we will nearly always stumble across fear in one guise or another. Our job is to expand our consciousness beyond the boundaries fear creates so we may liberate ourselves from its hold over us. So, how do we expand our consciousness?

The Law of Inertia

When we consider the law of inertia, we understand that once energy is in motion, it will continue on its course unless an opposing force that is equal or greater to it is applied. Thus, the energy of fear will continue on its course and intensify the experience over time unless an opposing force (such as intelligence, love, forgiveness, insight) is applied. Love, gratitude, and joy are all expansive emotions and serve as excellent counterforces to fear. Intelligence and wisdom serve to expand the mind, which is why education is so important in overcoming the world's evils. Forgiveness pulls the attention of the thinker out of the thought-form, causing it to break apart.

All these counterforces operate under the same law of inertia, moving our consciousness in a new direction.

It's important to be aware that the more the consciousness trapped in a state of fear contracts, the more it hardens and becomes inflexible. The light of awareness dims and can eventually go out. In extreme cases, this loss of light or love is so extensive that any hope of recovering the consciousness trapped in that state ceases to exist. It becomes nonresponsive to any counterforce. This extreme state is rare but very dangerous, as the consciousness (animating life) trapped in the thought-form becomes detached from the soul of the thinker and persists independently on the astral plane, generating only fear and attracting more of the same. This is part of the mechanics behind what we call our lesser "demons" and "devils." They are animated, detached thoughtforms that are one-note wonders of fearfulness, aggression, invalidation, hate, suspicion, and so forth. This state is entirely different from the case when the thinker *transforms* his consciousness by *removing* or drawing his attention out of fearfulness with love or intelligent thought. With loving intelligence, the animating life of the soul is withdrawn out of the thought-form; consequently, the positive nucleus is no longer present to hold the pattern together. Thus, the form breaks apart and is destroyed and the animating life liberated.

It is often the case that we shove chronic fear into our unconscious mind in an effort to be rid of it. But we are not rid of it, as part of our mind is still caught up in the fear. This is a problem in two ways. First, we've managed only to become *unconscious* of the source of much of our suffering, making it much harder to understand the source of our problems. Second, we haven't truly removed our attention from the thought; thus, we have failed to transform it as needed. This is why it is important for us to become aware of our fears and begin to dialogue with them. It is up to us to mentor our wounded self so that we can free the consciousness trapped there and integrate it into our higher Self.

The Shadow and the Ideal

As we do the investigative work of uncovering the thoughts and beliefs that are controlling us, we eventually become aware of a curious other duality—one that sits within the ego rather than between the ego and the soul. We come face to face with the dichotomy of "the shadow" and "the ideal." The shadow contains our deepest fears, shame, and feelings of unworthiness, while the ideal shimmers in our minds as the person we wish and hope ourselves to be. What is important to remember is that *neither* the ideal self nor the shadow self are the *true divine Self.* Both are personas we've developed to cope with the stress of our misperceptions.

Picture the ego as a line where the shadow self is at one end and the ideal self is at the other end.

The Shadow   The Ideal

Subconscious mind .... Consciousness mind

Everything on the continuum between these two poles comprises the ego mind, and our concept of ourselves moves up and down along that line in response to our experiences, thoughts, and beliefs at any given moment. We tend to own the part of the continuum that is near the ideal self and disown the part that is too close to the shadow self. The first step in healing the self is to turn the line into a circle and realize that the *entire circle*—the shadow and the ideal—is our ego mind. The second step is to realize that even the full circle is still not the true Self because both of these personas are responding to fear. The divine Self, or the soul, rests outside this polarization of the mind. It is consistent (unlike ego personas) and certain, works from knowledge, has personal power, and speaks to us through our intuition, which is experienced as a strong sense of clear, rational knowing. Learning to discern the difference between intuition and beliefs helps us recognize our soul.

In typical ego style, we project our ideal and shadow selves on others, and we constantly compare how well everyone is measuring up to our ideal. We like people who reflect back our ideal, and we dislike people who reflect back our shadow. For instance, when we encounter someone we admire and look up to, we are seeing that person through a projection of our ideals. That person is reflecting back to us what we aspire to be. Conversely, when we encounter someone we dislike or resist, we are seeing that person through a projection of our shadow self—the one we try to hide from the world and even from ourselves.

Let me give a personal example of how the shadow persona and the ideal persona color our world. Back in my singer-songwriter days, I had strong opinions about songwriters. I loved Patty Griffin (and still do) because her music really spoke to me. I had strong ideas about what made a song "good," and her music fit the bill to a tee. On the other hand, I greatly disliked Taylor Swift because her music did not speak to me. I saw Patty through the eyes of my ideal self ("I want to be like her; she deserves to be loved") and saw Taylor through the eyes of my shadow ("She's not good enough; she doesn't deserve to be so popular"). Even though I was embarrassed that I felt so jealous and bitter over Taylor Swift's success and fame, it was how I really felt at the time. Sadly, the feelings of jealousy, bitterness, *and* embarrassment added to the invalidation and worthlessness my shadow felt because my ideal did not approve of those feelings. (You can't win for losing with these two aspects!)

Interestingly, things changed for me one day when I heard Taylor Swift's backstory. Although I don't know if what I heard is completely accurate, I felt the gist of it rang true, and it was a transformational moment for me. Apparently, Taylor first went to LA and was not only turned down but also told she was no good and couldn't sing and that she should give up and go home. Well, she did leave LA, but she never bought into the notion that she wasn't good enough. She persisted with her dream. One day, while she was supposedly playing at a truck stop outside Nashville, she was "discovered" by the man who gave her a shot.

This story woke me up. Suddenly, I saw her through the eyes of my true Self. I recognized her as a spirit unabashedly shining her light out into the world, fully believing in herself and unapologetically bringing the gift of herself into her life. Wow! The jealousy and bitterness melted away, and I found myself internally thanking her for being herself in such a visible way. I still prefer Patty's music because it moves me, and I still don't prefer Taylor's music because it doesn't. But that's OK; besides, I'm not her target audience. Now I can appreciate both of these beautiful spirits for shining their light in their own way. From the vantage point of my soul, I know that my light is not dimmed but is enhanced because they inspire me. We all shine a little brighter when the Spirit of each person shines out into the world.

So, my initial relationship with these two women was experienced through my ego's beliefs and fears. This also works in reverse. Others will respond to us based on what they perceive we're sending out. Their perception will be dependent on their own ideas, values, and sense of self-worth. Let's say you're an outgoing person who talks a lot and gets a lot of attention. One person may respond very positively to these traits because she values them and perceives them to be attractive. Another person may respond quite negatively to these traits because he perceives them to be unattractive. These mixed reactions can create a lot of confusion and pain for us. This is especially the case if one of our own core pictures is that we must please others to be OK, to be safe, and to feel loved.

The perception barrier is in play at all times. Even when we begin to operate from the soul and we're sending love and light out into the world, we can experience a negative reaction. Another may feel exposed, jealous, or resentful of the light and unconditional quality of the love. Light is the great revealer, and love is the great connector. Sometimes another person feels our light and love exposing his darkness, and he wants to avoid us as a result.

This is why living from perception and projection is such a complex thing. Our idealized thoughts and beliefs create a set of rose-colored glasses, and our negative thoughts and beliefs create a set of dark-colored glasses. *Both sets create distortion.* Getting to the root patterns or blueprints takes intense inner work. Neither the shadow persona nor the ideal persona within the ego is operating from a divine knowledge of inherent self-worth, and they remain locked in mortal battle until we begin to break down these walls and defenses in our minds. The ideal stands vigil in front of our shadow, demanding that it stay hidden. From the shadow's point of view, the ideal functions like a bully, shoving the shadow away and shaming it. From the ideal's point of view, the shadow is like an albatross, constantly undermining its vision of perfection. In reality, they both want the same thing—to experience love, acceptance, power, value, safety, and the like. They just have different approaches for obtaining those ends.

To evolve and ascend into higher states of being, this battle must be resolved; we must heal our fragmented mind. The soul is oriented toward inclusion, and it is the source within us that can help us heal this wounded state. It sits outside both avenues of approach and sees the common ground. Therefore, it is in a position to help these warring parts of our consciousness find the narrow middle path—the integrated path—that leads out of this opposition. The higher Self's sense of worth is stable because it knows only love. It knows itself to be a loving expression within the greater whole of Creation and never forgets that everything it creates is simply a way to experience and learn about the inherent forces of creativity within us all. This knowledge is stable and eternal and does not change over time, although it does expand. Spiritually, our base of knowledge can grow as we create and learn new things, but whatever is true on the cosmic level never becomes untrue at some later time. For example, our knowledge of divine love can expand over the course of our evolution, but love at the divine level never becomes anything other than love; it never becomes fear, hate, or conditional.

Think back to our story about Rickie in chapter 5. Imagine her participating in a conversation with her boss about her work. She's speaking from a place of total certainty about her inherent worth as a human being. If she no longer needs someone outside herself to tell her she's OK, she's free to enter into negotiations, with a steady heart and clear mind. It's so much easier to be curious about the situation and remain open to seeing things in a new and different way. It's also easier to stand clearly in her truth and state her point of view without fear.

Dropping the Masks

Understanding how our thoughts and emotional reactions define our reality is the first step in moving out of suffering. *Both* the shadow persona and the ideal persona are resistant and afraid of the divine Self because the divine Self cannot be controlled, distorted, or made fraudulent by the ego. The divine Self can only tell the truth and behaves naturally, just as a young child does, without self-consciousness. It operates from pure intention and acts in accordance with its inner knowingness. This is what Jesus means when he says, "Except ye be converted, and become as little children, ye shall not enter into the kingdom of heaven."Matthew 18:3

This verse has been interpreted by the ego as a set of rules to live by, such as "don't be boastful; be simple, be trusting, and so forth." However, this interpretation is missing the larger point. Jesus is pointing out that our spirit is already in this state of innocence. He is saying the only way to be reconnected with the kingdom of heaven (which is the state of living within our divine mind) is to take off the masks we've created in our egos and access our authentic divine nature, which has no need to be boastful, manipulative, complicated, and so forth. The true, divine Self doesn't know the fear of the ego because it operates cocreatively within the whole of the Creation rather than as an independent island in resistance to the whole. As long as our identity remains trapped in our emotional responses to the external world, we cannot fully experience our true identity as spirit. In other words, as long as we identify ourselves as *being our emotions* rather than as *being a creative entity* that is experiencing things, we will remain unable to inhabit our true identity.

Let me share a story from own life that turned out to be a major turning point for me in my awakening and self-healing journey. One day, after a particularly powerful meditation, it dawned on me to ask my shadow a simple question: "What do you want?" My shadow replied, "I want to be loved. I want to be seen for who I really am." I thought, "Well, that sounds good to me, too." This gave me the courage to explore my shadow and try to figure out what she was trying to tell me. A technique for doing this began to unfold within my mind. From a place of unconditional love and curiosity, I asked my subconscious mind to show me what the problem was. The answer I got was that I craved a level of recognition but could not manifest it because I had judgments about it. Recognition was risky business. To be seen, heard, and known requires a certain vulnerability to rejection. ("Oh dear," said my inner child. "Anything but that!") It also requires a certain level of confidence. You must be able to put yourself in the center of your life and speak up, ask for what you want, and be assertive. And all these qualities, while present within me, had a stigma attached to them in my mind. They felt dangerous because they might be displeasing to others. Of course, they can be dangerous if not used in a balanced way. So, when I was very young, these qualities were the first to get shoved underground. And because energy follows thought, being assertive, confident, and bold enough to ask for what I really wanted always came at a high price for me. I noticed and began to cower from the competition, criticism, and rejection coming at me from others. Now, those reactions are common enough in the world. People do tend to be competitive, critical, and rejecting of others, especially if the other person is getting a lot of attention. But other reactions may have been happening, too—acceptance, admiration, and even inspiration. Yet I was focused on the negative reactions because I was afraid of them and because I believed I had to make everyone else happy in order to be "good."

Eventually, my physical body began to break down, too. In my twenties, I started suffering from chronic laryngitis. It took me years to understand that this was the result of my belief that it was not safe for me to ask for what I want or express myself in a way that put a spotlight on me. My ideal self believed I should be pleasing to others and that *they* got to determine what was pleasing. I felt compelled to be seen as always happy; humble; easy to get along with; sensitive to others' needs; and a giver, not a taker. Often, this was my authentic state. But when I didn't feel this way, when I was angry or hurt or wanted to have my own way on something, I found myself in a real bind. This internal conflict eventually made it impossible for me to be fully emotionally real. I'd try to stuff my "negative" feelings away until they would erupt over something relatively small. At that point, I would feel foolish and guilty, and both the shadow persona and ideal persona would get the results they believed in. Without a proper understanding and perspective from which to understand this inner conflict, I saw my deep desire to be seen as threatening to my ideal's sense of how to experience love. This is how the ability to assert myself out in the world came to be repressed and began to produce toxic results physically, emotionally, and mentally. Both aspects of me wanted to experience love:

the shadow wanted to be loved as is, and the ideal wanted to obtain love through pleasing others. A balance between these two approaches is what was actually needed.

I found it amazing that my compassionate interest in attending to my shadow without judgment is the very thing that ultimately led me to an avenue out of this dichotomy. I am naturally concerned about the welfare of others and interested in how my behavior affects those around me. I can count on this aspect to moderate my behavior and help me be self-reflective and sensitive to the needs of others. At the same time, I can direct this same compassion toward myself. I can count on this quality to be sensitive to my needs and to allow me room for self-expression. This higher point of view, which is not *identified* with my experiences, can help me understand my experiences and determine the quality of what I'm thinking and doing. There is a time and place for assertiveness, action, asking, and receiving. And there is a time for passivity, rest, listening, and giving.

What I experienced in that moment of clear connection with my soul is that both the shadow and the ideal are thoughtforms. They are both based on misperception, and they sit in opposition because they are the polarities within which the misperception exists. The shadow personifies our core negative belief, and the ideal personifies our adaptation. It is the aspect that is attempting to rectify the situation.

Our thoughts and emotions are the key to unraveling the story behind our ego. Both the shadow and the ideal are living amalgamations of emotionally charged thoughtforms—ideas about ourselves and the world around us. They're full of distortions, misunderstandings, and misperceptions. These thoughtforms contain our history and serve only to recreate it over and over again as we run our consciousness through them. When we begin to unearth the fears that underlie our ego, we see that both sides of the spectrum (the shadow *and* the ideal) have served as a barrier to our higher Self. When we trace our beliefs and our fears back through time, we can see for ourselves that this fearful orientation stemmed from our primal fear of death, pain (both physical and psychological), rejection, and sense of powerlessness caused by our loss of God consciousness. I believe the greatest torment for us is this loss of connection with the unconditional love of God that dwells within us in the aspect of our higher Self. Connecting with God internally heals us. We discover aspects of ourselves that empower us, and we actively begin to learn how to increasingly reveal our divinity externally.

The information our soul possesses can make us uncomfortable at times. Our true Selves have a much larger, interconnected, and relatively timeless perspective that puts the dramas we're experiencing in any given moment within any one lifetime into a whole-other light. The soul sees our experiences in the lower three worlds for the effects they are. Our experiences give us insight into the quality and clarity of our thinking and inform us about our ability to create intelligently from love. When we are in pain, we can be sure that our thinking needs adjustment. At first, it may be very unclear to us what that adjustment might be because we are a work in progress at the personality level. We are learning. The ego within us may feel angry about the concept of self-responsibility for our pain, but it's an important point to ponder. For when we truly understand it, we become empowered rather than the victims of our emotional and mental state.

Qualitatively, the love emanating from our soul is impersonal and impartial. When we live from this place, we can establish clear and healthy boundaries in a fair and forgiving manner. Why? The answer is that we no longer take other peoples' behavior personally, and we no longer believe that physical reality is the basis of our existence. We are able to think "cleanly" or purely without fearfulness distorting the creative process. That is what we're learning how to do right now in the evolutionary process—we're learning to become clear Thinkers. The soul is *light* and shines out into the world, attracting and connecting with the light in others. It also reveals where it is dark. This can make not only us but others around us uncomfortable if we are not ready to face that darkness and allow our inner light to heal it. When this resistance arises either internally or externally, we have the opportunity to learn how to remain steady in the light and maintain a loving attitude despite feelings of fear, rejection, or censure. In this way, we learn how move out of perception and projection, out of competition and ideas of relative worth, and into a place of intuitive knowing and clear-mindedness. We make room for our light to reveal our divinity and foster the light in those around us.

Facing the Adversary

The Adversary (also called sin, evil, the devil) is consciousness that sits in opposition to God (love, unity, at-one-ment). The adversarial mind is the result of our erroneous and narcissistic thinking. It is that which causes us to experience a lack of love and a perception of isolation or separation from others and from God. Theosophy teaches us that the soul on its own plane never loses its creative ability to extend love, and at that level we never become imperfect in any actual [77] sense. (This is an important point to ponder.) But in the lower levels of consciousness, we *can* and *have* used our creative ability inappropriately. We have misused our minds. Through the power of attraction (an energetic quality of love), we have generated thoughtforms that exhibit and reveal harmful, injurious, immoral, and inherently untrue thinking, resulting in fearful and painful experiences. This is an unfortunate misuse of the *energy* of love. (Please note the emphasis on the word *energy*.)

The central message of *A Course in Miracles* is that *nothing real can be damaged, and nothing unreal exists*. The Adversary tells us the opposite. It tells us that we are damaged, that

---

[77] Actual, existing in fact, real

separation is real, and that unity does not really exist. In my own process of facing the adversary, I came to see how my ego's ideas about good and bad, light and dark were all based in fear. I have come to realize that darkness is nothing more than erroneous thinking, nothing more than a lack of love. I am slowly learning how to love in the face of darkness, see beyond forms, and seek the light or soul in all things. This teaches me what *ACIM* writer Gary Renard calls "causal forgiveness." When we move our attention into the soul and realize that everything that is happening in the lower three worlds is a temporary state—more like a dream than any true reality—we can begin to withdraw our identity out of the world of effects. We can seek out the light in others; we can forgive their trespasses as we are forgiven ours and hold steady in our mind the higher truth that we are all within the brotherhood of souls.

Every one of us is learning how to stop miscreating and how to return to love. When we stop identifying with our experiences, we can forgive them because essentially they do not alter our divine reality as sons of God. This is an empowering realization. It is the Adversarial mind-set that promotes the idea that we are vulnerable, powerless victims. The soul empowers us to see this for the lie that it is and get on with the divine business at hand—learning how to extend love and work together as a coordinated whole humanity.

Light is the outward manifestation of love, and darkness is the outward manifestation of fear. Only love overcomes fear, and only light dispels darkness. This continues to be challenging, but I am learning. Each time I am able to face the darkness with a neutral mind, I increase my ability to shine the light of love out into the darkness, and it recedes. Just as a dark room is illuminated when we turn on a light, even a small light can have a tremendous effect. Even a seemingly small act of love can have a powerful transformational effect. And this love needs to be directed toward both ourselves and others. We are being asked to *awaken* from the ego, awaken out of our gigantic thought-form of separation and fear. This is different from trying to fix the ego or fix others. ACIM teaches us that any attempt to fix the ego is experienced as an attack by the ego. Thus, our soul does not attack us, nor does it attack others, for that would be the opposite of love. Awakening is moving out of the ego and no longer investing in the thoughtforms it holds. As we do this, those thoughtforms dissipate for lack of attention.

Let's take a look at a commonly held thought-form in the ego: the idea that we have all fallen from Grace. When this thought-form motivates us to seek reconnection with the divine, we begin to awaken to the realization that God is within us, and the thought is transformed from the fearful verdict the ego supposes it to be. When it makes us feel valueless and hopeless, it continues to vivify the ego, and it is harmful. In my experience, God (whom I can experience only directly through my own soul) doesn't sit in judgment of me because that is not the nature of God. It is the wounded ego that is judgmental and projects that state of mind on God. My soul is teaching me that my task is not to *fix* myself, others, or the world but to *awaken* to the living Love, Light, Power, and Presence of God-within-me and within all things. As we all do this, the world of the ego is healed. It melts away. Underneath all our pain is a genuine longing for love and connection, as this is our actual nature. When we experience loving connection within ourselves and with one another, the longing ceases and our inherent divinity is revealed.

Along the path of return, each of us must face the Adversary within and around us in order to move out of the world of effects and into the reality of the soul. As we learn to express the perfection of God-within-us, we return to a loving state of being because God *is* love. The ego strives to fill our sense of disconnection and emptiness with its own ideas about perfection, but the answers lie within the soul. When our struggle for perfection is nothing more than a consuming need to cover up our shadow, we are still investing in fearfulness and in the idea of separation. When our struggle for perfection inspires us toward self-discipline, dispassion, discernment, and decentralization, then we can be assured that we are using our creativity appropriately.

Chapter 7 Exercises

1. Fear
   - How has fear controlled your life? What have you not done? What do you avoid? What habitual reactions stem from fear?
   - What is the fundamental core thought in the center of your fear? (Take them one by one.)
   - Is it really the truth?
     o If so, what makes it true, and what are you invested in that makes it true?
     o What would need to be different for you to be free of this fear?
   - If not, what keeps you invested in it?
2. Who are you?
   - Are you the thinker of thoughts, the product of thoughts, or both?
   - If consciousness comes about through the merger of Spirit with matter, *who* is in charge?
3. What purpose do your thoughts and memories serve?
4. If you are all the forms you've created, what does this tell you about the possibility of change?
   - If you are your memories, how will change occur?
   - If you are your thoughts, can thoughts change? How do they change? Who is the agent of that change?
   - If energy follows thought to produce form, what happens to the form when you change the thought?
5. When an old way of thinking persists over time, even when you don't like it and you want to think differently, what do you think is going on?
   - What holds your attention in the old pattern?
6. What comes up for you when you consider the notion of the Adversary?
   - How does this state of mind work in your life?
   - How do you see it working in the world around you?
   - How do see yourself getting free of that state of mind?

7. How has forgiveness worked in your life?
   - What have you gained?
   - What do you find difficult to forgive?
   - What does this tell you about yourself and what you are working on as an evolving being?
8. What does the idea of "causal" forgiveness—forgiveness from the soul's point of view—bring up for you?
   - What comes up when you consider the idea that our lives in the lower three worlds are in many ways like a dream?
   - How do you see yourself waking up?

PART III: INTEGRATION

Reconstructing Me
Words & Music by Janet Lee Myatt © 2004

Stripped bare, standing alone in the cold, harsh light
I am shivering with fear and with delight
Break down as tears run down my face
I am no longer resisting the pain
I am under construction; beware
Don't expect me to be reasonable and fair

I'm reconstructing me
Uncovering something beautiful and free
I'm reconstructing me

The dam will break when the waters rise
My grief still takes me by surprise
Digging deep to find the pieces of my life
Discarding the undermining lies

Janet Myatt

I'm under construction; it's true
I'm difficult, wonderful and new

I'm reconstructing me
Uncovering something beautiful and free
I'm reconstructi ng me[78]

---

[78] Myatt, Janet Lee. "Reconstructing Me." Feels Like Thunder. 2005

CHAPTER 8 ~ DISCOVERING NEW WAYS OF BEING

Higher Power

Wherever I am, God is, and all is well.[79]

For those approaching the Path of Return, one of the most significant turning points occurs when we truly realize for ourselves that God is within us and within all things. Experiencing an intensely deep-felt connection with the Presence of God can change the course of our lives. Typically, when this happens, we want to strengthen this connection, and it becomes an important value in our lives. However, whether we know it or not, every moment of every day, God is present within us and within whatever situation, challenge, or experience we are having. Every idea, every thought, every emotion, and every action can lead us to God if we ask. This miracle may seem far fetched. We may wonder, for example, how a painful, negative, or unloving thought can lead us to God. God is *always* present, because only God is real. God is the life force and source of consciousness and energy within the entire universe. With our free will, then, we can choose to bring forth God's thoughts and God's presence in a situation, or we can choose to ignore it. A painful or unloving thought is simply our choice to ignore God's thought at that moment. It arises from our pain, from our ignorance, and from our orientation in selfish or separative thinking. The mind can

---

[79] Freeman

reveal, or it can divide. We have the choice to experience the larger God consciousness within us rather than remain invested in the smaller point of view of our separated self. We can always choose to turn our thoughts and our problems up to God and see what comes into our awareness.

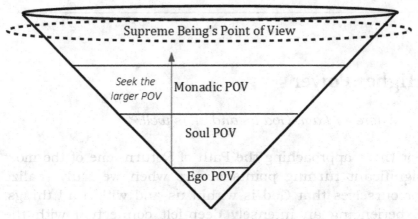

Figure 38: Connecting with God

When we are depressed, angry, or confused, we can stop and ask God to help us understand what's going on. There is absolutely no point in pretending we don't have the unloving, depressed, or angry thought or emotion. What we resist will persist. It is there for a reason—a very valid reason. We are in the process of learning something about the quality of our thinking, feeling, or being, and we are missing some vital piece of the puzzle, which God can help us discover if we ask. Our task in life is not merely to resist unpleasant emotions and pursue only pleasant emotions but to *learn* from our experiences and emotions—all of them.

Most of us greatly resist the fear, anger, and invalidation we feel inside. However, that energy has to go somewhere. It flows into our physical, astral, and/or mental body and causes disruption and imbalance in our lives. When we begin to understand that God is present in every situation, and we begin to ask God to show us the way, we begin to heal. And when we begin to think the thoughts of God and feel the love of God, we emerge from the constraints and neuroses of the ego. Let me quickly interject here that whether you call on this Higher Power by the name God or by some other name is irrelevant. What's important is acknowledging that a higher synthesizing, loving, intelligence exists and that we have access to it through our hearts and minds.

I have learned from my own experience that finding God in all things is not necessarily easy or blissful. Finding God requires us to stretch beyond our boundaries, beyond our comfort zones, and often beyond what we think we can handle. At first, it can feel painful, scary, and overwhelming to the ego and to the body. This is when it's helpful to remember to tell yourself, "Wherever I am, God is, and all is well." Even when we cannot feel the Presence of God because we are in such a contracted, small place of fear, we can willfully turn our thoughts to God and allow ourselves to be willing to move out of that fearful place. We can greatly help ourselves connect with this higher Source of light, love, and intelligence through practicing a form of meditation that works for us. Alignment is a key factor in receiving what we have asked for.

With integration work, I have found that we can simply let go of some things. We can realize the error of our thinking and move into a new orientation without much trouble. For example, one day, I suddenly realized with my entire being that drinking Diet Coke was bad for me. I threw the Diet Coke away, and that was that. After spending ten years or so drinking one or two a day, I stopped drinking them and never looked back. For other things, however, we will consciously have to undo or unravel. In those cases, we've tied up a lot of our consciousness in the issue, and thus it has become central to our journey. It holds a divine lesson we came here to learn in this lifetime. For instance, learning how to feel comfortable standing up for myself has been a gradual learning process for me. And it is a theme that continues to teach me lessons, even though I have made significant gains. Remembering that God is present can make the difference that leads us to a successful breakthrough. By allowing ourselves to connect with our divine mind, we open ourselves up to divine intervention, to "miracles." For instance, the right book or the right person may show up, and a new point of view emerges. Miraculously, an opportunity presents itself, a door opens or closes, and another one appears. Or we can have a sudden, clear insight that alters our perception and leads us to better outcomes. Remaining open to these kinds of divine interventions can bring about tremendous and powerful transformations in our life.

Here is an example from my own life. One day, I had a huge disappointment that caused me to feel completely powerless and taken advantage of. My chest felt tight and heavy, and that told me I was very angry. I developed a severe migraine, which told me I felt victimized and, again, powerless. I wanted to yell and scream at the people who had let me down and were putting me in such a terrible position. But, of course, I could not do this because I knew it would only make the situation much worse. I felt trapped and out of control.

This overwhelming feeling of powerlessness and entrapment provided the first clue on how to begin to move out of this incredibly painful place. I had to stop and acknowledge that I was not in control of the situation. "I have no control over this person," I said to myself. "If she chooses to behave irresponsibly, and if she chooses not to honor her word, there is nothing I can do about that." When I began, I still felt a lot of anger in my body. I repeated the statement several times until my body was able to realize the truth of what I was saying and finally begin to let go of the anger. I played out all the worst-case scenarios in my mind to their ultimate conclusion until my mind could acknowledge that I could not stop this person or *make* her do the right thing. I felt so small, sad, and completely invalidated after all I had done for this person. I wondered if I really had no other choice but to be a victim. I began to breathe into my body and seek out the larger lens of my higher consciousness. From there, I sought out the even-larger God consciousness my soul remains connected to at all times. I stated my intention clearly: "I am not in agreement to being a victim. I don't know how to proceed with this situation. I trust that You do. I trust that in this vast universe of love and light there is an answer that will bring my highest intention to fruition. I will get out of the way and allow You to work Your magic."

Throughout the day, as I would feel the hook of anger and helplessness make a grab for my attention, I gently reminded myself that I had control over only how *I* handled the situation and that I had no clear answer yet on what to do or say next. So, my job was to move forward with my day and trust that all would be well. Again and again, I turned the situation back over to God. I envisioned the problem as a ball of energy that I handed over to this Higher Power, and I said, "I'm willing to change, I'm willing to learn, I'm willing to see and do things differently to get where I want to go with this situation." Every time my wounded inner child wanted to play the pity harp, I gently reminded her that we had a choice: we could grow the negativity and the victim energy, or we could grow the faith and trust energy. Then, I gently turned my thoughts back to God and reminded myself that God was "on it."

An important element to this process was that I didn't tell myself that God was separate from me. I didn't pretend that some power "out there" was magically going to solve this problem for me. Instead, I *strengthened my connection* with this Higher Power, this Higher Intelligence, this loving Presence and allowed it to *emerge within me and within the situation.* I allowed it to take over while I managed my wounded self with continual reminders of what was possible. In this case, the less I did to try to change the situation, the better.

At the end of the day, God encouraged me to open up a discussion with my husband about the problem and get his input. This proved to be very productive and created a solid foundation for our intention to hold the other parties accountable for sticking with the original agreement they had made with us. This prompted my husband to speak to one of the individuals in a loving but firm manner. He made it clear that we were expecting him (and the other person involved) to hold up their end of the agreement and that there really was no other alternative. He did this in such a kind way—as he always does!

I began to see that all we had to do was move forward with the original agreement and trust that everything would fall into place. The first miracle for me was that my husband also saw this and was willing to stand side by side with me in a united way. In the past, he would have wanted more definite assurance from the other parties before proceeding. The second miracle happened the next morning when the other person involved in the situation finally agreed to keep her end of the bargain and even thanked me for all I had done for them.

Once again, I had the opportunity to learn this important lesson. I cannot control the world, nor can I control the people around me. I can control only what I do and how I do it. Trusting in a Higher Power sometimes feels as if we're "doing nothing about it," but this couldn't be more inaccurate. Trusting in a Higher Power means we're no longer putting the ego and the wounded self in charge. Instead, we're stepping into our true self—the self that exists within God, within a Higher Power, the self that is always cocreating within the larger context of divine love.

Forgiveness

Forgive us our debts as we forgive our debtors.^{Matthew 6:12}

We touched briefly on the idea of forgiveness in our discussion about fear, but I'd like to explore this essential divine characteristic more deeply here. As we travel the Path of Return, it is important for us to make room in our psyche for mistakes—our own and others'—and to be forgiving. The way humanity currently learns is through trial and error. This is true for all of us. We create our reality through the ideas and beliefs we hold in our minds, and we experience the consequences—good and bad, favorable and unfavorable, successful and unsuccessful. So, what is a mistake, really? At the most fundamental level, it's a negative result stemming from of our creative activity, our perception, or our current understanding of the reality we're in. When we suspend judgment and look at the situation with neutrality, we have the opportunity to figure out what we're meant to discover and take corrective measures. When we hurt someone, for example, we tend to feel guilty about it. When we use that guilt as a motivating force for self-examination, it is a useful emotional response *as long as we move through it by figuring out the underlying pattern and then arrive at forgiveness* for both ourselves and the other players involved. What underlying need/desire drove us to behave in a hurtful, harmful, or oblivious way?

Remember, God does not attack. God does not condemn us, because God is love. This means that the divine Self is able to embrace us and help us awaken when we allow it to. With honest, open self-reflection, we can ask ourselves if the ideas and beliefs we are operating within are grounded in true perception or misperception. What motivation prompted the behavior—love or fear, connection or disconnection, forgiveness or judgment? When we take the time to process our experiences in this way, we create room to move out of our own ideas and biases and see things with a larger perspective. Furthermore, the very process required to uncover this larger viewpoint is in itself a gift because it directs us toward our higher self. I have found that we don't really go looking for the higher self until the personality has run out of answers and is no longer adequately able to cope with the inconsistencies of living in its own ideality. Consequently, mistakes often play an important part in most of our key turning points. Compassion and forgiveness for ourselves and for others are essential elements in this process. When we make a mistake and we hurt others, they will have a reaction. When we can feel compassion for them *and* for ourselves, for their pain and ours, we will be able to move through the mistake rather than get locked into it through defensiveness or self-judgment. When our compassion extends to both ourselves and to the person we hurt, we can more readily invite forgiveness into our heart.

What about when people hurt us? If we follow the advice of our ego, we'll be tempted to take their behavior *personally* as an indication of our worth and sometimes of their worth, and we'll suffer either way. Many negative symptoms arise when we feel victimized. We'll either believe we deserved it because we're not good enough or judge ourselves to be superior, rendering the other person inferior and unworthy of our love and forgiveness. Both of these reactions increase our investment in separation from God and from one another, and they grow our experiences of fear and lack of love. Instead, if we realize that the other person is also struggling under the influence of a chaotic system and also ensnared in the pitfalls of his ego, we can depersonalize the experience and forgive him. We can choose to understand that he simply hasn't yet been able to transform his consciousness from a fearful orientation to a loving one. He is learning through his experiences, as we are. Sometimes this means that we will need to let the other person know how his behavior affected us, even as we practice forgiveness. We can speak our truth *and* forgive him because we understand the larger esoteric cause underlying his behavior. We still need to maintain healthy boundaries and, when appropriate, hold others accountable for their behavior with suitable consequences. But the key to transforming our consciousness out of chaos and suffering is to do this without taking their misdeeds *personally*. This allows us to avoid falling into the pitfall of a victim mentality.

And it allows others to learn through the same law of cause and effect we are all subject to.

This, then, is the difference between forgiveness at the *causal* level, which is transformational, and forgiveness at the *effect* level. Causal forgiveness forces us out the mind-set of our personality and into the mind-set of the soul, where there is no delusion that we are not all inherently OK. From this divine point of view, we are able to step out of the "story" our personality is ensnared within. We move our *identity* out of our emotional experience. From the soul's perspective, we're able to realize that every emotional experience is actually a transitory experience designed to teach us how to love better and reveal our inner Light. To understand this better, we can imagine that, from our soul's perspective, our personalities live in a state that is much like a dream. When we're dreaming, everything *feels* real to us. But when we awaken, we realize it wasn't "real"—at least not in the dense world we all call "reality." It was just an experience we were exploring on the astral plane. When we awaken, we move our identity out of the dream and associate with the reality of our waking consciousness. This same phenomenon exists between the soul and the personality.

By comparison, forgiveness from the personality level falls short of a truly transformational experience, but it can set us in the right direction. It falls short because when we remain *identified* with the effect, we believe we have been victimized, and we perpetuate the dream (or nightmare, as the case may be). We remain invested in the "reality" of the world of illusions we've made up in our minds.

I remember a situation with my family where a series of events led each of us to become very angry with each other. We were all blaming each other for the miserable state we were in, and we experienced an ugly scene. For several weeks, I stumbled around in a fog, bouncing between extreme self-recrimination and angrily castigating everyone else. I couldn't find my way out of the hole I'd fallen into. And even as I slowly and conditionally began to forgive the others, I remained stuck in a place where I could not forgive myself. I saw myself as a victim *and* an antagonist and was unforgiving of both roles. I continued to pray and ask for guidance. Finally, I felt the presence of Archangel Michael surround me and fill my mind. He asked me, "How do you feel about Lucifer?"[80] I replied, "I don't like him very much. He's caused a lot of problems in the world." Michael asked me, "What do you think God should do about him?" The first thing that popped into my head was, "God should get rid of him." But even as I thought it, I knew this wasn't what my heart believed. Michael replied, "How can God do this when he is one of God's beloved sons? Are you saying God should kill his own son? Would *you* kill one of your beloved sons?" I replied, "No, of course not. I can forgive *them*. It's myself I can't forgive." Michael replied, "Are you not also one of God's beloved children? Are you saying you're not worthy of His forgiveness? How can that be so? If He can forgive Lucifer, and He has, certainly He can forgive you. It is only your fearful self who cannot forgive your fearful self."

I began to feel God's love wash over me and flow through me toward all things regardless of their state of conscious awareness. In that moment, I felt compassion for myself and everyone involved, and I was able to forgive us all. I saw the deeper pattern of pain within each person and how it contributed to the result. I knew with great certainty that I could not go backward into the invalidating point of view that had caused my part in the drama, but I also saw that the entire event was inevitable, given each person's underlying thought patterns. The quality of the forgiveness I had been extending to the others in the previous days was nothing like the expansive quality of this experience. My initial forays had still been steeped within a victim mentality, and so the

---

[80] The whole conversation was based on the symbol of "Lucifer" as the archetype for the "fallen" self—the narcissistic, isolated, fearful, arrogant self sitting in opposition to God.

forgiveness felt contrived, and I still felt miserable. I had been *willing* to forgive to get out of pain but remained unable to forgive completely because I was still *identified with the effects* of the event. My willingness moved me in the right direction, though, and helped me open up to this profound causal forgiveness flowing from my soul. This experience opened my mind and heart in a way that allowed me to move out of a core picture I'd been carrying around in my subconscious mind for years—perhaps even lifetimes. Soul identification returns us to right-mindedness. We step out of the dream the personality is encased within, remember the inherent worth of everyone, and awaken to the Oneness of being.

High Compassion and Low Compassion

Our human compassion binds us the one to the other—not in pity or patronizingly, but as human beings who have learnt how to turn our common suffering into hope for the future.[81]

I had a good friend who told me she had been raped by a man who broke into her house and held her at knifepoint. I was filled with horror and fear, and I felt so badly for her. But she said something I have never forgotten: "I refuse to see myself as a victim because then I really would be hurt. I am OK. I've always been OK." By acknowledging her inherent worth and the fact that she cannot be damaged by the events of her life, she was able to refrain from identifying herself as a victim. Thus, she was able to free herself from the experience and move on with her life. Her acknowledgement moved me out of low compassion (i.e., seeing her as victim who must be somehow be permanently scarred by her experience) and into high compassion (i.e., recognizing the pain of the situation she went through but knowing her to be inherently OK). When we witness another's pain, we can feel empathy for them because we, too, have felt pain and know what it feels like.

---

[81] Mandela, Nelson.

We know how difficult it can be to navigate through it and arrive at understanding. However, it is important that we not invest in disempowering ideas about the person's experience. We need to refrain from picturing the other person as a victim and instead hold steady in our minds the image that they can successfully navigate their way through the painful experience. When we feel sympathy or empathy for another, we energetically tend to match the grief or pain. We need to be careful with this because it can quickly become harmful to both parties. First, it adds more negative energy to the other person's experience. Second, it brings the energetic vibration of our own vehicles down into a matching pattern, which becomes toxic to our own mental, emotional, and physical well-being. This does not serve the highest good for either party.

I recall a story of a young man who was badly burned in a military maneuver in Iraq. Most of his body was badly disfigured, especially his face. Before the accident, he had been the typical, good-looking, charismatic, popular football player in high school. After the accident, he believed his life was over. He slipped into a deep depression, resisted physical therapy, and wanted to die. His mother, however, refused to give in to his self-pity and his belief that he was a monster. She held steady in the light and told him repeatedly how valuable and beautiful he was, that his soul is what made him who he was, and that most people would be able to see this, too. She told him not to worry about those who couldn't see this in him. This young man eventually responded to his mother and began to heal. He then went on to play a significant role in a daytime soap opera about a burn victim, and then went on to win *Dancing with the Stars*, capturing the heart of the nation with the light and love that radiated out of him. His mother's high compassion saved his life.

Why is this important? Let me give an analogy. Let's say there is a cancer cell in the body. Next to that cancer cell is a healthy cell. The cancer cell has formed a negative pattern that is out of sync with the larger whole and is working at odds with it. And let's say that the cancer cell couldn't do any better at the time because it was overwhelmed by a negative agent of some sort. The healthy cell next to it recognizes the cancer cell's distress and wants to help. The healthy cell feels tremendous empathy for the cancer cell—it literally "feels his brother's pain." As a result, it begins to experience that same negative pattern within itself. Thus, we have two cells running the negative energy, and the pattern grows in strength, intensity, and impact. It becomes much harder for the surrounding cells to hold their healthy pattern. Let's say a third cell recognizes what's happening and chooses not to *feel the pain as its own.* Instead, it knows how challenged the other two cells are at the moment but also knows of the overall wellness of the whole. Instead of investing emotionally in the negative state of the two cancer cells, it acknowledges the situation and focuses its attention on the larger truth that millions of other cells in the system are all healthy. This focus allows it to extend this healthy pattern outward to the cancer cells. It has sympathy for the cancer cells, meaning it understands the difficulty without judgment, but it does not take the pattern into itself because it knows this will only grow the problem. Instead, it serves the higher good by maintaining a healthy vibration and focusing on the wellness of the larger whole. This allows that cell to broadcast to the two cancer cells the higher truth of the inherent healthy pattern. This gives the two cancer cells a much better chance of returning to wellness by matching the healthy pattern.

Let's take a look at one more area where neutrality, nonjudgement, and nonresistance can promote healing. When we are communicating with another person, and particularly if the other person is upset, paraphrasing is one of the very best things we can do to help him feel heard and understood. This powerful communication tool does not require agreement, sympathy, or problem solving on our part to work. It does, however, require a willingness to attend to the other person in a caring and open way even if we disagree with him. Paraphrasing has the power to transform lives because it helps us connect with others in a way that allows each person to experience feeling heard. An effective paraphrase names the other person's emotion and conveys to him what we understand he is saying and feeling.

Let's say your spouse is angry and hurt over something his coworker said. Instead of investing in negativity by calling the coworker a big jerk or trying to fix the situation, you can paraphrase: "You're hurt that Bill didn't recognize how hard you've been working on the XYZ project. He noticed only the one thing that didn't get done instead of all the other things that did." Notice that when you paraphrase, you're not agreeing or disagreeing with anything; you're simply acknowledging with kindness how your spouse feels. Chances are your spouse's shoulders will drop; he'll take a deeper breath and begin the healing process. You may have to go through several rounds of this if the pain is deep and if the situation is complex. But if you continue to listen actively, you create a whole-new energetic field where the other person can begin to decompress, let go, and even start to see the larger picture. Chances are he'll be able to figure out for himself what went wrong and what he might be able to do differently in the future. Paraphrasing is an active form of high compassion. It also works when you're the one the other person is having a problem with. Once he experiences feeling heard by you, he's much more likely to open up to listening to what you have to say.

High compassion is an act of doing no harm. It flows from the soul and leads us into forgiveness, inspiration, and intuitive knowing of a higher good. It connects us with our ability to see the larger whole and the broader truth, and it gives us access to the hidden keys that unlock us from our imprisoning deceptions. Low compassion is a psychological identification with the thoughts, feelings, or attitudes of the other person that keep both parties invested in the delusions that arise out of the separated mind. High compassion and causal forgiveness stem from the unified awareness that we are all divine beings having experiences in the lower worlds. And those experiences—no matter how horrific or beautiful— are temporary. All experiences are the avenue through which we learn about the quality of our thinking in the lower worlds, but they cannot damage or negate our divine status as ascending Sons of God. The soul *on its own plane* cannot be damaged, polluted, divided, broken, lost, or victimized. When we remember this, we can begin to work differently in the world.

Healthy Boundaries

That doesn't mean, however, that the rapist in the earlier example shouldn't have been sent to prison if he'd been caught. At the personality level of experience, his *behavior* was not OK. Obviously, his fearful personality was wildly out of control; consequently, he perpetuated grievous harm to others. At the form level, an appropriate consequence serves the highest good because it provides clear feedback about the quality of the person's thought patterns and emotional responses through the auspices of cause and effect. This is an extension of high compassion because the higher Self upholds the truth that the behavior was the result of wrong-mindedness and the misuse of creative power. The soul knows that the personality *is fully capable* of learning how to do better. That is what the personality is here to do.

Perfectionism

One of the energies that can get in the way of compassion and forgiveness is perfectionism. Perfectionism within the ego mind often creates a judgmental and intolerant attitude. As a recovering perfectionist, I came to this understanding very slowly. Perfectionism and intolerance are closely related in the ego mind. I have always had extremely high expectations of myself. Why? There are several answers to this question.

233

Janet Myatt

On one level, I have high expectations because a part of my consciousness has never completely forgotten the perfection of living in unity with God, and I yearn to experience that again. I feel great joy when I see and experience the perfection in something or someone. When I see others as they truly are—spirit to spirit—I recognize their perfection. On this level, there is no intolerance, no competition, and no fear—only joy. When competition and invalidation enter my psyche, I know I've dropped down into the consciousness of my ego. On the ego level, I place high expectations on myself in an effort to counteract my deepest core picture of not being good enough. I have come to understand that most human beings carry this feeling of not being good enough deep down inside; thus, it is a core picture for most of us, if not all. Jesus explains in ACIM that this is because we all intuitively know that we've lost touch with the part of ourselves that is Divine. We have a sense that something vital is missing. The part of our consciousness that resides in the ego was originally connected to our higher Self, and a residual memory of this remains with us to some degree. Thus, the ego knows that it is a fabricated construct and, as such, is vulnerable to being exposed as fraudulent.

While the ego is equally unaware of spirit, it does perceive itself as being rejected by something greater than itself.[82]

As discussed earlier, this is why self-esteem is an ever-shifting facade. I learned to cope with this feeling of not being good enough by being very critical of myself. My ego mind continually strove to figure out how to be perfect so I would become "good enough." This approach leads to judgment, invalidation, and competition and is based on a lack of love. It is definitely fear based. It creates a vicious cycle: If I'm perfect, I must be right. If I'm right, then I must be valid. I'm invalid if I'm wrong because if I'm wrong, I'm imperfect.

---

[82]   *ACIM*, p. 58.

Perfect = Right = valid. Wrong = imperfect = invalid.

Where is there room for growth in this kind of thinking? Furthermore, it set the stage for me to be critical not only of myself but of everyone else whom I perceived to be acting in an imperfect way. This fosters an environment of judgment, competition, and control. Numerous times, I have felt deep pain when someone who I believed was acting imperfectly got rewarded. I would wonder why I didn't get noticed or rewarded for all my good deeds and so forth. These experiences fed the core picture: "I'm not good enough." It was only when I came to realize that ego-level perfectionism was creating an awful trap that I opened myself up to the idea of being compassionate and forgiving with myself. I slowly came to realize that I'm here to learn; without a tolerance for mistakes, I wouldn't be able to do that. I also came to understand in my heart that everyone else is also here to learn and that they need room to make mistakes, too. As I became more compassionate and forgiving with myself, my capacity to do the same for others grew, and vice versa.

Is it wrong to want to do something right? Not at all. But if our motivation stems from fear and not from love, we will end up disappointed. When we are "giving to get," we are coming from a sense of lack and operating from fear—the fear that we don't have something we need, such as acceptance, love, and power. The Buddhists talk about having no attachment to outcome. They encourage individuals to pay attention to the path, to the journey. Focusing our energies on manifesting our highest intention in the present moment moves our attention off a future "gain" and puts us squarely into what is happening now. This gives us the power to adjust how and what we're manifesting in the moment. Are we connecting? Are we revealing our light? Are we being of service to others, helping them discover and reveal their light? Are we producing the effects we desire? If not, what do we need to do differently? What do we need to learn or remember to help us succeed?

Janet Myatt

This approach gives us room to work intelligently with our mistakes or missteps and with our successes.

When we allow the journey to teach us as we go, it is exactly right. There is a different brand of "perfect" when we operate from our soul and let go of our attachment to fear. We place ourselves faithfully in the hands of our own divinity and trust in the larger purity of God's goodwill flowing through the universe. When we allow ourselves to detach from the outcomes our egos have imagined and move into the intelligent flow of the greater field of life, we stop trying to control our path and instead let it unfold. When we allow ourselves to feel compassion for ourselves and the world around us, we no longer feel the need to judge or compete, and we gain greater clarity about what to do in any given situation. When we forgive from the causal level, we step out of the dream state of the ego's world of lack and step into the world of intelligent divine love. The more we do this, the more we begin to seek ways of serving the highest good for everyone.

Deprogramming the Mind

"There is no other teacher but your own soul." [83]

Another important attribute to develop in the process of awakening is the ability to question everything. We need to question our thoughts, beliefs, motivation, actions, habits, morals, ethics, codes of conduct—everything! This includes questioning the values and programming of our tribe, family, nation, religion, schooling, scientific theories, and anything else we can think of. Perhaps not all at once, though—that might render us incapacite. But systematically over time, we need to be in the habit of investigating the inherent quality of the underlying thoughts and beliefs in play within any given situation or experience we are involved with. We can get in

---

[83] Swami Vivekananda. Brainyquote.com

the practice of going within and uncovering the larger divine truth.

Let me give an example. Most people agree that loyalty is "good" and disloyalty is "bad." *Loyalty* is defined in the dictionary as "faithfulness to commitments or obligations... faithful adherence to a sovereign, government, leader, cause, etc."[84] But loyalty in the world of the ego is always relative and must be questioned. For example, a gang member shoots his neighbor in a drive-by. Is the gang member demonstrating loyalty to his gang? Yes. Would he be called disloyal if he refused to shoot? Yes. What if he found out the intended target was his cousin, and he warned the cousin? Would this be a betrayal to his gang? Yes. But what would God say? What would the *Divine* within that gang member say? How many countless wars have been fought in God's name? Was God present in any of those wars? When the 9/11 terrorists "sacrificed" themselves and thousands of other people in the name of their God, was God pleased? Was God present in that intention? What do we believe? Do we believe God was thinking those thoughts?

So, we cannot assume the programming handed down to us through our family, nation, religion, or educational system is inherently true. We can't take anything for granted on our journey back to wholeness. Examine and question everything, and talk directly to God. Then, wait patiently for an answer to emerge. It may take quite a while to unravel the truth from the lie and to distinguish the ego's answer from the Spirit's. This is a deeply internal and individual process that eventually helps us connect our personality consciousness with the greater consciousness of God. As I've said before, there is no one way to do it. And there is no "free pass" simply because we belong to a certain religion, nation, or tribe. We cannot say, "My religion says murder is OK if we're killing infidels. My family says those people are inferior, so it's OK to treat them

---

[84] Dictionary.com definition of *loyalty*.

as such. My nation tells me it's unpatriotic to question what it's doing, so I'll just look the other way." We can know we are on our true path only with direct one-to-one communication with the God consciousness within us.

This examination process extends beyond the big questions of religion and government. We live in a mental-emotional world full of dichotomies, or pairs of opposites: happy-sad, introverted-extroverted, leader-follower, assertive-passive, flexible-inflexible, detail-oriented–big picture, and so forth. Dichotomies create specific orientations along a continuum, but these segregated traits and approaches are not holistic. Each is missing elements found on the opposite side of the spectrum. Both sides have something valuable for us. So, when our characteristics, our "truths," and our values become fixed in one position, blinds spots and weaknesses form. For instance, the strong person may learn something valuable from experiencing a weakness. The leader may discover she can learn something amazing by following another. The do-gooder may need to let someone figure something out for himself. The analytical type may benefit from a more fluid, abstract approach to solve a tricky problem. The paradigms we live in and the corresponding mental/emotional structures that form the scaffolding of our consciousness actually imprison us when we cannot move through them.

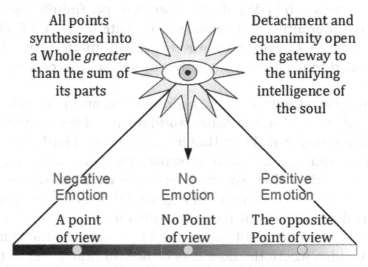

All points synthesized into a Whole *greater* than the sum of its parts

Detachment and equanimity open the gateway to the unifying intelligence of the soul

Negative Emotion

No Emotion

Positive Emotion

A point of view

No Point of view

The opposite Point of view

Figure 39: Moving out of Dichotomies

The point is, decentralizing out of our thoughtforms and our current ego identity involves finding a way to detach from our "givens" so that we can move into an entirely different frame of reference that sits *above* the pairs of opposites. From this higher plane, we can move out of our blind spots and see our weaknesses. We can learn something more about the *wholeness* that contains the dichotomy. Even more importantly, we slowly begin to see for ourselves that the paradigms we live in are relative and not absolute. This opens us up to discovering larger unified fields of consciousness and higher states of being. Each larger unity we discover liberates us from imprisonment in old forms.

This requires meditative, prayerful contemplation and discernment. It also requires great courage and fortitude because in our external life we will have to be willing to be rejected by our tribe, family, loved ones, and any other energy that seeks to control us through fear. On the internal planes, we will have to be willing to abandon our current paradigms *before* we have another to replace it with. I call this "jumping into the abyss." We can't go back over the same old ground because there's nothing new to learn there. We can't stay on the edge of the unknown indefinitely because we are inherently creative; we must create. Thus, we find we have to move forward and bravely set foot into terrain that is unknown to us. This is the only way we can discover it.

I remember standing in my bedroom one afternoon when it dawned on me that the entire world my mind believed in was not inherently true. I saw that it was a series of shifting walls of ideas and beliefs that imprisoned me. I also saw that the key to the door that would allow me to walk out was in my hand. It had been there all along, but I'd been too caught up in the drama of my situation and also too afraid to step out because of what might be on the other side. At the time, I had no idea where the door was or how to find it. Yet in that moment, I made a strong, clear, one-pointed intention to find out how to set myself free. Once this intention was set, I began to act on the guidance that followed. Certain events were set into motion that eventually led to a series of radical changes in my point of view. This process continues to this day.

Eventually, those who are awakening will be asked to lead by example to the best of their ability at any given time instead of just trying to fit in and play it safe. This is not always easy. It's simple, but not easy. It's simple in that all we have to do is go within and talk to God. But learning *how* to do this, how to actually recognize God's thoughts, and how to be courageous enough to act on what we discover takes practice. So, as we've seen, we can't simply make a list of behaviors, values, and ethics and label them "good" or "bad" and call it a day. Instead, we will have to move out of the push-pull of dichotomies and up into that higher point of view of the soul. From this vantage point, we will most likely notice that both "sides" of an issue are operating within a paradigm each believes to be true and that both are trying to do what they believe is right, fair, or just. Once we see this common ground, the battle lines can no longer be so sharply drawn, and new ideas have room to emerge.

The more we do this, the better we get at discerning the motivation underlying the paradigms involved. Behaviors, values, and ethics that stem from the separated self (the ego) will ultimately be connected to fear. Behaviors, values, and ethics that stem from the Spirit will be connected to love, certainty, and knowledge. As extensions of Divine Spirit, God's point of view is accessible to us via our soul. It can be hard to see the paradigms we operate within because they create the context of our lives—the set, the props, the costumes, the very theater within which we live. So, we can start only wherever we find things not working or no longer making sense and gradually work our way through the structure of beliefs we're entrenched within.

As we navigate our way through our thoughts and beliefs and bring them into alignment with God, we will begin to stabilize our mind, and this helps us create a bridge from the lower consciousness of the personality to the higher consciousness of the soul. This process is not linear. We don't question a belief, value, or ethic once and then never revisit it again. The process is spiral-cyclical, akin to peeling off the layers of an onion. We navigate through one layer and create a certain level of stability and equilibrium that enables us to open to new levels of awareness. Then, suddenly, something shifts, and the next layer of energy around that belief is exposed and must be examined. Sometimes, something will happen in our lives that causes our mind to contract back into survival, fear, competition, and uncertainty. When this happens, we can be certain that a new cycle of growth is beginning where we must once again question everything. Each time we go through the process, we become more competent and more aware of the pitfalls. We gain experience and discover what works for us and what is true for us, and we make better choices.

Eckhart Tolle portrays this phenomenon beautifully in his book *A New Earth*[85]. He shares a Buddhist parable of a

---

[85] Tolle, Eckart. *A New Earth*.

man who accidentally falls into hole while walking along his path. Down in the hole, it's dark and miserable, and he yearns to find a way out. He suffers and moans and cries for help, but no one comes to rescue him. After a long time of suffering, he eventually begins to seek his own way out. After an enormous struggle, he finally finds a way out and climbs back into the light. What joy! But one day, as he's walking along, he accidentally falls into the hole again. He's filled with despair. How could this happen again? As before, he suffers. Eventually, though, he stops lamenting his fate and once again finds his way out of the hole. Time passes, and the man continues on his journey. But one day, while he's walking along his path, he spies another hole. He struggles to go around it. Despite his best effort, however, he slips and falls in anyway. This time, he immediately focuses on how to get out and is able to do so with relative ease, and he moves along. Over time, the man begins to recognize the terrain most likely to harbor a hole. With this experience, he is able to avoid falling in one as he traverses through that particular terrain.

The journey back to wholeness is like this, and it will take patience and fortitude. It will require us to figure out what works for us and to figure out our own truth. Keep in mind, though, that we aren't really alone on this journey, for God is within us all the while. We have an inner guidance system and can learn to recognize and use it.

> *The light of God surrounds me. The love of God enfolds me. The power of God protects me. The presence of God watches over me. Wherever I am, God is and all is well.*[86]

---

[86] Freeman.

The Law of Momentum

When an idea reaches critical mass there is no stopping the shift its presence will induce.[87]

One of the many challenges I've dealt with on my journey is the fact that the ego is so deeply entrenched within us all. It exerts itself in most things most of the time because this is where the majority of our awareness lives. It prevails in every aspect of our lives—work, home, and even within sound, effective, deeply committed spiritual communities. The ego mind is ever present and causing us trouble. As I've pondered this over the years, the first thing I've learned is that inward change and outward change don't happen simultaneously. There is a lag. In our meditation and prayer states of mind, we are blessed with glimpses of a higher reality. In moments of divine connection, we feel the thrill of divine power and how easily and gracefully it can work in the world. But in between these moments of clarity, we spend the majority of our time living in the fear-based, competitive world of the ego. This does not mean we're not making progress through our meditation and reflection process. Every invalidating and untrue picture that we identify and pull our consciousness out of does cumulatively help us reveal the light of our soul more readily. Every negative belief and invalidating idea we surrender does advance the evolution of our consciousness. And every loving thought we invest in brings us in closer rapport with our divine Self. However, in my experience and observation, a lasting outward change does not become manifest until a significant reorientation out of our ego point of view occurs. For a long period, we experience an intermittent connection with our divine Self. During this time, persistently building and strengthening this connection builds the momentum needed to sustain a more consistent connection. Over time, the law of inertia works in our favor, and what we have set into motion remains in motion.

[87] Williamson, Marianne. BrainyQuote.comp

I am reminded of the hundredth monkey effect, in which a certain critical number (or percentage) of a population must learn a new behavior on their own before it miraculously spreads instantly to the rest of the group.[88] Within our minds, a similar cumulating effect is true when withdrawing from the ego and merging with the soul. We take a series of small steps through trial and error, we suffer setbacks, and we try again until we finally "get it," and a fundamental shift in our understanding occurs. For example, when I first started meditating, I had to remind myself to do it; some days, I would forget. When I did remember, I had to work through resistance, distractions, and a lack of concentration. Some days, it all worked beautifully, and I felt great. On other days, the whole thing was a struggle, leaving me feeling fuzzy and as if I missed the mark. But I hung in there, and it gradually got easier. After several years, I realized that it came naturally to me to ground, center in, and connect with spirit. Then, after several more years, it became clear to me that my life in general was a "waking meditation." I still do specific meditation practices on a daily basis, but most of the time now I am grounded and working from spirit, with occasional moments of disconnection rather than the other way around. The point is that the initial investment, as difficult as it was, paid off and yielded external change.

When the Going Gets Tough

"You must not turn aside, for then you would go after futile things which can not profit or deliver, because they are futile." 1 Samual 12:21

As we navigate our way through the veils of perception that separate us from the greater truth, we are truly tested. Because this is so, we need to be willing to persevere, even when the going gets tough. It's helpful to begin by working on the things we're most willing change and steadily work

---

[88]   Wikipedia.org. "100th Monkey Effect."

our way toward the central core of our ego. Again, each layer of misperception we shed helps us reorient our mind toward the greater truth of our divine nature. Some experiences are easier than others, but all transformative work requires that we meet our true Self on a deeply emotional, cognitive, and psychic level. This is often very challenging. It's important to take heart and validate our progress as we go, for we inevitably must come face to face with our deepest, most highly charged fears. If we've worked patiently and kindly with ourselves, we find ourselves better able to tackle this enormously difficult task. We don't start with our core pictures, but we do end up having to heal them sooner or later because we won't be free of our fear until we do.

It's helpful to know that sometimes we can temporarily become stuck in fear and resistance when we first enter into the very highly charged landscape of our innermost core-fear ideas and beliefs. We can experience "hitting a wall" and become tempted never to venture beyond it. This is because our core fears form the bedrock on which our ego is built. The ego perceives the idea of dissolving that bedrock as a direct threat, even though the ego is filled with pain. These moments require our loving patience. They are also the times when we need to become the most persistent in our pursuit of change and growth, for we can be sure we've hit the lodestone of our delusions. When I studied at the Berkeley Psychic Institute, I knew that the times I really didn't want to go in were the times I needed to make sure I showed up. Something that was stuck was about to get busted, and the resistance within me could be quite intense. Despite this resistance, I also knew I'd worked hard to find that stuck thing, and I didn't want to lose the opportunity to break through it. So, I'd go, feeling miserable physically, mentally, or emotionally, to be sure. But I'd go.

When we remain steadfast in our pursuit, we are rewarded by the discovery of the more unified and loving self waiting for us on the other side. So, instead of giving up when things get

Janet Myatt

tough, get excited! This is the marker you've been searching for. Behind that brick wall is truth, freedom, and wholeness. Reorienting our minds is hard work in the beginning, but the rewards are nothing short of "heaven on earth," as Jesus often speaks of in his ministry.

The Power of Present Time

Realize deeply that the present moment is all you ever have. Make the Now the primary focus of your life.[89]

The true Self and God live in present time. The ego has a hard time living in present time. It tends to live in the past and the future.

- Try it.
- Do it right now.
- Sit quietly for five minutes and keep your thoughts solely in the present moment.

I bet that was hard! Did your mind tend to wander? Did you start to think about what you could be doing instead? Did your to-do list pop into your head? Or did you wander back in time, thinking about something that happened earlier in the day or the week? Did a problem or feeling from the past keep grabbing your attention and pulling your awareness out of the present moment?

It can be quite a challenge to bring our mind into present time and keep it there. But, as we've seen, when we run our consciousness through all our preexisting pictures, ideas, or concepts, we're going to persist only in reprojecting the past repeatedly. This makes it difficult to create anything new. I call this "looping." It's akin to watching the same movie over and over again. Looping stifles inspiration, blocks illumination, and shuts off our intuition. And yet it is the basis of our

---

[89] Tolle.

reality. The ego is built on the countless ideas we've set into motion and continue to identify with. The thought of moving out of those loops is disorienting to the ego. It asks, "Who will I be if I step out of what I know and believe?" My question is, "How will we ever find out if we don't give it a try?"

For instance, if we believe money is scarce, this thought will circulate through our brain consciously and unconsciously. And because it is our "money blueprint," this is what we will continue to build, because there is no *new* information to create from. Disciplining the mind to attend to what is going on in our mind *right now* gives us the ability to change course if what we're thinking and feeling is not up to snuff. But we have to be willing to give up the old way of thinking. A magical moment can occur for us when we let go of our routine patterns and determine what we need right now. We can align and connect with Divine Mind to find inspiration. *Inspiration* is defined as a "divine influence directly and immediately exerted upon the mind."[90] This is where the magic of working cocreatively with the soul shows itself. The higher, holistic, integrative pattern is available to us. When we allow ourselves to move our identity into our soul, we become connected to the greater field of Life and begin to operate within the overriding divine plan that exists within the Mind of God. This makes it possible for obstacles to be overcome and new outcomes to occur.

I call this "syncing up with the grid." When we are aligned with Divine Mind, we are connected to the cosmic switchboard and easily find the information and support we need to create in concert with the greater field of life. When we are off the grid, we're imprisoned in the disconnected space that exists between the lines of force, and life becomes difficult and chaotic. The lines of force flow around us. But instead of riding the currents, we are tossed about in their wake. This level of creative work can be directed by the soul only in the

---

[90]   Dictionary.com definition of *inspiration*.

present moment because in reality we can create only in the present moment. Life is happening *now*. So, we're either creating something new in this moment or re-creating the same old thing by running our energy through a blueprint we created in the past. The old blueprint has power only because we continue to run our consciousness through it. But when we stop doing that (truly stop doing that), the blueprint ceases to exert influence; eventually, it will dissipate.

Let me direct our attention to the Law of Economy for a moment so that we can really begin to understand what is needed here. This law teaches us that energy will follow the path of least resistance. For example, if water is flowing downhill, it will tend to flow into the preexisting gullies and ravines and slide away from the high places. Our oldest, most entrenched thought patterns have the strongest charge because they have the largest nucleus. We've been placing our attention in them for a very long time. And they take up the most room in our consciousness because we continually add to them each time we have an experience that matches them. This means that the easiest thing for us to do is to slip into these enormous thoughtforms. Therefore, it will take a considerable amount of work on our part to change the inertia favoring that way of thinking and being. We will have to continue to take our attention out of the old pattern repeatedly and then deliberately place it in a new direction until that old form finally breaks up for good.

With our money example, if we want to change our reality regarding money, we have to become aware of the limiting belief and change it. And we will have to do this over time. If we continually enter into a present-time communication with Divine Mind and remain open to change, we will discover a new reality emerges. God will help us remove the obstacles in our minds that continue to create scarcity, fear, lack, separation, competition, and so forth. Opportunities that we would never have noticed before will suddenly catch our attention. Ideas will begin to bubble up that we may have discounted or ignored in the past. Or we may begin to realize just how much abundance we already have and release limiting beliefs about always needing more.

In this way, our reality begins to change. This is true for any problem we are facing. When I have a problem in my life that I can't figure out how to solve, I hand it up to God. I ask God to show me a new way of thinking, reacting, and believing. I allow my intuition to show me a new way to solve the problem, or my mind is illuminated in way that moves me out of distortion.

Another type of present-time experience has to do with creativity. Inspiration, illumination, and intuition all open up the channel in our mind, and we know what to say or do in the moment. I have learned to teach my classes this way. I've moved away from a strict curriculum and detailed notes. I set an intention, align, and allow my highest Self to come through in the moment. These classes are always powerful because I am cocreating them in the moment with the soul of every person there. The experience is invariably greater than the sum of the parts, and our shared experience is quite profound as a result.

Disengaging from the ego and engaging the soul is done moment by moment. This connection allows us to engage in authentic, original moments that often require us to think and act differently from how we did in the past. Our perspective broadens. When we focus our attention on a problem, without opening to the higher perspective of the soul, we tend to grow the problem. If we open our minds up to the larger point of view of our true Self and ask God to help us, we can have an ah-ha moment. In this way, Divine Mind can help us move mountains, see things we've never imagined possible, and create miracles. The more we live this way, the more we begin to reunify our consciousness and improve our experience of ourselves and our world. By creating a coherent, unifying,

Janet Myatt

and truthful whole, we gain a broader perspective, and our personal power and ability to transform grows.

Meditation

Spiritual meditation is the pathway to Divinity.[91]

In my experience, daily meditation and reflection are necessary for transformation to take place, for it is not enough simply to think about God. We must actually *experience* God. It is not enough to understand that spirit exists; we're experiential beings. If we don't experience it within ourselves, it never becomes real. When we see it, know it, communicate with it, validate it, experience it, and *become* it, Spirit becomes real to us. Meditation and prayer create the needed energetic alignment and mental discipline to enter the world of Spirit with awareness. It opens up avenues for significant change to take root in our daily existence. James Allen's *The Way of Peace* describes meditation in this way:

> *Meditation is the intense dwelling in thought upon an idea or theme, with the object of thoroughly comprehending it, and whatsoever we constantly meditate upon we will not only come to understand, but will grow more and more into its likeness, for it will become incorporated into our very being, will become, in fact, our very self.*[92]

When we consciously experience subtle energy and have awareness of the loving Presence of Spirit within us, we come to *know* it. We begin with faith and move toward the certainty of knowing beyond any doubt. So, faith is an important gift we can give ourselves to get us going and keep us going when things gets tough. *ACIM* defines *knowledge* as "absolute certainty." Meditation and reflection give us the opportunity to discover directly that God does indeed exist, and we can

[91] Allen, James. *The Way of Peace.*
[92] Allen.

know Him personally because we are a part of Him. When we pray or ponder on something, we are holding a certain vibration of energy that is open and receptive to change and assistance. Meditation is a mental discipline that alchemically transforms our energy matrix in a manner that enables higher vibrations of energy to flow into our minds and bodies. We literally tune in to these higher frequencies and allow them to become amplified within us so that we can see, hear, feel, sense, and/or know what is being broadcast to us. We literally build an energy bridge between the lower identity and the higher, creating a continuity of consciousness between the personality and the Spirit. When we finally encounter our divine Self and experience it within us, our entire paradigm shifts. We gain access to levels of information, insight, and interconnectivity that liberate us from the prisons we've experienced for so long.

In my work as a spiritual counselor and healer, I have seen for myself the enormous shifts that take place when people begin to meditate daily. In my view, this is because meditation trains the mind to be still, centered, quiet, and steadfast. We turn our awareness inward—away from the external, busy, noisy, and reactionary world around us—and literally raise our energetic vibration to come into alignment with higher mind, much in the way a radio dial can be tuned to receive specific signals. I highly recommend starting with the grounding and running energy meditation I learned at the Berkeley Psychic Institute. It's particularly amenable to those of us who live in the Western world because this technique keeps the mind engaged. In this Tree of Life–type of meditation, we actively use our creative imagination to picture the energy we are working with. And because energy follows thought and we create through our pictures, this is a very effective method for bringing our minds into the higher vibrational state needed to access our intuition and illuminate our minds. If you recall from our earlier discussion of how the mind works, this is precisely the energetic pattern we want to create—placing the lower mind in the receptive state and allowing the higher mind to be the active directing agent.

Once this technique is familiar and a part of our daily life, we can expand our practice to include other types of meditation and add additional energetic tools and techniques into our spiritual toolbox that will continue to enhance our transformational process and aid us on our journey back to wholeness. Because I have personally experienced and witnessed in others such profoundly life-altering improvements as a result of meditation, I can't stress enough the importance of finding a daily practice that works.

Walking the Talk

The process of rehabilitating the lower self through accessing the higher Self is a two-way street. Accessing higher mind through meditation, prayer, and deep reflection is deeply transformational, and we must also be able to apply what we experience in the higher planes in our external life. If we experience only our own divinity in meditation or prayer and never find a way to incorporate that consciousness into our everyday life, we will not precipitate the kind of transformational change we are seeking in our lives. If we don't walk the talk, we won't really get anywhere.

It is comforting to know that the soul on its own plane remains connected to the Divine Plan and continues to create regardless of what we do in our amnesic state at the personality level. The personality cannot damage the soul, but it can continue to ignore it and in so doing miss the chance to transform our life. However, once the personality seeks connection, the soul "enters into deep meditation and begins to respond to our call."[93] Once this connection is sought, the soul continues to reach out to us, to inspire and illuminate our minds, and to heal us when given the chance. It takes courage to act on the

---

[93]   Bailey. *A Treatise on White Magic.*

information, inclinations, and visions the soul communicates, and yet that is what we're here to do. The beauty and burden of physical reality is that it teaches us about the creative process. Therefore, we learn by doing.

When God, in the form of All That Is, exploded in the Big Bang, he did so out of a desire to *experience* all the creative potential within. Physical reality is highly experiential. Cause and effect is tangible and concrete. Consequences are experienced on a corporeal level, which makes the experiences deeply emotional and potent. When we do harm to ourselves and others, we not only see it but also feel it on a deeply emotional and physical level. The emotional impact of our choices is tremendous—both the positive and negative experiences. This is very instructive; however, once we closed our minds off from our true divinity, we forgot the purpose behind our creative activity here. We lost our so-called user's manual. Now, many of us are in the process of remembering. And as we do, we help ourselves and others rise up to new levels of understanding and healing.

Our journey requires faith and perseverance as we act on the ideas, insights, and epiphanies that are revealed to us in the still, quiet place within each of us. Master Djwal Khul teaches us that

- Alignment precipitates crisis,
- Crisis precipitates Light,
- Light leads us to revelation, and
- Revelation leads us to integration.

Meditation teaches us how to align and open the channel of consciousness that connects us with Divine Mind. This connection burns away our blinders, and we come to see the nature of our delusional way of thinking. This is quite uncomfortable but also a relief in the end because we are led to the Light of God. Light is the great revealer. It shows us our beauty but also our darkness, and it is uncompromising in this. At first, it is quite blinding, and it takes time for our eyes to adjust. But when they do, a new direction—a new path—is revealed. We see our next step. As we take it, we begin to integrate this new way of being into our consciousness. We become more than we were. We live in the moment, and we discover the interconnectedness of all Life. One day, we will all be fully awake conscious creators revealing God's plan and our divine nature. In the meantime, each of us who takes up this journey aids the Whole. And as the Whole is revealed, each part is illuminated and enhanced.

Chapter 8 Exercises

1. Try turning something that's troubling you over to a higher power. Be aware of your thoughts and emotions throughout the experience. Manage your fears by acknowledging them without investing in them. Throughout the day, find techniques for moving your mind into a receptive place, and pay attention to your higher intuition.

2. Select one thing that you feel resentful over and determine what belief or thought in your mind is making you feel like a victim. Begin to question that thought, and make room for a different point of view.
   - Try putting yourself in the other person's shoes and see what emerges.
   - Take a look at how in your own way you might do the same thing the other person has done. What is he or she mirroring back to you?
   - What can you bring forward in yourself to forgive this situation and forgive the other person?
   - See if you can look at the situation as a learning environment for all parties involved. Does this make it possible to forgive without any lingering feelings of being a victim?

3. Pick an area in your life that always seems to be challenging and keeps looping over and over.
   - How do you typically respond to this issue?
   - What would the opposite response look like?
   - What value, belief, or orientation creates the foundation of your approach?
   - Can you move out of it into a point of view that is not boxed in and can see things differently?

4. Think of one personality trait you have, and spend the day doing the opposite.
   - Note what fears and anxieties arise.
   - Note what opens up.

5. Are there any people you turn to for help when things get tough? If so, what is the quality of their aid? Do

they help you see things in a new way and help you discover your blind spots? Or do they feed the drama?

6. Experiment with living in the present moment.

- **Sensory** exercise: Take your shoes off and walk very slowly over various surfaces. As you do this, concentrate on what your feet are sensing. Don't allow your mind to wonder; remain focused on the sensations in your feet.
- **Emotional** exercise: Throughout the day, whenever an emotional response emerges within you, let it go. Imagine dropping it down your grounding cord until you feel like you're a pure, clean vessel of light. Who are you without these emotional reactions? How do you respond to life?
- **Mental** exercise: On another day, spend the day letting go of your ideality and ask your indwelling "thought adjuster" to illuminate your mind before you act. Observe what happens.

7. Make a commitment to putting something into motion that you feel is coming from your higher self.

8. Meditation:

- If you already meditate regularly, take a moment to validate all that you've gained from this practice, and then check in with yourself and see if you are ready to add new techniques and tools to your practice. Ask your higher self to guide you.
- If you are new to meditating, commit to meditating at least five days a week for the next thirty days and see what happens.
- Try one of the guided meditations on my website at janetmyatt.com or on my YouTube channel.

http://www.janetmyatt.com/guided-meditations/
https://www.youtube.com/channel/UCK3pdOAz
XyEqh4dUK3s6goQ

Part IV: Ascension

In the Stillness
Janet Lee Myatt © 2006

In the stillness, I can watch the blood flowing through me
In the stillness, I can hear my own true voice
In the stillness, I can see the traps I've stumbled into
In the stillness, I can see I have a choice

In the stillness, I can see all my temptations
In the stillness, I come face to face with my own fear
In the stillness, Death will shake his finger at me
In the stillness, I can hear God whisper in my ear

And all is well here in the stillness

In the stillness, I can see a brand-new future
In the stillness, I can face the great unknown
In the stillness, I can dare to come out of hiding
In the stillness, I can find my own way home
In the stillness, God reminds me to find the laughter
In the stillness, I know for sure I'm not alone

And all is well here in the stillness[94]

---

[94]   Myatt, Janet Lee. "In the Stillness." Janet Lee Myatt. 2010

CHAPTER 9 ~ THE SEVEN RULES FOR INDUCING SOUL CONTROL

An interesting way for us to go over a brief recap of what we've been looking at in this book is to consider the Seven Rules for Inducing Soul Control presented by Master Djwal Khul (DK) in Alice Bailey's book *Esoteric Psychology*, volume II.[95] These rules give us a glimpse into the larger purpose and creative objective of the evolutionary process we are engaged in. They also give us insight into the innate tendencies and traits of the soul. Awakening is no easy task, and it helps us gain some much-needed perspective when we consider the underlying principles inherent in the creative process. These traits are naturally being developed in humanity through the evolutionary process. Knowing what they are gives us the opportunity to call on them consciously and accelerate our development.

DK explains there are two broad objectives directing the evolutionary process of human consciousness at this time:

1. Expand human consciousness so that it can develop from the *"germ of self-consciousness (such as it was at individualization)"* and bring it up to *"complete group consciousness and identification"*—that is, up into the larger unified whole we exist within.
2. Bring the ascending energy of the human kingdo m *"into such close rapport with the descending energy of spirit*

---

[95]   Bailey. *Esoteric Psychology II*, pp. 214-225

*that another great expression—a group expression—of
Deity may emerge though man into manifestation."* [96]

The energies flowing on the planet and into the human
kingdom at this time are designed to help move us in this
auspicious direction. These rules give us a strong indication
of the tendencies that are being stimulated. They don't outline
in any specific manner what to do but instead point out what
these inherent qualities are and what their purpose is. It's
up to us to figure out how to work more consciously and
deliberately with them.

One—Synthesis

*"The tendency, innate and ineradicable, to blend and
synthesize."*[97]

DK tells us this rule is the basic underlying law of life itself,
and it is a quality of the first aspect of deity.[98] This tendency
draws us back to our discussion of the Big Bang and the
distribution of God into His Creation. Synthesis is the act
of combining constituent elements or abstract entities into a
single or unified entity. As we have seen, this is the nature of
at-one-ment and isolated unity.[99] God is the great synthesizer
of all that is contained within Him. All creative activity relates
back to Him. Within the Supreme Being—that is, He who
contains the entire Grand Universe and all the creatures
that populate it—various lesser isolated unities exist, from
superuniverses to the integrated personality of a human being.
And all these lesser unities are synthesized and coordinated
within the mind of God the Supreme.

---

[96] Ibid, p.215
[97] Ibid, p.220
[98] To review the seven qualities of God, refer to Figure 18.
[99] See At-one-ment in chapter 6.

On the form side, this tendency has to do with creating and destroying as old forms pass away to make room for new forms. On the consciousness side, this tendency is the basic cause of all great expansions of consciousness, be they individual, racial (the human race as a whole), planetary, or systemic. Specifically, as we acquire life experience, our capacity and ability to extend into larger states of awareness and identification grows. If this is true for us, it is also true for the larger systemic and cosmic beings within which we dwell. As above, so below. For instance, the mighty Entity ensouling our planet also gains creative life experience and expands in capacity and ability as a result of His creative work at the planetary level. This simply happens on an order of magnitude beyond our current ability to comprehend.

This tendency to synthesize and blend stems from an act of will. How does it pertain to us at the human level? When we choose to align our consciousness with the will aspect of God, we have the opportunity to sense His greater Purpose and Plan and begin to act accordingly. This calls for us to put aside purely selfish activity, activate a destroying or repulsing force within us, and apply our creativity in ways that draw us into the greater whole. We can see then just how important is this work of liberating our hearts and minds from that which separates us from God and from one another, as well as how important it is for us to use our will to serve the highest good of the whole.

Two—Hidden Vision

"The Quality of the hidden vision."[100]

This refers to the motivation that underlies the creative process, and it is related to the second aspect of deity: love-wisdom. It points us to *intention*—what is inspiring or motivating creative activity? In the lower three worlds of the personality, this

---

[100] Bailey. *EPII,* p. 221

quality is experienced as physical sight, emotional desire or our wish life, and intellectually as concrete rational knowledge or understanding. (We subconsciously understand this and often ask "do you see?" when we want to know if someone understands something.) This quality of the hidden vision is the underlying creative *urge* to experience something in a tangible way, and it is what precipitated consciousness itself.

For those on the path of return, it shows up as the aspiration to manifest the higher vision of intelligent, loving at-one-ment accessed through the abstract and intuitional mind of the soul. On the form side, it shows up as an increased vibration that reveals the light or higher intelligence within the form. Consciously, this is correlated with the principle of illumination—a holistic vision that unifies and transforms. Over time, the ascender realizes that what he or she is interested in experiencing and participating in changes. The desire nature expands out of a pursuit of purely selfish desires and transmutes into a great love of humanity. This in turn prompts a great desire to pursue that which serves the highest good of the whole.

So, rules one and two work hand in glove. As our inner vision expands and increases in vibration, the old forms will have to break apart. Newer forms are then created that can sustain the higher frequencies and reveal the larger vision. As I mentioned earlier, we are literally up-stepping matter by working with it. The last creative age impregnated matter with innate intelligence; in this creative age, we are impregnating matter with the ability to reveal love. How does that work? As *we* become attuned to love and inspired to express it, we create blueprints that call for a certain quality of matter. As we call that matter to us, we imbue it with the rate and vibration of love.

Over the course of our evolution, we have steadily been growing into an understanding of love. First, on a personal level, we have pursued what we love, what we desire for our self. Over time, this expanded to include love relationships with certain specific others, particularly our family and our tribe. Now, we're being called to expand our consciousness into a love for all, a love for the greater whole.

We can see just how important and stupendous is this work of transmuting our desire nature into the higher love nature. Consciousness that is vibrating as divine love takes us on a journey that moves us from conditional love to transcendent, unconditional, universal love. It moves us out of the wounded self into the free unlimited self. As we discover this unending source of divine energy within us, our cup runneth over; we feel no emptiness or neediness, we experience no deficit. In this way our divine nature is able to radiate out from our core into the world around us and connect with the same light in others. In this way, we build the kingdom of Heaven on Earth. Experiencing divine love opens the heart and mind to new ways of relating that create more individual freedom for everyone and at the same time establishes our inherent interconnectedness. When two candles light a room, one candle does not take light from the other. Instead, the two create a radiance that is greater than the sum each is putting out.

DK makes another fascinating point for us to consider. Moving away from fear and into the light of higher consciousness affects more than our individual experience, more even than the experience of the human kingdom as a whole, although that is our current evolutionary goal. In the long run, the light of humanity affects the greater system and even the universe, of which we are a small but vital part. He reveals that humanity as a whole has the opportunity to one day become a "station of light" and a "magnetic center" in the universe of such a potent and intense power that we (united and at-oned) will then be able to serve a mighty purpose within the life of God in this universe. Each person who adds more light into the system increases the total light radiating in that system. We are truly a part of a Grand Adventure, the

263

Janet Myatt

likes of which we cannot begin to comprehend fully. I find this inspiring, and it helps me move out of self-pity over the challenges in my life and inspires me instead to get on with my own healing and to be of assistance to others. We are all in this together, and we all count.

Three—Organizing Intelligence

"The instinct to formulate a plan."[101]

This refers to the creative intelligence or third aspect of deity inherent within us. It is instinctual, it governs all creative activity, and it is the basic cause of evolution on all levels—individual, planetary, and systemic. This is the ability to see the relationship of the parts to one another and to the whole and organize them in a fashion that brings them together to produce a result. In the lower nature, it can show up as manipulation—using intelligence to get what one wants at the expense of others. In the higher nature, it is that quality of intelligence that draws things together into a meaningful process or arrangement that produces at-one-ment. For instance, there is an intelligent design to the physical body that causes all the various systems and component parts within it to work as a unified whole. DK tells us it is this same tendency that first leads the human being into developing an integrated personality, and it later leads to the dissolution of that personality into the greater whole.

This rule also works in conjunction with the others. (And this is true of all the rules.) Aspiration alone cannot heal the world. It is a key component, to be sure. Yet without the addition of an intelligent, synthesizing plan willfully put into motion, it will remain an unfulfilled wish. The saying "If wishes were horses, beggars would ride" sums this up nicely. The beggar can sit on the side of the road and wish, or he can make a plan for how to go about getting a horse. The higher

---

[101] Ibid, p.221

264

abstract, intuitional mind provides the overlighting vision, the goal. It also connects us to our innate ability to figure out how to manifest it. And it gives us the ability to synthesize the lesser into the greater.

God's Plan is in the process of emerging into our collective consciousness, as those who are sensitive and actively tuning in are responding to it and acting on it. More individuals are taking an interest in the spiritual side of life; and as they do, new values are emerging, new groups are forming, and new agendas are being introduced in schools, governments, communities, corporations, and the like. This shows us that humanity is slowly but surely responding to the higher Plan. And as these smaller groups come into unified sync with the higher rhythms, they begin to function at a higher level of efficiency and produce better results. This increases their impact on the larger whole. As these smaller unified groups merge and meld into larger unities, their impact grows exponentially. Eventually, the attributes revealed by the expanding unified field will become so strong energetically that even the most disorganized and disconnected pockets within the whole will begin to feel the pulse and respond.

This instinct is the result of the development of the mind and the higher intellect in humanity. We can see that each person who uses his or her innate organizing intelligence to unify rather than manipulate or divide can and does make a difference. Furthermore, even small groups that are intelligently working for the higher good of the whole can and will have a greater impact in the long run, compared with larger groups that are not.

Janet Myatt

Four—Creative Imagination

"The urge to creative life though the divine faculty of imagination."[102]

This has to do with our ability to create mental-image pictures of things that do not yet exist in any tangible way, and it is related to the fourth quality of God: harmony through conflict. We have to be able to imagine something before we can build it. For instance, in terms of dense physical things, Edison first had to imagine the lightbulb was possible before he could set about the work of bringing it into manifestation. The Wright brothers had a vision that inspired them to work to make it real. In terms of subtle or intangible things, saints and sages have been inspired by internal visions of heaven throughout the ages, and these visions continue to capture the imagination of humanity and inspire us to make it real. This quality of soul gives us the ability to initiate the building process and put it in motion.

As usual, this ability is first used to envision our own personal desires without regard to the welfare of the larger whole. This often leads to conflict, warfare, and struggle as agendas are squared off against one another. But even so, the process of manifesting our vision gives rise to the world of meaning as we learn about the quality of our creativity through the effects we produce. For example, what does it mean to win? What does it mean to lose? What does it mean to love? What does it mean to hate? These experiences in turn eventually lead us back to the soul, because at some point we get tired of conflict and start to ask what the greater purpose and meaning of life might be. We begin to long for harmony and endeavor to create beauty. This innate tendency to imagine is what lies behind our great works of art, scientific breakthroughs, intellectual insights, and spiritual revelations and ultimately is that which enables us to envision and comprehend the

---

[102] Ibid, p.222

larger Plan. Comprehension leads to a building response that ultimately produces the revelation of God.

How can we stimulate and develop this ability? On the inner planes, meditation and creative visualization are powerful ways to strengthen this soul ability and bring it into alignment with the larger Plan. In our external life, looking for the larger interconnectivity between ourselves and others in everything that we do—both at home and at work—and envisioning a better world for all is an inherently useful way to develop this quality within us. Imagine a world where divisions between people dissolve and we begin to relate to one another as divine beings. Imagine manifesting a world that is full of abundance, cooperation, kindness, mutual aid, and service to one another. Imagine a world where the education system is one that recognizes the God consciousness within each child and is designed to support each child's highest good—where children are able to play, learn, and be creative according to their own design. Imagine knowing how to parent our children in a manner that nurtures them and helps them develop their inherent inner wisdom and maintain contact with their divine Self. Imagine a world of cocreativity rather than competition and control—where inclusive, unconditional love rather than separative, special love is the motivation behind our activities and where value and worth are known as inherent qualities in all rather than something relative to objective forms. Imagine living in a community where we know our neighbors and work collectively to help one another. Imagine a world where there is food, housing, employment, education, medical assistance, and transportation for everyone. Imagine a world where technology is developed and used only to benefit the health and wellness of our planet, bodies, and societies rather than to control or kill others.

If we can imagine it, we can build it. Manifestation happens when spirit is dedicated to bringing an idea into objective form. This is how we anchor, activate, and actuate the full potential of our souls. Despite whatever objections the rational mind might offer, it starts with a vision and a commitment to that vision. Many souls are highly motivated at this time to connect with one another so that we may evolve not only as individuals but also as a race. Humanity is at a crossroads, and the cosmic energies pouring on the planet at this time are sending us the required aid to take this step. In my experience, the biggest naysayers we have to overrule are within ourselves. So, the process of healing the negative ego is truly important work. And this process is ongoing, for each new level of awareness we acquire eventually brings us to new doorways that will require the next leap of faith. This inner visioning quality of the soul gives us the opportunity to change what we create individually and together and enables us to come into sync with the larger creative Purpose and Plan of the divine.

Five—Analysis

"The factor of analysis."[103]

This soul quality has to do with discernment and is related to the fifth quality of God: concrete knowledge. In forms, this quality shows up as the tendency to separate, divide, and create polarities or oppositions. In consciousness, it leads to wider comprehension and understanding and to increasingly larger identifications. DK tells us this is the factor that will ultimately cause the appearance of the fifth kingdom in nature: the *kingdom of souls*. Why? As we expand our conscious awareness out of the limitations of the individual ego, a twofold process ensues:

1. Imprisoning forms are identified and destroyed, making room for new forms to be built.

> This illustrates how this principle works within forms—consciousness separates from that which limits.

---

[103] Ibid, p.223

2. The liberated life energy is then free to join with the larger whole; therefore, the scope of what it can comprehend expands.

> This illustrates the life/consciousness side in action—consciousness merges into larger isolated unities.

Each expansion into larger forms of identification, along with the corresponding production of lighter vehicles of expression, enables the indwelling conscious life to comprehend, respond to, and reveal the Plan more coherently over time.

We touched on this quality when we talked about the importance of questioning everything—our internal assumptions and the barrage of programming entering our minds through our shared environment. The concrete mind is the seat of our internal "Analyzer." This innate ability to distinguish, discriminate, examine, and make rational is an integral part of what helps us get free of our delusions. It is the aspect of us that can ask good questions but cannot always provide good answers. However, the question posed sends us on a search for understanding. And this search provides the catalyst that eventually leads to revelation. The Analyzer seeks to understand the underlying cause of an effect. Once it comprehends a cause, it eventually begins to question that cause, too, as it comes to recognize that it is also an effect of something else, something still hidden. And so the treasure hunt continues. In our pursuit of meaning and quest for understanding, we steadily uncover each underlying cause until we finally run into God. As we penetrate the enshrouding veils that give form to That which is formless, we arrive one day at the moment where we finally recognize and know the Life that brought all forms into the light of day.

Janet Myatt

Six—Idealization

"The quality, innate in man, to idealize."[104]

This has to do with our innate tendency to strive toward perfection and is related to the sixth quality of God: devotion and abstract idealism. In chapter 8, we talked a bit about how this trait can be misused within the ego, producing critical attitudes, judgment, divisiveness, and competition. But at the soul level, it is the inherent drive to execute creative purpose as completely and perfectly as possible. It is that drive within us to know and reveal God and our innate "homing device"— that which propels us on the path of return.

On the form side, this quality operates as the force within procreative energy that seeks to generate perfectly built bodies—a baby with ten fingers, ten toes, a full set of working organs, and so forth. In the ego, it initially works out as the drive to fulfill material desires. In the concrete mind, it operates as ideologies, creeds, and dogmas. In the lower self, this trait first produces competition, intolerance, fear, and even cruelty as personal ideals clash and individuals and polarized groups compete for material resources, power, fame, and glory. And even within our own psyches, we saw that our internal shadow persona and ideal persona remain locked in mortal battle until we move out of our misperceptions. Thus, the way this quality manifests in the worlds of form depends on the evolutionary stage of the creative entity involved.

Eventually, this divine quality will be the force that helps us relinquish our delusions because it is the force that leads to sacrifice, one-pointed purpose, devotion, and forward progress. It is the underlying cause of the organization and cooperation between all parts within a system. Once an ideal is comprehended within the mind and activated by such a strong desire that we become devoted to its execution,

---

[104]   Ibid, p. 224

we begin to organize the required thoughts, actions, and materials needed to see it through to manifestation. We can understand this when we think about how hard we are willing to work to manifest our personal goals and ideals. We become committed to doing whatever it takes; we'll put in long hours, give up comforts, and expend enormous amounts of energy to achieve our ends. And this sacrifice and effort is necessary for us to do what's needed.

This same tendency to sacrifice and remain focused gives us the ability discover right-mindedness and right activity as we travel along the path of return and endeavor to comprehend and reveal God's Plan. DK states that this Plan is designed *"to awaken in man the following responses:— right desire, right vision and right creative activity based upon right interpretation of ideals."*[105] When our ideals carry the peace and stillness of God and are inclusive, centered, balanced, intelligent, loving, and rightly organized, then our devotion can see us through all the necessary steps to fruition. Jesus perfectly embodies this quality in his ministry.

Seven—Manifestation

"The interplay of the great dualities."[106]

"Through the activity engendered by this interplay, and through the results achieved (producing always a third factor), the whole manifested world is swept into line with the divine purpose."[107]

We've actually talked quite a bit about this rule already. In essence, this rule is pointing out that duality—or the interplay of two factors—works to produce something new: The Father plus the Mother produces the Son, spirit plus matter gives rise

---

[105] Ibid, p.224
[106] Ibid, p.225
[107] Ibid

to consciousness, energy plus ideas/thoughts produces form, and so forth. Basically, this rules speaks to the underlying cause of the appearance and disappearance of all forms, be they subtle or dense. And it promises us that as we engage in the creative process, we are fulfilling a larger divine purpose. We may not be able to comprehend the larger purpose of God, but we can look at how the creative process engenders growth. Clearly, we gain experience through the process of working with matter and creating forms of expression. Over time, we do manifest an ever-increasing awareness of, and conscious participation in, the larger creative process we are involved in. Participation in this process gives rise to something *new*; something emerges in the universe that would not have come about without the experience. For instance, the Monad on the front end of its evolution is untapped creative *potential*, not yet actual. It is the through the process of working with matter and forms that this potential is activated and brought into existence.

Let's look at this a little more closely. Confining the life essence of spirit within a form creates an experience of imprisonment within a fixed structure, producing a specific point of view. Experimentation begins, and the law of cause and effect comes into play. From within this fixed design, spirit experiences the results of its creativity as it works in the worlds of form. The limitations of form-experience induce a series of *"conscious adaptations of energy"* that eventually benefit both the evolving consciousness of the Spirit and the evolving consciousness of matter. Let's look at the benefit to spirit first.

1. Merging with matter produces consciousness itself.
2. As the consciousness develops, it begins to discern a sense of self—a sense of a personal existence separate from other selves. This is followed by a long evolutionary period of struggle where the indwelling consciousness operates within the limitations of identification with the physical body, the desire nature, and the world

of personal ideas and ideals. This struggle eventually results in the emergence of the integrated personality. This is something that did not previously exist in time and space and is the direct result of the creative activity of spirit working with matter.

3. Once the integrated personality awakens to an awareness of being both *self* and *not-self*, a struggle to become liberated from imprisonment in *not-self* (or form) ensues. The aspirational nature supplants the lower desire nature, and the quest for love and wisdom becomes the goal. Now the pair of opposites the consciousness is dealing with is the lower self and the higher self, or the vertical pair of opposites. And vertical merger requires resolution of the numerous horizontal pairs of opposites we deal with in our day-to-day life: good—bad, happy—sad, right—wrong, rich—poor, love—hate, competition—cooperation, I—we, and so forth. Resolution of these apparent oppositions comprises a series of at-one-ments. We come into an experience of that which is greater than and inclusive of all that sits along the polarized field. The tip of the upward-pointing triangle embraces, unifies, and uplifts that which has been sundered. Again, a new thing is born from the interplay of the dualities involved.

4. This struggle leads the evolving spirit through ever-expanding at-one-ments with higher and higher states of being. And all these growth experiences activate the formerly latent divine potential as these qualities are called forth, anchored on the physical plane, and made actual. From this interplay, a fully functioning creator is born.

Now let's consider the benefits to matter.

1. Impregnation by spirit precipitates adaptation as the directing life consciously modifies various grades of atomic energy to serve its immediate purpose and goal. It is through this process that the ensouling entity is

    able to organize and prepare the matter for the next higher expression.

2. Once a form has served its purpose, the ensouling life moves out of it, and it breaks apart. The liberated atoms retain their ability to respond in an organized way and can now be used to create more complex forms.

3. Over time, all the atomic matter involved in the creative process is improved as it is brought into alignment and attuned to the higher rates and rhythms of higher consciousness.

Once again, we see a third factor arise out of the interplay of two factors. On the form side, the new factor is more complex forms that can increasingly reveal higher amounts of light, love, and intelligence. Spirit is then able to use this illuminated field of substance to clothe itself and reveal its divinity in tangible ways.

This rule nicely encapsulates the overall theme and purpose of this book. And all the rules for inducing soul control succinctly summarize what we've been examining throughout the book. Everything that has been discussed here is meant to serve as a catalyst for personal growth and provide signposts to aid in the awakening process. There aren't any simple exercises to employ or specific disciplines to follow. It is up to each of us to figure things out as we go—we are creators, after all! However, there is an underlying order to the creative process and to the great divine purpose of God. These rules give us an overview of the inherent qualities within us and within the greater Whole. They are qualities and tendencies that we can count on to influence and shape us as we evolve. We can entrust ourselves to the larger Plan that underlies our journey and seek out ways to align and fulfill our part, knowing that we have within us everything we need to do this great work.

Entering the Kingdom of Heaven

I hope that you will do whatever you need to do to discover the greater you. You'll be so glad you did, and you'll help change the world. Facing our fears is never easy, but it is necessary in order to be free and enter into the Kingdom of Heaven, which is none other than our divine mind. The mind, our free will, and our loving essence are our greatest gifts. When we choose to do the work of reorienting our mind out of our body-identified ego personas and into the Spirit-identified world of God, we transform ourselves, others, and the world around us. We cannot fix the ego because, in the end, it is not real; we can only transcend it with love, compassion, and forgiveness. Just as collectively we cannot fix the world as we currently view it, we can only transcend this viewpoint. All the light we gain through meditation, prayer, and thoughtful reflection enables us to access levels of divine love, compassion, and forgiveness for ourselves and others. And it is this work that creates the bridge that leads us out of the world of misperceptions and into the world of true perceptions. From there, it is a short leap of faith into the one-minded reality of God we are all inherently a part of. The journey back to wholeness is exhilarating, exasperating, joyful, frightening, amazing, and difficult, but it is the most important work we'll ever do. I invite you to embark on it and share your experiences with others so that they, too, can experience the wholeness of our shared divinity. Each one of us who takes this journey clears the way for the entire human race to ascend and create Heaven on Earth.

May it be with the blessing of the Supreme Being that you find your truth, your peace, your light, and your love, and that you live your life joyfully.

Om, Peace, Amen, Namaste.

Chapter 9 Exercises

I recommend spreading these meditation exercises out over the course of at least one week. All these healing requests and reflections are meant to be done in meditation. Then, over the course of the days and weeks that follow, take note of what comes up for you.

1. Synthesis. Ask for a synthesis healing to help you bring the various parts of yourself into a unified and coordinated whole and help you better comprehend how you fit into a larger whole.
   - Take note of what emerges in your consciousness.
2. Hidden Vision. Take a look at what motivates you. You will probably discover more than one thing. Take a look at each thing as it comes up.
   - How does it serve your life?
   - How does it serve the greater good?
3. The Instinct to Formulate a Plan. Ask for a healing on this ability.
   - Allow yourself to become aware of instances where you use your intelligence get what you want without consideration of the impact on the greater whole. Especially look at where you manipulate others and rationalize your behavior.
   - Allow yourself to become aware of how this divine ability enables you to know what needs to be done to fulfill a creative purpose. Especially look at those magical moments where everything fell into place seemingly without effort.
   - What makes the difference between these two ways of using this ability?
4. How has creative visualization worked in your life? Have you ever had a dream or an aspiration that you could see clearly in your mind's eye? How did this affect your activity in life?

- As you imagine a better world, what comes up for you? Is there something in this vision that you can directly contribute to?

5. Allow your higher mind to reveal to you how this process of uncovering the root cause of effects leads you out of limitations. Ask your Higher Self to lead you out of a current distortion that is limiting you. What needs to be destroyed? What do you discover when you let go?

6. Ask for a healing on the concept of sacrifice and see what opens up for you. Reflect on things you have given up in order to serve a higher purpose. What's next for you?

7. Ask for a healing on your integration process. Become willing to let go of any pain, resentment, and fear associated with your awakening. Reflect on what you have gained. What "new thing" has come out of your struggle?

Part V: Closing Remarks and Appendices

Secret Soul

Words & Music by Janet Lee Myatt © 2003

Becoming visible in an unkind world
Saying hello to that little girl inside
I am a window I can look right through
The shadows disappear and lead me to my mind
And in the center a burning flame
No more playing this hiding game

And now I know
I must reveal my secret soul

Becoming visible to the untrained eye
Dropping my shield and casting my dye I am real
I am a wonderer and I have been here before
A million lifetimes a million doors and I am real
Now I remember what I thought I forgot
I am a precious child of God and I am real

I may not know it all, I may not get it right
I may look like a fool, but then again I might
Just take you by surprise
My eyes are open wide, I am just like a child
I'm going for the prize, I will no longer hide

Gently she calls me to gather
The missing pieces of my dream

And now I know
I must reveal my secret soul
And now I know
I must reveal my secret soul
My secret soul

CLOSING REMARKS

Finding Our Truth

I hope that you have found this book useful and that is inspires you to ask questions, go within to find your answers, and feel passionate about seeking the greater truth about yourself, others, and the universe you are a part of. It has been my intention to share my experiences with you and to discuss the hidden nature of things as I currently understand them. I encourage you to use the information in this book to search deeply within yourself for your truth. I also encourage you to seek input from a wide variety of sources, including all the world's religions, spiritual and esoteric writings, and the recent discoveries emerging within the scientific community. The mystical heart of Divine Truth can be found beating underneath all the man-made veils and distortions that overlay these paths. And when we peer through many different lenses in our quest for knowledge and awareness, we begin to move around our own built-in biases and prejudices and ultimately uncover our own God consciousness. We are each unique creations within the Creation, and no one path would ever serve everyone in the same way. God is much too creative for this! But each path can serve anyone who seeks the truth. One thing all these traditions and paths can agree on is the power of meditation, prayer, and quiet reflection—and more than anything, the power of love. God is within us, so that is where we must go to reconnect and develop our consciousness. I wish you the very best on your journey. I hold a vision of us all standing in the Light of our God consciousness and cocreating a world that is in accordance with highest good of all.

Many blessings!

Appendix A ~ Guided Meditations

Basic Cleansing and Centering Meditation

Use this technique at the start of your meditation practice. It is designed to still the body and the mind and increase the communication between the personality and the soul. I encourage people to do this basic technique first because it "cleans out" all your energetic bodies and increases the quality and strength of your meditation practice. Just this technique alone, done for twenty to thirty minutes daily, will produce a noticeable transformational change in your consciousness.

For you to get the full benefit from these exercises, I recommend doing them in a quiet place where you won't be disturbed. Take a moment to sit quietly and go within. If you like to take notes, make sure you have a pen and paper next to you.

Letting Go—A Self-Healing Technique

- Ask your inner wise self to come forward in your mind.
- As you consider the questions in each exercise, allow your mind to drift lightly in a nonjudgmental space. Then, notice whatever you notice. With awareness, you regain the power of choice. You can let go of what no longer serves you and call in what will.
- To help you do this, imagine a golden ball of energy in the center of your chest. This is your divine Spirit, your highest creative essence. Breathe into this golden ball

283

of energy and watch it expand outward. Continue to breathe into this golden ball as it expands to fill your entire body.

- Continue expanding this golden ball until you are sitting in a huge golden bubble of your own highest creative essence. Begin to release down your grounding cord feelings, beliefs, and memories you're ready to let go of. Let them simply fall away like veils; allow them to drop down your grounding cord to be recycled by Mother Earth.

- Continue to release until you feel light and full of your own divine love. Notice the greater truth of who you are. Begin to communicate with the "you" who has been sitting in all those beliefs. Allow that self to experience the divine love and unending acceptance of your greater self. Allow any limiting beliefs and blueprints to dissolve gently in the golden radiance of your divine energy.

- Create the intention to mentor the smaller self. Make a promise that the greater you will bring the patterns and blueprints that currently control and limit the smaller you into the light. Let your inner child know that he or she is not alone. You are there, you have always been there, and you will always be there. Breathe!

- When you feel ready, come out of trance. Pat your body. Breathe deeply into your body. Stand up and stretch. Write down anything you want to remember or validate, including any next step that you can take to support this spiritual goal.

The Trinity Meditations

The meditations below are designed to help you connect with your inner wisdom and increase your ability and capacity to expand your consciousness in ways that help you strengthen your connection with the divine.

Experiencing God the Father—
Igniting Divine Creativity

In the meditation, I invite you find a quiet place where you can sit quietly and go within. Create the intention that you will experience God the Father energy and bring your communication with this aspect of God fully into your awareness and into present time.

Part 1

- Begin by focusing on your breathing. Gently breathe in and out, calming the body and the mind.
- To help you come into present time, create a line of energy from the base of your spine down into the very center of the Earth.
- Allow this line of energy to be nice and wide—at least as wide as your hips—and set it on release.
- Begin to release your day, your week, your work, your chores, your dreams...
- Let the energy of all the people you interact with release down this grounding cord.
- Release your to-do list. You can pick it up later.
- Let your body know that nothing effortful is required of it at this time; you will be sitting quietly for the fifteen minutes or so.
- Breathe!
- Now, focus your attention on your heart. Imagine that golden spark that is *you*, and begin to breathe into this spark. With each in-breath, imagine that golden energy getting bigger and bigger, filling up your body, and activating within every cell in your body—every neuron, every synapse happening in the brain—all being flooded with this golden energy of your own highest creative essence.

- Settle the body even more deeply as you bring this energy forward in your awareness and breathe deeply now. In and out. Deep breaths.

Part 2

- Open your mind to an all-embracing, welcoming, loving Presence within you.
- Allow the energy in your body to come up a light, easy, amused vibration. Let go until you find a lightness of being.
- Now, imagine you are a powerful engine, and turn on the ignition switch!
- Feel Life energy flowing through your veins, pumping through your heart, filling your mind.
- On the in-breath, allow this energy to rev up; on the out-breath, allow it to flow out into your world.
- Using your intention, seek a connection with the flow of universal intelligence and ask for your part in the larger plan to come into your mind. Become aware of any place in your life where you are ready to initiate something new—a new project, a new direction, a new way of relating or understanding, a new level of consciousness. What are you ready to ignite and manifest or reveal in objective form?
- Now ask, what needs to be destroyed, let go of, or resolved. To clear the way for something new, we often have to be willing to let go of the old. What is getting in your way or limiting you from moving in this new direction?
- Resolve to let it go right now, and bring in a new flow of creativity, certainty, and direction.
- Allow any fear, uncertainty, anxiety, or self-judgment to be liquidated by this loving radiance flowing into your mind.
- Allow your intention to vibrate within the greater harmony of God's will. Come into agreement to working cocreatively with the Universe to manifest this idea in whatever manner serves the highest and best good of all.

286

- Ask for the opportunities, resources, guidance, and help you need to come your way.
- Allow yourself to remain open to cosmic guidance, to see things differently, to do things differently, and to understand things differently.
- Commit to remaining open to change and keeping an open mind.
- Further commit to being courageous and boldly moving in the direction your inner guidance points you.
- Take a moment to experience this alignment and feel the power of this level of communication and creative integration with the greater whole.
  o Feel the loving Presence of this energy. Feel the enthusiasm for creativity. Feel the support of the entire universe within you, lifting you up, working cocreatively with you.
- Allow your heart and mind to expand with gratitude and the grace of this unlimited divine love.

Part 3

- When you feel ready, return your awareness to your body, breathe deeply, and exhale. Begin to pat your body gently and allow your attention to return to your physical surroundings.
- Open your eyes.

Experiencing God the Son—Interconnectivity

- Begin this meditation by following the steps outlined in Part 1 above, and then continue with the following steps.
- Imagine you are a shining star radiating light and love. Say out loud several times "I Am" at a steady, rhythmic pace.
  o Allow your body, your feelings, and your thoughts to all come into sync with this rhythm.

- When you are ready, imagine the night sky and place yourself in this starry field. Pay attention to all the other shining stars that exist in the universe with you as you come into connection with the whole.
- As you move into an experience of unity with the whole, imagine that you are part of a universal symphony. Together you and all the other players in the orchestra are producing beautiful music. *Be* the beautiful music you create together. Feel the *oneness* of the music within you.
  o What do you experience?
  o What happens to your sense of self?
- Now pay attention to the conductor of the symphony. Experience how much easier it is to play your part at the right time and at the right pace if you're following the conductor's lead.
  o Imagine facing away from the conductor as you wear soundproof headphones. How much harder would it be to stay in sync with the whole symphony? What happens to your part? What happens to your experience?
  o Return your attention to the conductor, and come back into sync with the whole.
- Notice that you can be aware of yourself, others, and the whole all at the same time. The emphasis changes depending on where you are placing your attention.
  o Listen to your sound. Imagine you are playing the violin.
  o Listen to others' sounds. Listen to the trumpets. Now focus on the drums. Now pick out the piano.
  o Listen to the whole sound—all the instruments together
- When you are ready, return your attention to your body and to the room you are in.
- Have the intention of making room for an expanded understanding of yourself as an evolving "Son" of God and your experience of the interconnectedness of the greater field of Life.
- Open your eyes, pat your body, and take a deep breath.

Experiencing the Infinite Spirit—Healing the Mind

- Begin this meditation by following the steps outlined in Part 1 above, and then continue with the following steps.
- Bring the top of your head up to a golden color.
- Ask for the Infinite Spirit to fill your mind.
- Imagine that your mind is made up of a huge conglomerate of geometric shapes. You have thoughts that look like squares and thoughts that look like triangles. You have circles, pentagrams, octagons, parallelograms, and all other sorts of shapes in various sizes, colors, and hues. Some have clear edges, and some are fuzzy and indistinct.
- Ask the Holy Spirit to give your mind a healing. Allow Divine Mind to clear out the old and make room for the new.
  - o Have the intention and willingness to allow your mind to come into alignment with the coherent, overarching divine plan of the Creator.
  - o Let go of fearful, outdated, painful, and limiting thoughts, ideas, beliefs, and programming by allowing anything that does not serve the highest good to be cleared away.
- Imagine these shapes transforming before your very eyes. See a beautiful, coherent pattern emerge out of the chaos.
- Allow the walls that imprison your mind to fade away, and see yourself stepping into a larger understanding of yourself, others, and the world around you.
- Let go of divisions, prejudices, competition, and selfishness and step into a new paradigm, a new orientation that is based on divine qualities such as
  - o cocreativity,
  - o service to others,
  - o compassion,
  - o forgiveness,
  - o unconditional love,

- o   healthy boundaries,
- o   fluid thinking,
- o   accuracy,
- o   precision,
- o   courage, and
- o   openness.
- Which of these qualities capture your attention at this time?
- What other divine qualities come to mind? Take note of them.
- What divine qualities are you already using in your life?
- What divine qualities are you here to learn about and develop in this lifetime?
- Take a moment to reflect on your life and see how all the circumstances of your life (the positive and the negative) have conspired to help you develop and employ these qualities.
- Take a moment to be grateful for your life and the experience you are gaining.
- When you feel ready, picture your mind now revealing a beautiful kaleidoscope of colorful shapes. Allow this kaleidoscope to be dynamic and responsive to your developing intuition rather than fixed and rigid.
- Return your awareness to your body and the room you are in. Take a deep breath and open your eyes.

Shadow Work Technique

Before you begin this technique, take a moment to identify one major repeating pattern in your life that you'd like to heal. Reflect on your life and, working with your inner wisdom, allow your intuition to bring the pattern to the front of your mind. (In my case, it was people-pleasing—a constant, driving, overpowering need to please others, even at my own expense.) What constant, driving, overpowering response pattern stands out for you?

1. Ground and run energy until you are quite centered, relaxed, and connected to your intuitive, wise self. Use one of my <u>Grounding and Running Energy</u> audio-guided meditations if you like.
2. Connect with your higher self.
   - Use imagery that works for you, such as walking through a nature scene you enjoy and arriving at a beautiful house.
   - Enter into the house and ask to meet your higher self.
   - Ask your higher self to help you uncover the root cause of the repeating pattern of limitation in your life. (*How you connect with your higher self is less important than simply creating the intention to do so and opening your heart and mind to this unconditionally loving Presence within you.*)
   - Create a comfortable chair to sit in and create a screen out in front of you.
3. Ask for the earliest memory of whatever feeling underlies your core issue to appear on the screen in front of you. This may show up as an actual memory or a collection of vague memories or feeling-tones merged into one symbolic scene in your mind. (*Core pictures tend to be tied to worth and/or safety—Am I loved? Am I valued? Am I safe?*)
   - Allow a very young version of yourself to appear on your screen, and allow yourself to remember what she was feeling—not what you think she *should* be feeling but what she was *actually* feeling at the time, unedited by your adult mind.
   - What was happening in her life at that time?
   - How did she feel about herself, others, and the world?
   - What conclusions did she make?
   - How did she cope with her feelings? What did she decide was the best way to handle the problem as she saw it? (*Hide, confront, please, tune out, eat, be*

291

cute or funny, seduce, rescue, play dumb, freeze, take on adult responsibilities, etc.)

    o *The point here is for you to uncover the unconscious beliefs involved in your repeating pattern and to uncover how you've been coping with it. Coping strategies are things such as becoming a people pleaser, a rescuer, a bully, a wallflower, an overachiever, a pretender, and so forth. There are countless coping strategies. The trick is to uncover yours.*

4. Let your younger self know that she didn't do anything wrong. You know that she was always doing the very best she could to cope with situations she couldn't fully understand and that you love her unconditionally. Let her know that she is worthy simply because she exists as a precious child of God within the Creation. She is loved by you and loved by God no matter what.

5. Take this younger self into your arms, and allow unconditional love from your higher self to pour through your heart into the heart of your younger self. Give her all the love and attention she needs, and let her know that she deserves your love and attention. Let her know that you are there and that you (*the higher self*) have *always* been there. Allow your younger self to take this in, and allow her to talk to you if there is anything she wishes to say to you.

6. Forgiveness steps:

- Invite the Spirit of the other person to be present in front of you.

- Tell the other person exactly how you felt *at that time* about the situation and let him know what you needed and what you feel he did that was wrong or lacking in some way. Get it all out. Cry, yell, stomp your feet if necessary, but get the emotion and the personal truth you experienced *out*. Let the inner hurt be expressed to the spirit of the other person. It is important to allow this core issue to be aired and brought out into the open light of day. You won't be left in this state, but you need to get it out of the vault.

- If the other person has done wrong or given you a burden that was his to carry, imagine placing it in a ball of golden light, and give it back to him. Let him know that it is his burden and that you know he can carry it and take care of it himself. (*Even if you've bought the notion that he cannot take care of his issue, move your mind out of that prison; instead, validate that he, too, is a fully capable spirit on a journey of self-discovery. He will never learn what he set out to learn if you keep trying to do it for him. Holding on to his stuff is just another coping strategy for attempting to gain a false sense of being in control. You don't actually have free-will authority over his stuff. We learn under the law of cause and effect. Let him have the effect of his behavior as you understand it.*)
- Now, ask the other person if he has anything he'd like to say to you. Listen and attend. (*Often, the other person acknowledges his trespass or ignorance and expresses remorse. If not, it's OK. Give him a chance to speak, too.*)
- If you have a reply, then speak your truth.
- See if you can understand the larger context of the situation. What was happening with the other person at the time? Did he know how to do better? Was he also suffering? Was he also limited and afraid or ignorant in some way—as are we all? (*Again, the important point here is not to take on his limitation or try to fix it for him but rather to understand what happened and forgive him.*)
- Now, allow divine forgiveness from your higher self to flow down into your mind and into your heart, filling you up with unconditional love and forgiveness for yourself and the other person. Then, allow this golden stream to flow over to the other

person. Allow this unconditional divine love to flow effortlessly through you and out to him.

- To whatever degree you can, allow yourself to forgive him fully. Allow the story to end. Acknowledge that this chapter in your life is done. Imagine getting to the end of a book and writing "The End" on the last page. Give that book to your Record Keeper,[108] and have her file it away.
- Let the other person know you forgive him and that this story is over.
  - o Pick up a golden stick representing this issue.
  - o Break the stick and say, "I forgive you, I release you, all is well."
  - o Throw the broken pieces into a golden fire and allow them to burn completely.
- Place the Spirit of the other person in a beautiful golden ball of light.
  - o With your God-hand, pick up the golden ball with the spirit of the other person inside and hand the ball up to God. As you do this, repeat, "I forgive you, I release you, all is well."
  - o Let the light go up to God.

7. Bring your younger self into your heart, and let her know that she is safe with you. Imagine putting her in the passenger seat of your life, and let her know that she is no longer in charge. She no longer needs to protect you or try to make things better. Let her know that you—the healing adult self and the higher self— are now in charge and she can be a kid. Assume the role of the divine parent and promise to take loving, good care of her. She may not always get her way, but under your care she will be loved and attended to in a manner that will bring her into the light of higher understanding and forgiveness that will liberate her from fear.

---

[108] Your Akashic Record Keeper is a specific type of ministering spirit that helps you keep track of all your life experiences.

8. Bring your attention back to the room you're in and into your body. Create a huge golden ball of light above your head, and have your higher self fill it with love, acceptance, and any other divine quality you like. Pull it into your body, filling up every cell in your body until everything comes up golden. Allow your heart to be filled with light, love, and power. Make room for a "new normal" in your life.

9. Reach over and touch the ground. Open your eyes. Take a deep, cleansing breath and enjoy the rest of your day.

Be aware in the coming days and weeks of your inner child's response to life, and take a moment to make new choices that will both free you from limitation and heal the wounded self. It's not about repressing this aspect; it's about healing it. Call on your higher self to guide you in new ways of thinking, responding, and feeling in those situations that challenge you. Be willing to change your mind and your emotional state to allow new perspectives to enter.

APPENDIX B ~ MY STORY

I was always an intuitive and psychic child, but I didn't have a vocabulary that could explain my experiences. I just knew that I felt very different from everyone else, different from my family in a way that was inexplicable. I know it frightened my family, and it frightened me, too. I could sense and see energy and beings that others seemed to think were not real, not there. I knew I wasn't crazy and that what I saw and sensed was really there, but I didn't know what to do about it. I was terrified and alone, even isolated.

Nighttime was particularly difficult for me. I was afraid to be alone in my room and afraid of the window—I always asked my brother to pull down the shade for me. I often begged him to sleep in my room, bargaining with him, offering to do some of his chores if he'd agree. I saw or sensed scary, dark, impossible beings, such as the "lion man"—a being with the lower body of a human and the head of a male lion. Whenever he appeared, he was always angry and aggressive, hanging out in the hallway outside my bedroom. I would shift from being fast asleep to being awake in a heightened state of awareness. In this state, I would begin to sense the lion -man's presence in the hallway. I would hear him creeping to my doorway until finally I was fully awake and screaming. My poor mother wouldn't know what to make of my terror and my certainty of the bad thing that was in the house. She would hold me until I fell back asleep or she took me into her bed.

A recurring nightmare of being burned alive at the stake haunted me for many years. I had a strange aversion to nuns, priests, and Catholic churches. They frightened me, and I was inexplicably afraid of Spain. I couldn't understand how anyone would want to go there, and I knew I certainly never wanted to set foot in the place. Many years later as an adult, I finally understood that my nightmare and odd aversions stemmed from a soul memory of being burned at the stake as a heretic by the Inquisition in the Middle Ages. I was killed for being psychic and speaking about things that ran counter to the Church's doctrines. As terrifying as that experience was, I now know that at the moment of my death I saw the glory of God in all things. I saw that my intuitive knowing had been true—*we are all* divine beings. I desperately wanted to tell the people who had sentenced me to death about this great love. I wanted the hatred and fear to stop. Both the trauma and the mission of that lifetime were bleeding through into this lifetime.

Once again, I could see things that others could not, and I felt an urgent need to remember and understand the deeper truth of things. This quest has proved to be a great gift to me. At the same time, one of my great challenges this lifetime has involved learning how to speak my truth fearlessly, especially when I sense others might find it upsetting or uncomfortable.

On the upside, as a child I also had encounters with beneficent beings. I remember having a conversation with Jesus as I walked home from school in the fifth grade. I was upset that people thought he was the *only* Savior and that other enlightened masters, like Buddha, didn't count or weren't "the real thing." I remember, vividly, Jesus telling me that Buddha was his brother and that he brought enlightenment to his part of the world. He told me that they worked together and for me not to worry too much about it. He told me that all paths eventually lead to God and one was not necessarily better than another. It was really more about finding a path that fit the person seeking to know God.

I *knew* this was true; it resonated deeply within me. As a result, I never believed otherwise, no matter who tried to get me to see it differently or how certain they seemed to be about it. As an adult looking back, I find this internal certainty remarkable; after all, I was just a child. I see now that this was one of the first pillars of truth remembered by me in this lifetime. It has defined the course of my life and continues to guide me to this day.

When I was twenty, my boyfriend's father married a woman who was a psychic minister. My boyfriend was teasing me about being afraid of the dark at my age, and this woman asked me if this were true. I said yes and explained why. It was such a relief to me when she didn't laugh at me or act as though I were crazy. Instead, she explained briefly and simply that a spirit in the body has seniority over any spirits hanging around that don't have a body. All I had to do was acknowledge them and tell them to leave, and they would be compelled to do so. She presented this information to me as a spiritual law, and I took it as such because it resonated. I recognized the truth of what she was saying and consequently regained a level of power over my life. I saw that I had a *choice*, and I could banish these beings with my will.

That's not to say I was never frightened again by energy or beings that I encountered, but I never felt so completely out of control and powerless again. I had a vocabulary for what I was experiencing, and I had a new tool: conscious intention backed by certainty. This was one of my first powerful steps out of fearfulness.

In 1981, I graduated from the University of California, Berkeley, with a degree in psychology. A year later, I decided to pursue my master's degree. In 1985, I graduated from San Francisco State University with an MA in educational psychology. Three months later, I moved to Los Angeles to take a position as a corporate trainer with a large bank. It was an excellent job, and it enabled me to get away from a painful breakup with a man I had been deeply in love with—or at least I thought so at the time.

Several key turning points happened during my time in L.A. As a corporate trainer, much of my time was spent teaching classes. I was also in the process of trying to put a band together with a good friend who had moved to Southern California several years before me. But I had been suffering from chronic laryngitis for over seven years, and this was making both of these endeavors quite difficult. This was a very frustrating and upsetting situation for me, not to mention physically painful as well. I went to see a fancy specialist, who spent less than five minutes with me and informed me I had polyps all up and down my vocal cords. He said I would probably have to give up teaching, and definitely singing, and that I would most likely need surgery. I was devastated. I had been singing and performing since I was six years old. How could this be? How could the two things that were so vitally important to me be going away? I remember speaking to a woman at my job about it, and she shared with me how she'd had to give up her dream of becoming a professional ballerina because of an injury. The message was "bad stuff happens, and you just have to accept it and move on." Well, I didn't agree. It just didn't resonate as truth to me. I knew that I was not going to accept it. I was going to find a way to heal myself.

Shortly after that, my mother came for a visit. While I was at work, she wandered into the Bodhi Tree Bookstore, which was a famous New Age bookstore at the time. As she wandered around, she noticed a book by Louise Hay entitled *You Can Heal Your Life*, and she felt strongly that she should buy it for me. This book changed the course of my life. I came to understand that underlying all illnesses is a belief, *and those beliefs can be changed*. I decided to give it a try. I repeated the positive affirmation suggested in the book for laryngitis: "It is safe for me to ask for what I want; I am free to express myself; I love and approve of myself; all is well." I repeated this affirmation day and night whenever I could think to do so. I began to drink herbal tea and to envision that I could and would heal my vocal cords.

A year later, I needed to have a physical. While I was there, I asked the doctor to look at my vocal cords. He told me they looked perfectly healthy. There might be just the very beginnings of a small polyp forming on one vocal cord, but that didn't look serious and would probably not become a problem. He asked me why I had wanted him to take a look. I told him about the chronic laryngitis and the prognosis of the specialist from the year before. He looked completely perplexed and asked me if I could explain how I had healed myself. I laughed and said, "You don't want to know because you won't believe me." He said, "Give me a try." So, I told him about the book and the positive affirmations. He was amazed. *I* was amazed that I had done it and felt motivated to keep working at healing my life and myself.

Another significant experience happened during my time in Los Angeles. I was on a weekend getaway with a man I was dating, his sister, and her boyfriend. The setting was in the mountains, quite beautiful and peaceful. I was reading several New Age books. One afternoon while Mark and his sister played tennis, I sat on the sidelines reading *One* by Richard Bach. The story sparked something within me. Suddenly, I felt myself sitting in an intensely bright column of light. I felt myself expand and become very light and filled with an immense love and joy. I knew with absolute certainty that God existed and was present and that I was connected to God, an inseparable part of God. I felt myself begin to glow.

My aura (an energy field that radiates from each of us and sometimes is said to have a particular color) became so bright and clear that Mark and his sister stopped playing. Mark said, "What's going on? Are you OK?" I don't remember exactly what I said, but I remember smiling and saying something about everything being fine. They both stared at me a few seconds longer before returning to their game. It was if they saw *something* but didn't know what it was they were seeing. However, they seemed to know that it was somehow beautiful or special. And *I* knew it was beautiful and profound and that

I would never be the same again. The relationship with Mark soon fizzled, but the mystical experience remained with me. A connection with God had been restored that would not be severed again. What joy!

In the 1980s, the New Age movement was in full swing in Los Angeles, and there was ample opportunity to experience new things, new perspectives, and new points of view. I went to see various trance channelers at house parties and listened to what they had to say about life, the universe, and how things work. This opened my mind to many new ways of thinking about life, and I felt a deep resonance with what I was hearing, even when I didn't fully understand it. They talked about how we are the creators of our own reality and about how God *is* creativity. They offered up mind-bending information on how time and space actually exist all at once and how unseen dimensions interpenetrate the world we experience with our five physical senses. I remember experiencing a quickening sense of excitement as I sensed what they were saying was true. But I also felt profound confusion. Why was my life so challenging if I was the one creating it? Why couldn't I find love? Why was I so lonely?

Eventually, I asked for a private session with one of the trance channelers, a man named Steven Hewitt, who channeled a being called "Friend." In the session, I asked about the broken relationship that had contributed to my decision to move away from Northern California. Despite dating other people in Los Angeles, I was still having a hard time getting over the man. Friend explained that I was confused about love. He told me that I was in a situation where I had loved the other person more than I loved myself, and this situation had created a void. He helped me understand that I needed to fill myself up with an abundance of self-love, and only then would the opportunity to love another person, truly, manifest in a manner that would be sustainable. He explained that the ex-boyfriend was a spiritual teacher of mine. He told me that we knew each other from numerous past lives and that we

302

often traded turns being teacher and student to one another. Even though I *knew* I was hearing the truth, I confess that I didn't immediately embody the lesson because I didn't yet know how. I had more to learn about myself and about love and consequently went on to have several more unsuccessful relationships before I eventually met my husband. But the seed was planted in my mind, waiting to burst through in time.

The last of these unsuccessful relationships ended so badly and caused such deep hurt that I sank into a deep depression. I felt powerless to create what I wanted in my life and wondered why. If I truly was the creator of my life, *why* couldn't I create the kind of relationship I wanted? Why couldn't I be loved the way I wanted? What did I have to do to become good enough?

I remember sitting on my bed so full of anger, sadness, and despair, promising myself that I would never again get involved with a man who didn't appreciate me or want the same things I wanted: a marriage, a family, and a home. I vowed that if I couldn't have what I wanted, I would remain single and put all my time, attention, and creativity into a career and friends, and I would learn how to be happy that way. I would live my life on my own terms and never again try to settle for less or try to be what someone else wanted me to be. The seed planted by Friend was beginning to germinate at long last.

This new vision of my life helped me realize that I needed to steer clear of the "broken" men—that is, men who were eternally needy because someone or something had let them down, broken their heart, or disappointed them. This type of man knew how to take but not how to give. I saw that I had gone from one relationship to another trying to fill up each broken man with my love. I could see their pain and wanted to take it away because I wanted my own pain to go away. I had a belief deep within me that I wasn't really good enough, and I had tried to become good enough by giving all my love away to someone who had the same belief. It never worked. Never.

I could always see their innate value, but I could not see my own. It wasn't until I began to challenge this belief within my own mind that I was able to create the kind of relationship I was seeking.

This was a huge turning point for me. Invest in me? Believe that I'm good enough? That I'm worthy? It was a new feeling within me, but it was right. During this time of reckoning, I was sitting on my bed, vowing to put myself front and center in my life, when an angel appeared at the foot of my bed. There she was, shining her loving light into my room and telling me everything was going to be OK. She said I was ready to have what I wanted because I finally understood *I* was important and that what *I* wanted was important. Now that I could see I *deserved* to have what I truly wanted, I was on the path to having it, and it was coming very soon. She was right. Less than two months later, I met my husband, Greg.

The circumstances of that meeting were divinely guided. By this time, I was back in Northern California, working temporary jobs while pursuing a career in music. My brother lived about an hour from me, and I was visiting him for the Presidents' Day weekend. I was planning to stay until Sunday evening. But when I awoke Sunday morning, my inner voice told me that I had to leave *right then* and go out the Crystal Springs Reservoir. Even though I had lived five minutes away from the reservoir for some time, I had never ventured over there. Yet the voice (which I now understand was my higher Self) was insistent, persistent, and urgent. So, as crazy at it seemed, I packed up and left. The voice told me to go *straight* to the reservoir, but I wanted to stop by my house and collect some things first because I didn't know why I was going there or what I'd be doing when I got there. All the while, the voice kept urging me: "Hurry! Hurry!" As I drove into the reservoir's parking lot, I saw a cute guy in an orange sports car drive in and park. I remember thinking, "Oh, he's so cute, but I look like a wreck!" I had on no makeup; I was in my ratty old ski sweater and gray leggings—not looking my best. I gathered my beach chair, coat, Diet Coke, and a backpack full of books and headed to the trail. I looked ridiculous. Everyone was walking, jogging, or biking past me as I trudged along as if I were on a weeklong camping trip. The cute guy from the orange sports car was behind me, chuckling to himself. As he started to pass me, he smiled and said, "Don't tell me, the tent's in the backpack." I blushed and laughed and had to stop to shift things around, for everything was slipping and sliding. He was so full of light and amusement, and he seemed so genuinely nice, that I found myself falling into step with him. We ended up walking along the trail, talking and laughing until my arms gave out and I had to sit down. We eventually walked back to park entrance, reluctant to part. So, we agreed to get together the next day for a bike ride. The rest, as the saying goes, is history. I remember bursting into my band rehearsal that night and telling my two girlfriends, "I've met the man I'm going to marry!" It just popped right out of my mouth. And even though it scared me to believe it, I *knew* it was true.

I'm sure the angel played her part in the whole thing and made sure Greg and I were both there at the same time. I'm so thankful I listened to my inner voice. Over the years, I've learned to tune in to that certain niggling feeling in my gut. For when I don't tune in and listen, I miss out on opportunities, or I get myself into a jam that could have been avoided. On the first night of our honeymoon, Greg confessed that he'd also heard a voice in his head that day at the reservoir. His voice said, "Speak up now or be alone forever." From that day on, "the voice" has been present at various significant times in my life and is now very much a part of my daily life. I have learned that this is the voice of God-within-me; when I listen, my life becomes divinely directed.

Greg and I got married in October 1990. Within a year, our first son, Shaun, was born. Shortly after, I developed a fear of bridges, despite the fact that I had grown up on an island where I had to cross several small bridges to get just about anywhere. I was especially fearful of driving in the right lane closest to the water.

One day, I was traveling over the Dumbarton Bridge, heading to a friend's house to go over song choices for her wedding. I usually tried to be in the fast lane near the center of the bridge. For some reason, though, I had to be in the right lane that day. As I nervously neared the apex of the bridge, my consciousness split into three realities. One part remained in present time, driving the car without incident. The second part went into an alternative scenario where the car skidded out of control and I was killed at the bottom of the bridge. The third part moved up into a magnificent column of white light and began to ascend. This white light was beautiful beyond words. I felt myself surrounded by unconditional love and filled with a peace that is hard to describe. I felt a deep yearning to follow the light and return home. The complete release of fear, responsibility, and limitations was alluring. I became aware that I had a choice at that moment. I could follow the car crash scenario and pass over into this amazing place, or I could choose to stay.

I thought of my little son and my husband, and I fiercely wanted to remain with them. I remember telling God, "I understand." God was showing me that the only thing that matters in the end is the love we experience and the love we feel for others. No amount of money or worldly success would trump love. That revelation allowed me to feel validated over my choice to be a stay-at-home mom. I had been feeling a lot of stress over not returning to "work" and felt subtly criticized when people asked me what I did. I wondered why they thought I'd ever stopped working; being a mother was the hardest (and best) job I'd ever had. I was grateful to be alive, and a peace settled over me. And I had new understanding about death after that; I knew it would be OK when the time came.

My fear of bridges persisted, however, until I finally recalled a past-life experience where my infant son and I were killed in a carriage accident that took place on a bridge. We were both thrown from the carriage into the chilly waters below and drowned. Becoming a mother in this lifetime activated the soul memory. Once my mother's instinct to protect my child kicked in, bridges seemed dangerous. After I accessed the soul memory, I was able to understand my anxiety and put things into perspective. The fear subsided.

As the years went by, Greg and I had two more beautiful boys. I continued to seek out opportunities to be involved with music and find ways to express my creativity. When my third son was six months old, I went to see a numerologist who had been recommended by a friend. I was at a crossroads in my life and unclear about what was next for me. I had been in a touring gospel choir before the birth of my third son but decided to retire after he was born, as the commitment was more than I could handle. I was also in an acoustic duo that was floundering. We'd been together for over five years and didn't have a clear vision of where we were headed. I needed some insight and direction regarding my path.

The reading proved to be very interesting. The numerologist told me it was clear I needed to be expressing myself artistically, but I had gotten a bit off track. She said I should be writing and performing my own music and that I needed to be in a position of leadership to develop those abilities. I told her that I was a musician, but I didn't write and had never been the designated leader of the projects I was involved in. She reiterated that it was very important that I begin writing my own music and leading my own project. It was my destiny to stop hiding behind others and learn how to lead and express my own truth, even if it scared me to do so. I was stunned. I had always yearned to write my own music but had given it up in my early twenties after being disappointed with the results of the few songs I had written. I wasn't sure exactly what to do with the information. The thought of giving up the duo was just too much to consider, so I put it out of my mind. A couple of months passed. One afternoon, I was lying down, trying to nap with the baby, when a song began to circle around my mind. The words and melody started to spill into my mind. Soon, I was humming and scrambling for pen and paper. Within an hour or two, a fully formed song was born. And I liked it. When my duo partner came over for a rehearsal later in the week, I played the song for her, and she liked it, too. We began to include it in our set list. My songwriting and leadership journey had begun. The music poured out of me. I soon got involved in arranging, producing, and recording my music. Within a year, my singing partner moved to Nashville with her boyfriend, and just as the numerologist had predicted, I became focused solely on my own music. Everything I learned at this time about creativity, leadership, and speaking my truth helped set the stage for the work I am doing today.

As I was diving into songwriting and music, I was also exploring my spiritual and psychic abilities. A woman from the choir I had been in was a psychic and a therapist. She didn't do a lot of predicting; rather, she read auras and worked with the spiritual body. She was an energy worker. She helped the spirit heal itself so the spirit could heal the body. I became intrigued. I had an insight that it was vitally important to my health and well-being for me to understand the world of spirit. There was a reason for my abilities. So, in 2002, I began a long period of intensive spiritual training at the Berkeley Psychic Institute, which is the seminary for the Church of Divine Man. After completing their intensive two-year clairvoyant program, I was entitled as an associate minister of the church in 2004. I continued at the institute for another six years, working as a spiritual counselor, healer, and teacher while pursuing my graduate studies there. After completing the teacher's program in 2010, I was awarded my minister's license. During my eight years there, developing my psychic and energetic healing abilities, I worked with all kinds of people—highly paid executives, professionals, students, and everyone in between. This was my road to becoming a spiritual counselor and teacher.

This training helped me learn how to open up to new levels of consciousness. All the early lessons of my life began to make sense: I could sense negative beings, see angels, and communicate with Jesus as a child because I am psychic. Love is not about trading a sense of worth with another; it is an outpouring of recognition, affinity, and communication that stems from our own internal sense of value and recognition of our divine Self. When I yield my life to the higher power within me, I get better results, and the twists and turns in my life take on greater meaning and purpose. Challenges in life give us an opportunity to grow and activate our divine potential. God really is at work in all things. More recently, I have learned that I am God in Action. I really do create my life, and I have the ability to change what isn't working and manifest good things. All I need to do is to listen to my inner guidance.

In the fall of 2010, my family and I moved to Livermore, California. This external move foreshadowed a significant internal shift within me, and the spring of 2011 was a time of accelerated spiritual growth. I was filled with a burning desire to bring my life into alignment with my divine purpose and yield my life completely over to God. Whenever I meditated or prayed, I asked God to reveal to me what I should be doing and to lead me into work that would be in alignment with the greater field of life. I no longer cared specifically what that work would be. I completely lost interest in pursuing music as a career and opened myself up to whatever the Universe wanted to show me.

The Universe responded quickly with a series of intense mystical experiences. They occurred so frequently that I was compelled to write down the revelations in order to assimilate them into my daily life. Circumstances began to happen in a synchronistic, spontaneous, and effortless way. My job was to recognize and act on the opportunities the Universe presented. Once I opened myself up to the process of discovering my deeper calling, it happened naturally, but

309

it was not always comfortable. In fact, there were times when it was quite challenging because I continually had to stretch myself beyond my comfort zone and let go of repeating patterns of limitation and fear in order to do this work.

The first pointer from the Universe was a humorous one. One afternoon, out of the blue, a woman I'd never met before called me at home and asked me to give her a psychic reading. Her last name was Stranger, and she had a strong southern accent. I thought she said, "This is a stranger calling you, and I'd like a psychic reading." I was so surprised that I blurted out, "How do you know I'm psychic, and how did you get my number?" It turned out she was a home health aide for my husband's aunt, and she had been reading my Christmas letters to Aunt Maye for the past several years. I immediately knew the Universe was up to something and I'd better pay attention. I did give the woman a reading and wondered what would come next.

Within a few weeks, I was again presented with an unusual situation. A woman at the gym I had recently joined was in great emotional distress one afternoon. She was clearly suffering, and the woman she was talking to about it was making her feel worse. Because I was also in the spa with them, I was inadvertently included in the conversation but was reluctant to say anything. As I was getting dressed, my inner voice began to urge me to reach out to this woman and tell her I was a psychic and a healer. Simultaneously, I heavily resisted this idea—it seemed unethical, as if I would be soliciting her. I began to walk out of the locker room when a force within me began to push me back. The voice said, "You asked to live a divinely guided life, and I am offering you that guidance right now. I can't make you act on it, only you can do that. What do you really want—to live the life you've asked for, or play it safe?" I stopped and gave myself a moment to gather my courage. I turned around, went back into the locker room, and offered the woman my card. Her eyes filled with tears, and she said, "I called you to me. I called you to me. I've been asking God to send a psychic to me. Thank you. When can I see you?" We made an appointment for the next day.

My life was never again the same. That same woman basically helped me launch my spiritual counseling business. She came to see me off and on for several years, and she told everyone she knew about me. From there, my client base slowly built. She also asked me to teach her friends and her how to meditate, so I began teaching out of my home. All that led to the work I do today. I am so grateful to her. And I am also grateful that I *listened* and that I *acted* on my inner divine guidance—that I allowed myself to step well outside my comfort zone and take a chance.

In 2012, I decided to take another chance. I was working with a unique client helping her access her inner wisdom. My own inner guidance told me to begin channeling the Supreme Being in our sessions because it would be safe for me to do so. I asked my client if she would be comfortable with this idea, and she agreed. This opened up a whole-new dimension to my work. I soon began consciously channeling other high-level divine healing personalities, such as Archangel Michael and Ascended Master Saint Germain, in addition to the Supreme Being. This new connection opened me up to information that was previously sitting just outside my conscious awareness. It gave me access to points of view that are much larger than my own, and my ability to grow in spiritual understanding and awareness was profoundly enhanced as a result.

I realize now that these loving Presences have been around me all my life. Along with my own higher Self, they have been gently guiding and assisting me and helping me turn my mind inward toward the divine Presence within me and within all things. All the events of my life have led me to the revolutionary understanding that *I Am God in Action.* Wow! And we are *all* God in Action. This profound revelation continues to transform my life each day. Clearly, it didn't come to me all at once. I had to work my way up to this epiphany slowly and arduously. But everything that has happened to me—the good, the bad, and the ugly—has served this path. Everything I do from here forward is about learning how to use the creative forces of God-within-me wisely and in alignment with the greater field of life.

APPENDIX C

Index

Index of Diagrams

GLOSSARY

Adversary: That state of being that sits in opposition to God, to at-one-ment or unity, to God's will and purpose. Selfishness, narcissism, that which is obsessed with form at the expense of soul.

Affinity: Feelings of acceptance. Connected to the fourth chakra.

Ascension: The process of spiritual awakening having to do with the evolution of consciousness. A series of initiations or large expansions of consciousness that happen in a particular order.

Astral Body: A subtle energy body that enables us to feel, to be sentient. Associated with the five physical senses and characterized by sensation, feeling, emotion, and desire. The precursor of intuition and a spiritual awareness of unity. Also known as the emotional body and the desire body.

Atonement: Unity. A conscious comprehension of the innate state of at-one-ment of all component parts within a whole. To come into energetic and psychological sync with the greater whole within which we live and breathe and have our being.

Awareness: Intelligence or thought that we remember and use in our daily life. Awareness expands as we tap into our greater consciousness but for the most part is currently limited to our daily experiences in physical reality.

Belief: An opinion or conviction not immediately susceptible to rigorous proof. Acceptance of "an alleged fact or body of facts as true or right without positive knowledge or proof." [109]

Big Bang: The creation of the Grand Universe (the Universe of universes). The creative thrust or outward, externalized manifestation of God's creativity.

Causal Body: The energetic body of consciousness that comprises the Soul during our evolutionary cycle of growth in the lower three worlds. Unlike the lower three bodies (or vehicles) used by a personality during an incarnation, the causal body persists over the entire course of our human evolution, developing over many incarnations, and is therefore relatively immortal. It is the storehouse of all our divine qualities—potential and actual—and develops through our creative activity in the lower three worlds. Once we have completed our normal human evolution, we begin our superhuman evolution, and the causal body dissolves, as it is no longer necessary.[110]

Central Universe: The first universe ever created by the Paradise Trinity: God the Father, God the Son, God the Infinite Spirit. Fully evolved and established in eternal homeostasis of Light and Love and Goodwill.

Chakras: Vortices of electromagnetic energy. The mechanism whereby we translate thought into form. That which produces all our vehicles of expression—physical, astral, mental. Part of the subtle body where lines of force (vital energy, prana), called nadis, intersect to form an energy center whereby energy is distributed to surrounding areas of the body, acting under the direction of the soul. All the energy centers condition the glandular system and our overall physical, mental, and emotional health and well-being. Where the flowing lines of

---

109   Dictionary.com —Belief
110   Powell. *The Causal Body.*

life force energy (or nadis) cross twenty-one times, we have a major center or chakra. Where they cross fourteen times, we have a minor chakra. Seven crossings result in energy points.

Consciousness: Intelligence or creative thought that exists both within our daily awareness and beyond it in our subconscious and superconscious mind. Currently, we access only a small portion of this powerful continuum of creative energy.

Create: To actualize or make real. A commitment or intention to make real a plan or idea. A direct manifestation of intention that originates in Divine Mind.

Divine Spark: A free-standing creator, a creative expression of God, bestowed with a unique point of view at the time of its creation and made in the image of God with free will.

Ego: Self-awareness; a recognition that one exists as a self separate from other selves.

> My use of the word *ego* refers to the psychological state of the lower self— a state of mind composed of a set of conflicting concepts and beliefs about the self made up to fill the void caused by misidentification with form.

> Theosophy discriminates between the word ego with a capital E and lower case e. *Ego* refers to the self-aware soul, the Higher Self. Also known as the Solar Angel; *ego* refers to the personality or the lower self

Etheric Body: The energetic counterpart of the dense physical body—the source of our animating life energy. The blueprint and energetic scaffolding from which the dense physical body emerges.

Evolution: A period devoted to the development of consciousness and form, culminating in a balancing of the energies of consciousness and form within the creative unit.

Existential: To exist and to have always existed in the past, present, and future. A state of being separate from or outside the experience of time.

> **Existential presence of God:** The quality of God that has always existed and always will and is not experiential. It is a pre-personal state and is the Source of All That Is. Eternal.

Experiential: That which is directly gained from what one has observed, encountered, undergone, perceived, understood, and remembered. A totality of perception and knowledge gained through creative activity.

> **Experiential presence of God:** The evolving, personalized quality of God that experiences Itself through Its creations. A qualitative state of God that is actualizing in the present but of unending existence throughout all future eternity.

Four *D*'s, the

> **Decentralization:** Movement out of a limited identity into increasingly larger and holistic states of awareness and being.
> **Discernment:** Keen observation of our thoughts and emotions resulting in an ability to make better choices.
> **Discipline:** Ability to adhere to a set of beneficial internal rules or laws
> **Dispassion:** Neutrality, equanimity, and ability to move out of emotional addictions and reactivity.

God the Father: The First Source and Center. The Creator of all things. Absolute intention and pure divine love; the igniting intelligent energy of the universe. That which is at the center of everything and extends divine will, power, and drive throughout the universe. The bestower of personality status on the evolving Sons of God. In Theosophy, it is the First Logos, which is will and purpose.

God the Infinite Spirit: The Third Source and Center. The Infinite Spirit is the God of Action; the God of Spirit—That which creates; the intelligence of energy and matter; Divine Mind; the source of intelligent action and activity in all things. It is the bestower of mind to all living beings and has oversight over the domain of the intellect. It is the organizing principle of creation and ensures that God's will is carried out. In Theosophy, the Spirit is the Third Logos, which is intelligent activity.

God the Son: The Second Source and Center. God the Son is the spiritual personalization of God the Father. He is the knowable personal identity of God, the pattern personality, the master design from which all of us are made. The Son is the Word of God, the "I Am." He is the force of attraction in energy. In Theosophy, He is the Second Logos, which is love-wisdom.

Grand Universe: The Universe of universes, encompasses all living creation, including all seven superuniverses plus the original central universe that exists at the hub of the wheel of spiraling superuniverses.

Grounding and running energy: A meditative practice that consciously enables us to work with our energetic bodies by aligning, balancing, and restoring our energy field to healthy rates and right rhythms.

Higher Self: Levels of consciousness that exist between the Monad on its own plane (which is entirely formless) and the incarnated personality in the lower three worlds. It includes the Spiritual Triad and the Soul (which includes our own higher mental body). Planes of consciousness and creative activity include Atmic, Buddhic, upper Manasic (mental).

Initiation: A specific series of expansions of consciousness that happen in a stepwise manner whereby spirit is successively liberated from imprisonment in form and released from the limitations of the ego. Developing divine power and knowledge to be of service to humanity in alignment with God's will and to serve the highest good of all.

Integrated personality: Coordination and mastery of the physical, etheric, astral, and mental aspects into one coordinated whole.

Intuition: A direct perception of truth independent of any reasoning process. In Theosophy, it is defined as "pure reason," which means a level of pure knowing that's not colored or distorted by perception and bias.

Involution: A period devoted to the attainment of the ability to build the physical forms (or vehicles of expression) through which spirit manifests. Its purpose is to carry divine Life slowly into dense matter and develop material forms in successive stages until a physical form is developed that is capable of serving as a vehicle of expression for a self-conscious being.

Knowledge: Certainty. A stable, consistent awareness and understanding that is unchanging, eternal, and connected to God.

Make: To fabricate something to fill a specific need done from a sense of lack. "When we make something to fill a perceived lack, we are tacitly implying that we believe in separation."[111] Creative activity is a manifestation of God. The ego identity is made up within our own separated mind—that which is no longer at-oned.

Mental Body: A subtle body and the vehicle of expression for the mind. The lower mental body is the concrete mind, which is composed of all the thoughtforms sitting in the rational

---

[111] *ACIM*, p. 44.

mind. The upper mental body is the abstract, intuitional mind; soul mind.

Misperception: Thoughts and ideas that foster and promote fear.

Monad: A divine creative entity; a metaphysical entity imbued with divine will, love, and intelligence. Also called a Divine Spark, a Son of God, a divine Self. From the human personality's point of view, the Monad corresponds with the Father aspect of deity as It is the most immediate Source of Life and Consciousness.

Multidimensional Self: Another term for the Spiritual Triad and Soul. The levels of consciousness and creative activity that operate in higher dimensions of time and space.

Nadis: Subtle threads of vital force that form channels along which more subtle energies flow. These threads underlie and penetrate the entire body and the nervous system. Where nadis cross one another, energy centers are formed.

- Twenty-one crossings = a major chakra or energy center
- Fourteen crossings = minor chakra
- Seven crossings = energy point

Paradise Trinity: *The Urantia Book* uses this term to refer to the original Father, Son, and Infinite Spirit of all Creation. The Paradise Trinity exists at the center of the Grand Universe, and they are the First Cause and Center, the Second Cause and Center, and the Third Cause and Center. Thus, they are the cause of all creation and exist at the center of all things.

Perception: A transitory, subjective reality that is based on inner experiences.

Personality: The consciousness of the incarnated human being.

Plane: A state of consciousness

Prana: Vitality, Life energy.

Projection: The outward expression of an inward state of mind.

Shadow Self and Ideal Self: Polarized self-images or personas within the ego.

> **The shadow** contains the aspects of our self that we reject, fear, and feel ashamed of and lives primarily in our unconscious mind.
> **The ideal** consists of what we wish our self to be to ensure love and acceptance and lives primarily in our conscious mind as a fantasy.

Shadow Work: The conscious activity of healing the wounded self.

Soul: In human terms, the soul is the consciousness and creative activity that exits between the incarnated personality and the Monad. During our human evolution, it is the repository of our life experience, the essence of the casual body, and that which causes incarnation. Universally, it is the consciousness, or innate divine intelligence, that exists within all things irrespective of the experience of "self" consciousness. The soul of matter would be its innate ability to respond to the Thinker.

Spirit: A divine being endowed with the qualities of will/purpose, love-wisdom, and intelligence.

Spirit-personality: Another term for Monad, Son of God, Divine Spark. Our true, inherent, original divine Self at the point of our inception in the mind of God. A creator with unlimited potential, an evolving being with many levels of consciousness contained within it.

Subconscious: Intelligence or thought that exists below or outside our daily awareness.

Superconsciousness: Intelligence or creative thought that exists above or beyond our daily awareness and existing at a higher vibration. Higher intelligence, divine mind.

Superuniverse: Seven superuniverses spiraling around the central universe, composed of a vast number of smaller local universes.

Thoughtforms: The merger of life energy (spirit) and manas (mental matter) producing a mental form that contains a level of consciousness.

Trinity: The Three aspects or personas of God:

God the Father	First Logos	Will (will to good, or intelligent will)
God the Son	Second Logos	Love - Wisdom (intelligent love)
God the Infinite Spirit	Third Logos	Active Intelligence (intelligent activity)

True Perception: Thought and insight that foster and promote love.

True Self: A broad term referring to those aspects of self that lead the personality out of the separated ego and reconnect us with our spirit—the part of our consciousness that remains aware of its interconnectedness with God.

Universe: A level of creation. Seven superuniverses are in the Grand Universe, numerous universes are within a superuniverse, and numerous local universes are within a universe.

Author's Note

In the Works Cited section, I've listed many excellent resources of spiritual and metaphysical information. I encourage you to seek out these sources and read them for yourselves. I frequently found myself challenged by the ideas and concepts presented in these great works, but that was only because I was used to thinking in a different and more limited way. Over time, I learned that I needed to open my mind and heart continually to things that were sitting beyond my understanding in order to discover the deeper meaning and purpose of my life. All these revelations sit in the superconscious mind, waiting to be revealed; no one is left out of the loop. Every one of us has access to this information if we but seek it out, and these books helped provoke me into doing just that. Thus, they may serve you in the same way. And what has continued to delight me is the discovery that the mystical heart of all the great religions and spiritual paths in the world are beating to the same divine rhythm and broadcasting the same great truths. The truth will never be forced on us, because we have unlimited free will to do whatever we please with our creative power. So, we will always have to choose to seek it out and be willing to travel the unknown byways and pathways within ourselves that will reunite us with our divinity. In my experience, only then will you find the answers to the mysteries revealed to us.

Works Cited

A Course in Miracles. 1975. Glen Ellen, CA: Foundation for Inner Peace.

Allen, James. *The Way of Peace.* Accessed December 1, 2011. www.worldspirituality.org/power-of-meditation.html.

Amaraea. 2010. *Divine Human Blueprint Course Material.* Self-published. www.Divine-Blueprint.com.

Ashley, Nancy. 1984. *Create Your Own Reality, A Seth Workbook.* New York: Prentice Press.

Bailey, Alice A. 1925. *A Treastise on Cosmic Fire.* New York, NY: Lucis Publishing Company.

— 1934. *A Treatise on White Magic.* Lucis Publishing Company.

— 1962. *Esoteric Psychology - Volume II.* New York: Lucis Publishing Co.

— 1950. *Glamour, A World Problem.* New York: Lucis Publishing Company.

— 1927. *The Light of the Soul.* New York: Lucis Publishing Co.

— 1972. *The Rays and The Initiations.* New York: Lucis Publishing Co.

Deepak Chopra, Debbie Ford, Marianne Williamson. 2010. *The Shadow Effect.* New York: Harper Collins e-Books.

Dictionary.com. *Belief.* Accessed August 8, 2016. http://www.dictionary.com/browse/belief?s=t.

— *Inspiration.* Accessed March 19, 2012. http://dictionary.reference.com/browse/inspiration?s=t.

— *Loyalty.* Accessed November 11, 2011. http://dictionary.reference.com/browse/loyalty?s=t&ld=1136.

Freeman, James Dillet. 1941. *The Prayer for Protection (also known as the Unity prayer).* Accessed July 30, 2012. www.beliefnet.com/Prayers/Christian/Travel/Prayer-For-Protection.aspx.

Hay, Louise. 1984. *You Can Heal Your Life.* Santa Monica, CA: Hay House, Inc.

King, Godfrey Ray. 1934. *Unveiled Mysteries. Kindle Edition.* Chicago, Ill: St. Germain Press.

Krishnamurti, Jiddu. 2012. *BrainyQuote.com, Xplore Inc.* Accessed June 29, 2012. www.brainyquote.com/quotes/authors/j/jiddu_krishnamurti.html.

Mandela, Nelson. 2016. *BrainyQuote.com, Xplore Inc.* Accessed 06 05, 2016. http://www.brainyquote.com/quotes/keywords/compassion.html.

Myatt, Janet Lee. "I Am Love." *Tattooed Heart.* 2005. http://www.cdbaby.com/cd/janetleemyatt1.

Myatt, Janet Lee. "In the Stillness." *Janet Lee Myatt.* 2010. http://www.cdbaby.com/cd/JanetLeeMyatt.

Myatt, Janet Lee. "Recontructing Me." *Feels Like Thunder.* 2005. http://www.cdbaby.com/cd/janetleemyatt2.

Myatt, Janet Lee. *Secret Soul, 2003.*

Myss, Caroline. 1996. *Anatomy of the Spirit.* New York, NY: Three Rivers Press.

Powell, A.E. 1926. *The Astral Body.* Wheaton, IL: The Theosophical Publishing House.

Powell, A.E. 2011. "The Causal Body (Part 1 of 2)." *A Publication of the Theosophical Society.* Accessed Jan. 30, 2013. http://hpb.narod.ru/CausalBody1.htm.

— 1925. *The Etheric Double.* Wheaton, IL: The Theosophical Publishing House.

— 1927. *The Mental Body.* Wheaton, IL: The Theosophical Publishing House.

Prophet, Elizabeth Clare. *Inner Perspectives: 6.1 Spiritual Alchemy & St. Germain.* Accessed June 14, 2013. http://www.summitlighthouse.org/Reading-Room/inner-perspectives/61-Spiritual-Alchemy.html.

Roberts, Jane. 2011. *The Seth Material (Kindle Edition).* Location 4234: New Awareness Network, Inc.

Roberts, Janet. 1974. *The Nature of Personal Reality.* New York: Prentice-Hall.

Robinson, Diana. Accessed June 11, 2013. http://www.flickr.com/photos/martian_cat/8429322217/.

Stone, Joshua David. 1994. *The Complete Ascension Manual.* Flagstaff, AZ: Light Technology Publishing.

Swami Vivekananda. *Brainyquote.com.* Accessed October 3, 2016. http://www.brainyquote.com/search_results.html?q=spiritual+self+reflection.

Tolle, Eckhart. 2005. *A New Earth.* London, England: Penguin Books, Ltd.

Urantia. 1955. *The Urantia Book.* Chicago, Il: Urantia Foundation.

Wikipedia.org. *100th Monkey Effect.* Accessed January 29, 2012. https://en.wikipedia.org/wiki/Hundredth_monkey_effect.

— *Adi.* Accessed March 1, 2016. https://en.wikipedia.org/wiki/Adi_(metaphysical_plane).

— *Anupadaka.* Accessed March 1, 2016. https://en.wikipedia.org/wiki/Anupadaka.

— *Atma.* Accessed March 1, 2016. https://en.wikipedia.org/wiki/Atma.

— *Fear.* Accessed November 13, 2011. http://en.wikipedia.org/wiki/Fear.

Williamson, Marianne. 1992. *A Return to Love.* New York: Harper-Collins Publishers.

Williamson, Marianne. 2016. *BrainyQuote.com, Xplore Inc.* Accessed August 13, 2016. http://www.brainyquote.com/quotes/quotes/m/mariannewi146987.html.

Acknowledgements

I want to thank all of the amazing, beautiful spirits I have had the great priveledge to work with as a spiritual counselor, teacher and healer. In my humble opinion, good teachers remain students at heart and recognize their students as some of their greatest teachers. Likewise, healthy healers know they receive a healing every time they have the opportunity to give one. It's a divine recipriocal process of learning, growing, and healing. I wrote this book not only to help myself better understand what I am learning, but also to help my students and clients on their journey. So in truth this book would not exist but for this reciprocity and all of the blessings my students and clients have bestowed upon me through their presence in my life.

I must single out a few people who were particularly instrumental in helping me see this book through to completion. *Thank you* Peggy Prien, Michelle Phillips, Suzanne Ross, Shaun Myatt, Julie Stein, Kate Mackinnon, and Lauren Doko for your unwavering support and encouragement.

I would also like to humbly acknowledge and thank Ascended Masters Djwal Khul, Saint Germain, Jesus, Mother Mary, and Archangel Michael for your words, inspiration, love, and healing. Above all, I thank the Supreme Being for loving us all so perfectly no matter what.

Printed in the United States
By Bookmasters